MASTERING AWS

A Comprehensive Guide to
Amazon Web Services

Edwin Cano

Copyright © 2024 Edwin Cano

All rights reserved

No part of this book may be reproduced, or stored in a retrieval system, or transmitted in any form or by any means, electronic, mechanical, photocopying, recording, or otherwise, without express written permission of the publisher.

First Edition, 2024

To all cloud enthusiasts, developers, and innovators who dream of building the future in the clouds.

This book is dedicated to those who challenge the boundaries of technology, continually learn, and inspire others with their vision and determination.

To my family and friends, whose unwavering support and encouragement make every endeavor worthwhile.

And to the incredible AWS community, whose shared knowledge and collaboration empower endless possibilities.

This work is for you. Let your journey to mastering AWS be a rewarding and transformative experience.

"The cloud is not just a technology; it is a foundation for innovation, agility, and limitless possibilities."

These words remind us that the journey to mastering AWS is not just about tools and services but about unlocking creativity and potential in the ever-evolving digital landscape.

— ANONYMOUS

CONTENTS

Title Page

Copyright

Dedication

Epigraph

Introduction

Overview of AWS ... 1

Part 1: Getting Started with AWS ... 22

Chapter 1: AWS Fundamentals ... 23

Chapter 2: AWS Identity and Access Management (IAM) ... 42

Chapter 3: Cost Management and Billing ... 67

Part 2: Core AWS Services ... 92

Chapter 4: Compute Services ... 93

Chapter 5: Storage Services ... 118

Chapter 6: Database Services ... 144

Chapter 7: Networking and Content Delivery ... 174

Part 3: Advanced AWS Solutions	204
Chapter 8: Security and Compliance	205
Chapter 9: Monitoring and Management	233
Chapter 10: DevOps and Automation	264
Chapter 11: Big Data and Analytics	293
Part 4: Specialized AWS Services	320
Chapter 12: Machine Learning and AI	321
Chapter 13: Internet of Things (IoT)	339
Chapter 14: Serverless Architecture	356
Part 5: Case Studies and Real-World Applications	374
Chapter 15: Building Scalable Web Applications	375
Chapter 16: Disaster Recovery and Backup	393
Chapter 17: Migration to AWS	409
Conclusion	425
Appendices	444
Afterword	469
Acknowledgement	473
About The Author	477
Praise For Author	481

INTRODUCTION

The rapid advancements in technology have shifted the landscape of how businesses operate, innovate, and grow. At the center of this transformation is cloud computing—a paradigm that eliminates the constraints of traditional infrastructure, enabling scalability, agility, and cost-efficiency. Amazon Web Services (AWS) has emerged as the leading cloud provider, offering a comprehensive suite of services that power startups, enterprises, and governments worldwide.

This book, *Mastering AWS*, serves as a gateway to understanding and utilizing AWS to its full potential. Whether you're a professional aiming to enhance your technical skills, a business leader seeking to drive innovation, or a student exploring the possibilities of cloud computing, this book is crafted to guide you step-by-step through the AWS ecosystem.

Why AWS?
AWS is a pioneer in the cloud computing space, providing an unmatched array of services for compute, storage, databases, machine learning, IoT, and much more. Its global infrastructure ensures reliability, while its pay-as-you-go pricing model makes it accessible to organizations of all sizes. AWS has become synonymous with innovation, enabling companies to experiment, iterate, and succeed faster than ever before.

What Will You Learn?
This book covers a wide range of topics, including:

The fundamental concepts of cloud computing and AWS architecture.

Setting up and managing your AWS account securely and efficiently.

Deploying scalable applications using services like EC2, Lambda, and Elastic Beanstalk.

Harnessing data with storage solutions such as S3, RDS, and DynamoDB.

Advanced topics like AI/ML with SageMaker, IoT solutions, and DevOps practices.

Cost management strategies and real-world use cases to maximize the value of AWS.

Who Is This Book For?
This book is designed for readers at all skill levels:

Beginners will appreciate the step-by-step explanations and foundational concepts.

Intermediate users will gain insights into best practices, cost optimization, and advanced features.

Experts will find value in the comprehensive coverage of AWS services and practical examples.

How to Use This Book
The chapters are structured to provide a logical progression from basics to advanced topics. Each chapter includes practical examples, hands-on exercises, and tips to help you apply the concepts effectively. You can read the book sequentially or jump to specific sections based on your interests and needs.

A Journey to Mastery
Mastering AWS is not just about learning how to use its services; it's about understanding how to leverage the cloud to solve challenges, innovate

faster, and achieve your goals. By the end of this book, you'll have the knowledge and confidence to harness AWS for any project or initiative, whether you're launching a startup, optimizing enterprise operations, or exploring cutting-edge technologies.

Let's begin this exciting journey into the world of AWS, where the only limit is your imagination.

— Edwin Cano

OVERVIEW OF AWS

History and Evolution of AWS

The Birth of AWS

- **2003:** AWS began as an internal initiative within Amazon to standardize their IT infrastructure for better efficiency. The idea was to provide services like storage and computing to external developers and businesses.

- **2006:** Amazon Web Services officially launched, offering a suite of cloud-based services including **Amazon S3 (Simple Storage Service)** and **Amazon EC2 (Elastic Compute Cloud)**. These were pioneering steps in the cloud computing industry.

Early Growth and Innovation

- **2007-2008:** AWS gained traction among startups due to its cost-effective and scalable solutions. Companies like Dropbox and Airbnb were early adopters.
- **2010:** Amazon.com migrated its retail infrastructure to AWS, proving its reliability at scale.

Expanding Service Portfolio

- AWS consistently introduced new services to meet the growing needs of businesses:
  - **2011:** Launch of Amazon CloudFront for content delivery and AWS Elastic Beanstalk for easy application deployment.
  - **2012:** Introduction of Amazon Glacier for long-term storage and AWS Marketplace for third-party applications.
  - **2014:** Release of AWS Lambda, which introduced serverless computing.

Global Expansion

- AWS expanded its global footprint by establishing **Regions and Availability Zones** worldwide to provide low-latency services and ensure data redundancy:

- **2012:** Opened AWS regions in Brazil and Sydney.
- **2016:** Launched regions in Canada, the UK, and South Korea.

Dominance in Cloud Computing

- By the mid-2010s, AWS became the dominant player in the cloud market, holding a significant lead over competitors like Microsoft Azure and Google Cloud.
- AWS achieved major milestones, including the introduction of:
  - **AWS Snowball** for data migration (2015).
  - **Amazon SageMaker** for machine learning (2017).
  - **AWS Outposts** for hybrid cloud solutions (2018).

Major Innovations and Recognition

- **2020s:** AWS introduced cutting-edge technologies such as:
  - **Graviton processors** for cost-effective compute performance.
  - **AWS Local Zones** for ultra-low latency.
  - Advanced AI and ML services like Amazon Lex and Rekognition.

Present Day

- AWS remains the leader in cloud

- computing, serving millions of customers globally across industries, from startups to enterprises.
- It continues to drive innovation in areas like quantum computing, IoT, and sustainability with initiatives like **AWS Clean Energy Accelerators**.

Impact on Cloud Computing

- AWS has transformed how businesses operate, enabling agility, scalability, and cost efficiency.
- The success of AWS catalyzed the growth of the entire cloud computing industry, with its model being replicated by many competitors.

AWS's evolution is a testament to Amazon's commitment to innovation, customer focus, and industry leadership. It continues to shape the future of technology and business.

Benefits of Using AWS

1. Scalability and Flexibility

- AWS provides **on-demand resources** that allow businesses to scale up or down depending on their needs.
- Supports dynamic scaling for applications, making it ideal for businesses with fluctuating workloads.

- Flexible deployment options: public cloud, private cloud, or hybrid cloud.

2. Cost-Effectiveness

- Pay-as-you-go pricing ensures you only pay for the resources you use.
- Eliminates the need for upfront investment in hardware and data centers.
- Offers cost-management tools like AWS Budgets and Cost Explorer to optimize spending.

3. Global Infrastructure

- AWS operates in multiple **Regions** and **Availability Zones** worldwide, enabling low-latency connections and data redundancy.
- Global reach allows businesses to deploy applications close to their users, improving performance.

4. Broad Range of Services

- Over 200 fully-featured services for compute, storage, databases, AI/ML, IoT, analytics, and more.
- Enables businesses to find tailored solutions for their specific needs.

5. High Availability and Reliability

- AWS ensures 99.99% uptime with its

robust infrastructure.
- Data redundancy through multi-AZ deployments ensures service continuity in case of failures.
- Disaster recovery solutions like AWS Backup and cross-region replication add extra layers of protection.

6. Strong Security and Compliance

- AWS follows a **shared responsibility model**, offering industry-standard security measures like encryption, firewalls, and monitoring.
- Compliance with global standards such as GDPR, HIPAA, and ISO certifications.
- Tools like AWS Identity and Access Management (IAM) and AWS Security Hub enhance security management.

7. Innovation and Cutting-Edge Technology

- Access to advanced technologies like serverless computing (AWS Lambda), AI/ML (SageMaker), and quantum computing (Amazon Braket).
- Frequent updates and new services ensure businesses stay at the forefront of technology.

8. Developer and Ecosystem Support

- Extensive documentation, training, and

a vibrant community of developers and partners.

- AWS Marketplace provides access to third-party solutions for seamless integration.
- Developer tools like AWS CodePipeline and AWS CloudFormation make DevOps more efficient.

9. Faster Time-to-Market

- Pre-configured services like Elastic Beanstalk and Lightsail simplify application deployment.
- Automation tools enable rapid provisioning and scaling, reducing time-to-market for products and services.

10. Sustainability Initiatives

- AWS is committed to renewable energy and aims to achieve **100% renewable energy usage by 2025**.
- Offers tools like the **AWS Customer Carbon Footprint Tool** to help businesses track and reduce their carbon emissions.

11. Support for Diverse Workloads

- Suitable for startups, SMEs, and large enterprises.
- Supports varied use cases like

website hosting, data analytics, mobile app development, and enterprise IT modernization.

12. Hybrid and Edge Solutions

- Services like AWS Outposts and Local Zones enable seamless hybrid cloud setups.
- Edge computing solutions allow processing closer to data sources for real-time performance.

AWS empowers businesses with scalable, secure, and innovative solutions, making it a leader in cloud computing for organizations of all sizes.

Common Use Cases for AWS

1. Hosting Websites and Web Applications

- AWS provides a scalable and cost-effective infrastructure for hosting websites and web applications.
- Services used:
    - **Amazon EC2**: For virtual server hosting.
    - **Amazon S3**: For storing static assets like images, videos, and files.
    - **Elastic Load Balancing**: For distributing traffic.
    - **AWS Lightsail**: Simplified hosting for small-scale websites.

2. Application Development and Deployment

- Developers can build, test, and deploy applications quickly with AWS.
- Services used:
    - **AWS Elastic Beanstalk**: Simplified application deployment.
    - **AWS CodePipeline**: Continuous integration and delivery (CI/CD).
    - **AWS Lambda**: Serverless computing for event-driven applications.

3. Data Storage and Backup

- AWS provides secure and scalable storage solutions for structured and unstructured data.
- Services used:
    - **Amazon S3**: Object storage for files and backups.
    - **Amazon Glacier**: Archiving data for long-term storage.
    - **AWS Backup**: Centralized management of backups across services.

4. Database Management

- AWS offers a range of database services for relational and NoSQL databases.
- Services used:
    - **Amazon RDS**: Managed relational

databases.
- **Amazon DynamoDB**: Scalable NoSQL database.
- **Amazon Redshift**: Data warehousing for analytics.

5. Content Delivery and Media Streaming

- AWS accelerates content delivery and supports live and on-demand video streaming.
- Services used:
  - **Amazon CloudFront**: Content delivery network (CDN).
  - **AWS Elemental Media Services**: For video encoding and streaming.

6. Big Data Analytics

- AWS enables businesses to analyze massive datasets efficiently.
- Services used:
  - **Amazon EMR**: Big data processing with Hadoop.
  - **AWS Glue**: ETL (Extract, Transform, Load) for data preparation.
  - **Amazon Athena**: SQL queries for data in S3.

7. Machine Learning and Artificial Intelligence

- AWS offers tools and pre-trained models for building AI/ML applications.

- Services used:
  - **Amazon SageMaker**: End-to-end ML model development.
  - **AWS Rekognition**: Image and video analysis.
  - **Amazon Polly**: Text-to-speech conversion.

8. IoT (Internet of Things)

- AWS supports IoT device management and data processing.
- Services used:
  - **AWS IoT Core**: Connect and manage IoT devices.
  - **AWS Greengrass**: Extend AWS capabilities to edge devices.
  - **AWS IoT Analytics**: Analyze IoT data.

9. DevOps and Automation

- AWS simplifies DevOps practices with tools for automation and deployment.
- Services used:
  - **AWS CodeBuild**: Build automation.
  - **AWS CodeDeploy**: Deployment automation.
  - **AWS CloudFormation**: Infrastructure as Code (IaC).

10. Gaming

- AWS provides low-latency solutions for

multiplayer and mobile gaming.

- Services used:
    - **Amazon GameLift**: Dedicated game server hosting.
    - **Amazon DynamoDB**: For game leaderboards and session management.
    - **Amazon S3**: Storing game assets.

11. Disaster Recovery and Business Continuity

- AWS ensures data recovery and business continuity during disruptions.
- Services used:
    - **AWS Elastic Disaster Recovery**: For rapid recovery of applications.
    - **Cross-Region Replication**: For redundancy and resilience.

12. Enterprise IT Modernization

- AWS helps businesses migrate legacy systems to modern cloud infrastructure.
- Services used:
    - **AWS Migration Hub**: Centralized migration management.
    - **AWS Outposts**: Hybrid cloud solutions for on-premises workloads.

13. E-Commerce Platforms

- AWS supports scalable, secure, and globally available e-commerce

platforms.
- Services used:
    - **Amazon Aurora**: For high-performance relational databases.
    - **Amazon CloudFront**: For fast content delivery.
    - **AWS Lambda**: For event-driven tasks like cart management.

14. Mobile and Web App Development

- AWS provides backend services and tools for developing and scaling apps.
- Services used:
    - **AWS Amplify**: Backend development for mobile and web apps.
    - **AWS AppSync**: Managed GraphQL API.
    - **Amazon Cognito**: Authentication and user management.

15. Video Conferencing and Collaboration Tools

- AWS supports real-time communication applications.
- Services used:
    - **Amazon Chime SDK**: For building voice, video, and messaging apps.
    - **Amazon CloudFront**: To deliver real-time media at scale.

AWS's versatility and extensive service portfolio

make it suitable for almost any workload, from startups to large enterprises.

Understanding Cloud Computing Concepts

1. What is Cloud Computing?

Cloud computing refers to the delivery of computing services over the internet ("the cloud"). These services include servers, storage, databases, networking, software, analytics, and more. It eliminates the need for businesses to own and maintain physical data centers or servers, offering flexibility, scalability, and cost-efficiency.

2. Core Characteristics of Cloud Computing

- **On-Demand Self-Service**: Users can access resources such as servers and storage whenever needed without human intervention.
- **Broad Network Access**: Services are accessible over the internet from various devices like laptops, smartphones, and tablets.
- **Resource Pooling**: Resources like storage

and processing power are pooled together to serve multiple users (multi-tenancy).

- **Rapid Elasticity**: Resources can be quickly scaled up or down based on demand.
- **Measured Service**: Cloud usage is monitored, controlled, and billed based on usage.

3. Key Cloud Service Models

1. **Infrastructure as a Service (IaaS)**:
   - Provides virtualized computing resources like servers, storage, and networks.
   - Example: Amazon EC2, Microsoft Azure Virtual Machines.

2. **Platform as a Service (PaaS)**:
   - Offers a platform for developers to build, test, and deploy applications without managing underlying infrastructure.
   - Example: AWS Elastic Beanstalk, Google App Engine.

3. **Software as a Service (SaaS)**:
   - Delivers software applications over the internet on a subscription basis.

- Example: Google Workspace, Microsoft Office 365.

4. Deployment Models

1. **Public Cloud**:
   - Services are available to the general public over the internet.
   - Examples: AWS, Microsoft Azure, Google Cloud.

2. **Private Cloud**:
   - Dedicated to a single organization for exclusive use.
   - Offers enhanced security and customization.

3. **Hybrid Cloud**:
   - Combines public and private cloud environments, allowing data and applications to be shared between them.

4. **Multi-Cloud**:
   - Utilizes multiple cloud service providers to avoid vendor lock-in and enhance redundancy.

5. Advantages of Cloud Computing

- **Cost Savings**: No need for upfront investments in hardware or IT infrastructure.
- **Scalability**: Easily scale resources to handle varying workloads.

- **Accessibility**: Access services and applications from anywhere with an internet connection.
- **Business Continuity**: Ensures data recovery and continuity in case of disasters.
- **Rapid Deployment**: New resources can be provisioned quickly to meet business demands.

6. Common Cloud Computing Use Cases

- Web hosting and application deployment.
- Data storage, backup, and disaster recovery.
- Big data analytics and machine learning.
- IoT (Internet of Things) device management.
- Collaboration tools and communication platforms.

7. Challenges of Cloud Computing

- **Security and Privacy Concerns**: Potential data breaches and unauthorized access.
- **Downtime**: Dependence on internet connectivity and potential service outages.
- **Vendor Lock-In**: Difficulty in migrating

data and applications between providers.

- **Cost Management**: Unmonitored usage can lead to unexpected expenses.

8. Cloud Computing in AWS

AWS is one of the most prominent cloud providers, offering a comprehensive suite of services under all service models (IaaS, PaaS, SaaS). It enables organizations to deploy, scale, and innovate using cutting-edge technologies.

By understanding these core concepts, businesses and individuals can make informed decisions about adopting cloud computing and leveraging its benefits.

How to Use This Book

This book, Mastering AWS, is designed as a comprehensive guide to help readers of all experience levels, from beginners to advanced users, understand and leverage the power of Amazon Web Services (AWS). Below are suggestions on how to navigate and make the most of this book.

1. Identify Your Learning Goals

Before diving into the book, clarify your

objectives:

- Are you a beginner seeking an introduction to cloud computing and AWS basics?
- Are you a developer aiming to deploy applications on AWS?
- Are you an IT professional looking to master specific AWS services?

This book is organized to cater to various goals and experience levels.

2. Follow a Structured Approach

The book is divided into logical sections to guide you progressively:

- **Beginners**: Start with foundational chapters like *Understanding Cloud Computing Concepts*, *History and Evolution of AWS*, and *AWS Basics*.
- **Intermediate Users**: Focus on chapters discussing *Core AWS Services*, *AWS Use Cases*, and *AWS Best Practices*.
- **Advanced Users**: Explore specialized topics like *Serverless Computing*, *Advanced Networking in AWS*, and *Security and Compliance*.

Each chapter builds on the previous ones, making it easy to follow a structured path.

3. Practical Application with Hands-On

Exercises

- Many chapters include **step-by-step guides** and **real-world scenarios**.
- Set up an AWS Free Tier account to experiment with services as you read through the chapters.
- Follow along with the provided exercises to solidify your understanding.

4. Use as a Reference Guide

- If you are an experienced AWS user, this book can serve as a **quick reference manual** for specific services or concepts.
- Use the detailed index and table of contents to locate the topics you need without reading the entire book.

5. Leverage Visual Aids and Examples

- The book includes **diagrams, screenshots, and case studies** to illustrate key concepts.
- Refer to these visual aids to gain a better understanding of complex topics.

6. Apply Learnings to Real-World Projects

- After completing the chapters, try applying your knowledge to personal or professional projects.
- The case studies and examples provided in this book can serve as templates or

inspiration.

7. Engage with AWS Community and Resources

- Use the knowledge gained from this book to explore additional AWS resources like AWS Documentation, AWS Forums, and webinars.
- Join online communities to stay updated on new features and best practices.

8. Revisit for Certification Preparation

- If you're pursuing AWS certifications, this book can serve as a study guide for foundational, associate, and professional-level exams.
- Focus on chapters aligned with the certification syllabus and practice using AWS tools.

9. Take Notes and Track Progress

- Use the notes sections at the end of each chapter to jot down key insights and your personal observations.
- Track your progress through the exercises and revisit chapters as needed.

This book is a roadmap to mastering AWS, whether you're looking to build a foundation, deepen your expertise, or implement AWS solutions in your work. Adapt it to your pace and objectives, and enjoy your journey into cloud computing with AWS!

PART 1: GETTING STARTED WITH AWS

CHAPTER 1: AWS FUNDAMENTALS

Key Concepts: Regions, Availability Zones, and Data Centers

Amazon Web Services (AWS) operates a global cloud infrastructure that ensures availability, scalability, and reliability for its users. Understanding how AWS organizes its infrastructure through Regions, Availability Zones, and Data Centers is fundamental to leveraging the platform effectively.

1. Regions

- **Definition**: A Region is a physical geographic location around the world where AWS clusters its data centers.

- **Key Characteristics**:
  - Each Region is independent and isolated from others for **fault tolerance**.
  - Named based on their geographic area (e.g., us-east-1, ap-southeast-1).
  - Regions are designed to meet **data sovereignty** and **compliance** requirements.
  - Each Region contains multiple Availability Zones for high availability.
- **Examples**:
  - **North America**: us-east-1 (N. Virginia), us-west-1 (N. California).
  - **Asia Pacific**: ap-southeast-1 (Singapore), ap-northeast-1 (Tokyo).
  - **Europe**: eu-west-1 (Ireland), eu-central-1 (Frankfurt).

Use Cases for Regions:

- Choose the nearest Region to reduce **latency**.
- Select specific Regions for **compliance** with local regulations (e.g., GDPR in the EU).
- Use multiple Regions for **disaster recovery** or **global applications**.

2. Availability Zones (AZs)

- **Definition**: An Availability Zone is one or more discrete data centers with redundant power, networking, and connectivity within a Region.
- **Key Characteristics**:
  - AZs are physically separate and isolated from other AZs in the same Region.
  - Connected through low-latency, high-speed private fiber links.
  - Typically named as a, b, c within a Region (e.g., us-east-1a, us-east-1b).
  - Provide high availability and fault tolerance by allowing resources to be distributed across multiple AZs.
- **Examples**:
  - Deploy an application across **two or more AZs** for redundancy.
  - Use **Elastic Load Balancing** to distribute traffic across AZs.

Use Cases for AZs:

- High availability for critical workloads.
- Resilience to failure of a single data center.
- Disaster recovery within the same Region.

3. Data Centers

- **Definition**: A Data Center is a physical facility that houses servers, networking equipment, and storage systems.
- **Key Characteristics**:
  - Each AZ comprises one or more Data Centers.
  - AWS maintains stringent security, climate control, and redundancy measures for each Data Center.
  - Not directly visible to AWS users but forms the building blocks of AWS infrastructure.

Use Cases for Data Centers:

- Not directly managed by users but essential for ensuring reliability and scalability of the cloud infrastructure.

Key Differences Between Regions, AZs, and Data Centers

Feature	Regions	Availability Zones (AZs)	Data Centers
Scope	Geographic areas	Logical groupings of data centers within Regions	Physical buildings with servers
Fault Tolerance	Isolated for regional disasters	Resilient to individual data center failures	Single point of failure
Use Case	Data locality and global distribution	High availability within a Region	Operational infrastructure

Best Practices:

1. **Use Multi-Region Architecture**:
   - Deploy applications in multiple

Regions for global reach and disaster recovery.
- Example: Host a primary application in us-east-1 and replicate it in us-west-1.

2. **Leverage Multiple AZs**:
    - Distribute resources (e.g., databases, applications) across multiple AZs to ensure high availability.
    - Example: Use Amazon RDS Multi-AZ deployments for automatic failover.

3. **Understand Data Sovereignty**:
    - Store sensitive data in Regions that comply with local laws and regulations.

4. **Optimize Costs and Performance**:
    - Select Regions based on proximity to end-users to reduce latency and data transfer costs.

By understanding these key concepts, AWS users can design systems that are resilient, scalable, and aligned with business and regulatory requirements.

AWS Management Console, CLI, and SDK

AWS offers multiple tools for interacting with its cloud services. These tools cater to different use cases and preferences, allowing users to manage their resources in a way that best suits their needs. The three primary tools for managing AWS resources are the AWS Management Console, AWS Command Line Interface (CLI), and AWS Software Development Kits (SDKs). Here's a breakdown of each:

1. AWS Management Console

- **Definition**: The AWS Management Console is a web-based graphical user interface (GUI) that allows users to manage AWS services visually.

- **Key Features**:
    - **User-Friendly**: Easy to navigate with point-and-click capabilities for creating, managing, and monitoring AWS resources.
    - **Real-Time Monitoring**: Offers dashboards, metrics, and logs to monitor the status and performance of resources.
    - **Access to All AWS Services**: Provides access to almost all AWS services with features like EC2,

S3, RDS, Lambda, and more.
- **Resource Creation & Management**: Create, configure, and manage resources directly through the GUI. Includes step-by-step wizards for launching instances, setting up storage, etc.
- **IAM and Access Control**: Supports Identity and Access Management (IAM) to set up fine-grained access policies for users and groups.

- **Use Cases**:
    - Ideal for **beginners** and users who prefer working with a GUI.
    - **Exploring AWS services** and experimenting with different configurations without writing code.
    - Managing **small to medium-scale environments** or for users who do not require automation.

- **Limitations**:
    - Less efficient for managing large-scale environments or automating repetitive tasks.
    - Not suitable for **scripting** or managing resources at scale.

2. AWS Command Line Interface (CLI)

- **Definition**: The AWS CLI is a unified tool that provides a command-line interface for interacting with AWS services. It allows users to automate tasks and manage resources via text-based commands.

- **Key Features**:
    - **Cross-Platform**: Available on Windows, macOS, and Linux.
    - **Powerful Automation**: Supports automation of complex tasks with scripts. Can be easily integrated with **bash scripts** or **batch jobs**.
    - **Full API Access**: Provides access to almost all AWS services via text commands, making it suitable for advanced users and developers.
    - **Configuration Profiles**: Supports configuration of multiple profiles for different AWS accounts and regions.
    - **Command Structure**: Commands follow a consistent structure: aws <service> <operation> <parameters>, e.g., aws ec2 describe-instances.

- **Use Cases**:
    - **Advanced users** who are comfortable with command-line operations.
    - Ideal for **automating repetitive tasks**, provisioning resources, and managing large-scale

environments.
- Suitable for **scripting and DevOps workflows**.

- **Limitations**:
  - Requires familiarity with **command-line syntax**.
  - May not be as intuitive for **non-technical users** compared to the Management Console.

3. AWS Software Development Kits (SDKs)

- **Definition**: AWS SDKs are a set of libraries and tools for integrating AWS services into software applications. They provide language-specific APIs that abstract low-level AWS API calls, making it easier to interact with AWS resources programmatically.

- **Key Features**:
  - **Language Support**: AWS SDKs are available for multiple programming languages, including:
    - **Python (Boto3), Java, Node.js, Go, Ruby, C#, PHP, Swift**, and more.
  - **High-Level Abstraction**: Simplifies the process of interacting with AWS services by abstracting AWS API calls and handling retries, error management, and session

management.
- **Integrated Features**: SDKs integrate with other AWS tools and libraries, such as **Amazon S3** for storage, **Amazon DynamoDB** for databases, and **AWS Lambda** for serverless functions.
- **Efficient Resource Management**: Provides methods to manage resources like EC2 instances, S3 buckets, and Lambda functions directly from within applications.

- **Use Cases**:
  - **Developers** building applications that require AWS services like storage, compute, and messaging.
  - Integrating AWS functionality into **custom applications** or creating **serverless architectures** using AWS Lambda.
  - Writing **automated systems** that interact with AWS resources programmatically.

- **Limitations**:
  - Requires programming knowledge and familiarity with AWS APIs.
  - SDKs are not suited for tasks like **ad-hoc resource management** or **quick configurations**.

Comparison of AWS Management Console, CLI, and SDK

Feature	AWS Management Console	AWS CLI	AWS SDKs
Interface Type	Graphical User Interface (GUI)	Command-Line Interface (CLI)	Programmatic API (Language-Specific)
Best For	Beginners and visual learners	Advanced users, DevOps, Automation	Developers building applications
Ease of Use	Highly intuitive and user-friendly	Moderate (requires command knowledge)	Advanced (requires coding skills)
Automation & Scripting	Limited automation capabilities	Ideal for scripting and automation	Full programmatic control and integration
Access to AWS Services	Access to most AWS services via GUI	Access to almost all AWS services via CLI	Access to AWS services through SDK libraries
Platform Support	Web-based, no installation required	Cross-platform (Windows, macOS, Linux)	Multi-language support (e.g., Python, Java)
Scale Suitability	Best for small-scale or manual management	Suitable for small to large-scale environments	Best for custom applications and large systems

When to Use Each Tool

- **AWS Management Console**:
    - Use when you need to **quickly explore services**, manage resources manually, or troubleshoot in a **visual interface**. Ideal for beginners or those who prefer a GUI over text-based commands.

- **AWS CLI**:
    - Use when you need to **automate tasks**, manage resources programmatically, or work in environments where **efficiency and speed** are critical. Best for users comfortable with the command line and automation scripts.

- **AWS SDKs**:
    - Use when building **applications** that integrate with AWS services. Ideal for **developers** who need to

programmatically interact with AWS resources from within their own software applications.

By understanding the strengths and appropriate use cases for each tool, you can choose the right interface for your tasks in AWS and work more effectively within the cloud environment.

Setting Up Your AWS Account

Setting up an AWS account is the first step in utilizing Amazon Web Services for your cloud computing needs. This section will guide you through the process of creating and configuring your AWS account, including setting up security features and managing billing.

1. Creating an AWS Account

- **Step 1: Visit the AWS Website**
    - Go to the AWS homepage and click on the **"Create an AWS Account"** button.

- **Step 2: Sign Up for an AWS Account**
    - **Enter Account Details**: Provide your email address, password, and choose an AWS account name.

- **Account Type**: Choose between an **Individual** or **Company** account. Most users opt for the individual account unless they are setting up AWS for a business or enterprise.

- **Billing Information**: Enter your **credit card** or **payment method** details. AWS offers a **free tier**, but it still requires a valid payment method for verification purposes.

- **Identity Verification**: AWS will ask for a **phone number** and send a verification code via text message or voice call.

- **Step 3: Choose a Support Plan**
  - AWS offers different support plans:
    - **Basic Support**: Free and includes 24/7 access to customer service, documentation, whitepapers, and the AWS Trusted Advisor.
    - **Developer Support**: Paid plan for development support with pricing based on usage.
    - **Business Support**: Offers 24/7 access to AWS engineers, best practices, and a faster response time.
    - **Enterprise Support**: Aimed

at large organizations needing critical support and dedicated AWS experts.

- **Step 4: Set Up MFA (Multi-Factor Authentication)**
    - It is highly recommended to enable **MFA** on your root account for **security**. This adds an extra layer of protection by requiring both your password and a temporary security code sent to your mobile device.
    - AWS offers options to use an MFA device such as an **authenticator app** or **SMS**.
- **Step 5: Review and Confirm**
    - Review all the details and confirm the creation of your AWS account. AWS will send a confirmation email to the address provided.

2. Logging Into the AWS Console

Once your account is created, you can log in to the AWS Management Console.

- **Go to the AWS Console**: Visit AWS Management Console and log in with your account credentials.
- **Root User vs IAM User**:
    - By default, you will log in as the **root user** of the account. It's best practice to create **IAM (Identity**

and Access Management) users for day-to-day management, especially to avoid using the root account regularly.

- **IAM users** are more secure as they allow you to assign fine-grained permissions to different users based on roles.

3. Setting Up IAM Users and Permissions

- **Step 1: Create an IAM User**
    - Go to the **IAM Dashboard** in the AWS Management Console.
    - Click on **"Users"**, then **"Add User"**.
    - Enter a username and select the type of access for the user (Programmatic access for CLI/API access, and/or AWS Management Console access).
    - Choose permissions. You can either assign **existing policies** or create custom permissions for the user.
        - For new users, it's recommended to assign them the **"AdministratorAccess"** policy if they need full access to all AWS services (use sparingly for sensitive accounts).

- **Step 2: Assign Permissions**
    - **Group Permissions**: You can add the user to a **group** (e.g., Admin,

Developers, ReadOnly) and assign permissions at the group level.

- **Inline Permissions**: If you need more fine-grained control, you can create inline policies specific to that user.
- **Multi-Factor Authentication (MFA)**: Set up MFA for additional security.

- **Step 3: Access Keys and Credentials**
    - If the user requires **programmatic access** via CLI or SDK, you can create an **Access Key** and **Secret Key** for them. These keys are essential for interacting with AWS services programmatically.

4. Setting Up Billing and Cost Management

- **Step 1: Set Up Billing Preferences**
    - Go to the **Billing and Cost Management Dashboard**.
    - Configure your **billing alerts** to monitor costs and usage. AWS allows you to set up **spending alerts** that notify you when you exceed certain thresholds.
    - You can also **enable AWS Budgets** to keep track of your estimated costs and actual usage.

- **Step 2: Explore the Free Tier**
    - AWS offers a **Free Tier** for new accounts, allowing you to

use a limited set of services at no charge within specified usage limits. Some services, like Amazon EC2 (t2.micro), Amazon S3 (5GB), and Lambda (1M requests/month), are free within certain limits.
- It's important to understand the Free Tier limits to avoid unexpected charges.

- **Step 3: Set Up a Payment Method**
  - Ensure your payment method is correctly linked, and keep track of usage to avoid surprises in your billing.
  - Set up **AWS Cost Explorer** to visualize your spending patterns and identify areas for optimization.

5. Securing Your AWS Account

- **Step 1: Enable Root Account MFA**
  - Protect your root account by enabling **MFA**. AWS recommends enabling MFA on the root account for added security.

- **Step 2: Use IAM for Access Control**
  - Avoid using the **root user** for everyday tasks. Create IAM users and assign the **least privilege** access policies to them.

- **Step 3: Enable CloudTrail Logging**
  - AWS CloudTrail tracks all API

calls made within your account. Enabling it ensures an audit trail of all activities, improving security and compliance.

6. AWS Account Management Tips

- **Track Your Usage**: Regularly monitor your **AWS usage** via the **AWS Cost Explorer** or **Billing Dashboard** to prevent cost overruns.

- **Set Up Email Notifications**: Configure email notifications for billing alerts and usage reports to stay informed.

- **Review Permissions Regularly**: Periodically review IAM policies and permissions to ensure that they are still aligned with best security practices.

- **Use Consolidated Billing**: If managing multiple AWS accounts, consider using **Consolidated Billing** to combine bills and gain volume discounts.

Summary

- **Creating an AWS account** is the first step to accessing the wide range of cloud services AWS offers.

- **IAM** users and permissions help you secure and manage access to your AWS resources.

- Regularly monitor and configure **billing**

and usage alerts to stay on top of your costs.

- Make security a priority by enabling **MFA** on your root account and using IAM users with appropriate permissions.

By following these steps, you'll be well on your way to managing your AWS resources effectively and securely.

CHAPTER 2: AWS IDENTITY AND ACCESS MANAGEMENT (IAM)

Users, Groups, and Policies

In AWS, Identity and Access Management (IAM) allows you to securely control access to AWS services and resources. The basic components of IAM are Users, Groups, and Policies, each serving a specific function to help manage permissions in a scalable and secure way.

1. IAM Users

An **IAM user** is an entity that you create in AWS to represent a person or application that interacts with AWS resources. IAM users have specific permissions to access AWS services.

- **Types of Users**:
    - **Root User**: This is the primary account holder, which has unrestricted access to all AWS resources. It's crucial to secure the root account by enabling **multi-factor authentication (MFA)** and using it only for account management tasks.
    - **IAM Users**: These are created within the AWS account and assigned specific permissions. IAM users can have access keys for **programmatic access** or a password for **console access**.
- **Creating an IAM User**:

    1. Navigate to the **IAM Dashboard** in the AWS Management Console.

    2. Select **Users** and click **Add User**.

    3. Enter a **User Name** and select the type of access needed:

    - **Programmatic access** for access via AWS CLI, API, or SDK.
    - **AWS Management**

Console access for browser-based access.

4. Configure permissions (more on that in the Policies section).

5. Review and create the user. The user will receive an **Access Key ID** and **Secret Access Key** (if programmatic access is enabled).

2. IAM Groups

An **IAM group** is a collection of IAM users that share the same set of permissions. Groups allow you to assign a set of permissions to multiple users at once, simplifying access management.

- **Benefits of Using Groups**:
    - Easier to manage: Instead of assigning permissions to each user individually, you can create groups for users with similar roles (e.g., Admin, Developer, or ReadOnly) and assign permissions at the group level.
    - Centralized management: Any permission granted to a group automatically applies to all users within that group.

- **Creating an IAM Group**:
    1. Go to the **IAM Dashboard** and click on **Groups**.

    2. Click **Create New Group** and enter the group name.

3. Attach existing IAM policies that reflect the permissions the group requires. For example:
- **AdminAccess** for full administrative privileges.
- **PowerUserAccess** for users who need broad access but do not need permissions to manage users or billing.

4. After creating the group, you can add users to the group by selecting **Add Users to Group** from the group page.

- **Best Practices for Groups**:
  - Assign users to **groups based on roles** (e.g., Admins, Developers, Analysts).
  - Use **least privilege access**: Grant only the necessary permissions to each group.

3. IAM Policies

An **IAM policy** is a document that defines permissions for AWS resources. Policies specify what actions are allowed or denied on which resources, and under what conditions.

- **Types of IAM Policies**:
  - **Managed Policies**: These are pre-defined policies provided by AWS,

which you can attach to users, groups, or roles.
- **AWS Managed Policies**: Pre-built by AWS and recommended for most use cases (e.g., AdministratorAccess, ReadOnlyAccess).
- **Customer Managed Policies**: Custom policies created by you to define specific permissions tailored to your needs.

◦ **Inline Policies**: These are policies created specifically for a user, group, or role and are embedded directly into that entity. Unlike managed policies, inline policies are not reusable and are typically used for very specific use cases.

- **Creating and Attaching a Policy**:

    1. Go to the **IAM Dashboard** and select **Policies**.

    2. Click **Create Policy**.

    3. Use the **Visual Editor** to specify actions, resources, and conditions, or write the policy in **JSON format**.

    4. Review the policy and click **Create Policy**.

    5. After creating the policy, you

can attach it to a user, group, or role by selecting **Attach Policy**.

- **Policy Structure**: Policies are defined using JSON (JavaScript Object Notation). A basic policy structure includes:
    - **Version**: Specifies the policy version.
    - **Statement**: A list of individual permissions. Each statement includes:
        - **Effect**: Allow or deny the action.
        - **Action**: The AWS service action (e.g., s3:ListBucket).
        - **Resource**: The resources the policy applies to (e.g., an S3 bucket).
        - **Condition** (optional): Conditions under which the policy applies (e.g., only allow access from a specific IP range).
- **Example Policy** (Allowing Read-Only Access to S3):

json

Code

```
{
  "Version": "2012-10-17",
  "Statement": [
```

```json
{
    "Effect": "Allow",
    "Action": "s3:ListBucket",
    "Resource": "arn:aws:s3:::example-bucket"
  },
  {
    "Effect": "Allow",
    "Action": "s3:GetObject",
    "Resource": "arn:aws:s3:::example-bucket/*"
  }
 ]
}
```

4. IAM Roles

An **IAM role** is similar to a user but is meant to be assumed by trusted entities like AWS services, applications, or IAM users from different accounts. Roles are typically used for granting access to resources without sharing long-term credentials.

- **Use Cases for Roles**:
    - Allowing an **EC2 instance** to access other AWS resources (e.g., S3 buckets, DynamoDB).
    - Granting permissions to **cross-account access**.
    - Enabling **AWS Lambda functions**

to execute actions on other AWS services.

- **Creating an IAM Role**:

    1. Go to the **IAM Dashboard** and click **Roles**.

    2. Click **Create Role** and select the type of trusted entity (e.g., AWS service, another AWS account).

    3. Attach the required policies to define the permissions for the role.

    4. After creating the role, you can assign it to an EC2 instance, Lambda function, or other AWS services as needed.

5. Best Practices for IAM Users, Groups, and Policies

- **Use the principle of least privilege**: Assign only the permissions necessary for each user or group to perform their job functions.

- **Create IAM groups based on roles**: Instead of assigning permissions directly to users, use groups to simplify access management.

- **Enable MFA** for all IAM users, especially those with administrative access, to add an extra layer of security.

- **Monitor and audit IAM activity** using **AWS CloudTrail** to track changes to IAM configurations and detect any suspicious behavior.
- **Review permissions regularly**: Periodically audit user permissions and ensure they still align with the least privilege principle.

Summary

- **IAM Users** represent individuals or applications that interact with AWS resources.
- **IAM Groups** allow you to organize users with similar permissions, making it easier to manage large teams.
- **IAM Policies** define the specific permissions granted to users, groups, or roles, allowing you to control access to AWS resources.
- **IAM Roles** are used for granting permissions to AWS services or other accounts to perform specific tasks.

By understanding and using IAM effectively, you can securely manage access to your AWS resources and ensure that users and applications have the appropriate permissions.

Best Practices for Securing

Your AWS Account

Securing your AWS account is crucial to ensure that your resources, data, and services remain safe from unauthorized access and potential threats. AWS provides a variety of tools and best practices to help secure your account, ranging from enabling multi-factor authentication (MFA) to regularly auditing your usage. Below are some key best practices for securing your AWS account:

1. Enable Multi-Factor Authentication (MFA)

MFA adds an extra layer of security by requiring a second form of authentication, such as a mobile device or hardware token, in addition to your password.

- **Why MFA is important**:
  - Even if an attacker gains access to your password, they cannot access your AWS account without the second factor.
  - It helps protect high-privilege accounts like the root user and IAM users with administrative access.
- **How to enable MFA**:
  1. Sign in to the **AWS**

Management Console.

2. Navigate to **IAM** > **Users** and select the user.

3. Click on **Security Credentials** and then **Manage MFA Device**.

4. Follow the instructions to set up MFA using either a virtual MFA device (like Google Authenticator) or a hardware MFA device.

2. Use the Root User Sparingly

The **root user** has full administrative access to all AWS resources, so it is vital to secure this account and use it as little as possible.

- **Best practices for the root user**:
    - **Enable MFA** for the root user immediately upon account creation.
    - **Create individual IAM users** for day-to-day administration and limit the use of the root user for critical tasks such as billing and account management.
    - **Use IAM roles and permissions** to assign access to users and services instead of using the root user for regular activities.

3. Follow the Principle of Least Privilege

Grant only the necessary permissions that each user or service needs to perform their job or task. This minimizes the impact of any potential security breaches.

- **How to apply the least privilege principle**:
  - **Use IAM groups** to assign permissions to users with similar roles.
  - **Avoid giving full access or broad permissions** like *:* (all actions on all resources). Instead, define explicit permissions for the resources a user needs.
  - **Review permissions regularly** to ensure users and services still require access to resources.

4. Use IAM Roles for Service Access

For services that need to access AWS resources (e.g., EC2 instances, Lambda functions), use **IAM roles** instead of embedding access keys directly into the services or applications.

- **Benefits of IAM roles**:
  - Roles allow temporary credentials to be assumed, reducing the risk associated with long-lived keys.
  - You can control the permissions granted to services on a granular level (e.g., only allowing an EC2 instance to access a specific S3 bucket).

5. Implement AWS Identity Federation

If you use external identity providers (e.g., Active Directory, Google), **AWS Identity Federation** allows users to access AWS resources without the need to manage separate AWS credentials.

- **How identity federation enhances security**:
    - It leverages existing corporate authentication methods, reducing the need for additional passwords and improving password management.
    - Allows for **single sign-on (SSO)**, streamlining access across multiple AWS accounts and services.

6. Regularly Rotate and Manage Access Keys

Access keys are used for programmatic access to AWS services. Regularly rotating these keys helps mitigate the risk of key compromise.

- **Best practices for managing access keys**:
    - **Rotate keys regularly**: Ensure that access keys are rotated frequently to limit exposure.
    - **Delete unused keys**: If a key is no longer needed, ensure it is deactivated and deleted to reduce the attack surface.
    - **Use IAM roles** instead of access keys for services wherever possible.

7. Use AWS CloudTrail for Logging and Monitoring

AWS CloudTrail provides visibility into your AWS account's activities by logging all API calls made within your account.

- **How to use CloudTrail for security**:
    - Enable **CloudTrail logging** for all regions to capture a complete history of activity across your AWS account.
    - Set up **CloudTrail trails** to send logs to an S3 bucket for long-term storage and analysis.
    - Use **Amazon CloudWatch Logs** to create alerts based on CloudTrail events, allowing you to monitor suspicious or unauthorized activity.

8. Set Up CloudWatch Alarms and Metrics

CloudWatch provides a centralized way to collect and monitor metrics and logs for AWS resources. By setting up **CloudWatch Alarms**, you can get notified about unexpected activities.

- **How to use CloudWatch for security**:
    - Set up alarms for unexpected resource usage, such as a sudden spike in EC2 instances or S3 storage access.
    - Use **AWS Config** to track changes to AWS resources and ensure compliance with your security

policies.

- Set thresholds for alarming on certain activity levels (e.g., too many failed login attempts, or API calls exceeding normal usage patterns).

9. Enable AWS Shield and AWS WAF

AWS Shield and **AWS Web Application Firewall (WAF)** provide protection against common web exploits and DDoS (Distributed Denial of Service) attacks.

- **AWS Shield**: This service provides protection from DDoS attacks, ensuring that your AWS resources are not easily overwhelmed.
  - **AWS Shield Standard** is included at no additional cost.
  - **AWS Shield Advanced** provides enhanced protection and features like 24/7 DDoS response team access.
- **AWS WAF**: This helps protect your web applications by filtering and monitoring HTTP requests based on customizable rules.
  - Use WAF to block malicious traffic, such as SQL injection or cross-site scripting (XSS) attempts.

10. Use VPCs, Security Groups, and NACLs

Virtual Private Clouds (VPCs) allow you to isolate your AWS resources and define secure network boundaries.

- **VPC Best Practices**:
    - **Use private subnets** for sensitive workloads, ensuring that they are not exposed to the public internet.
    - Use **security groups** to control inbound and outbound traffic at the instance level, and configure **Network ACLs (NACLs)** for an additional layer of security at the subnet level.
    - Limit internet access to instances by placing them behind **Elastic Load Balancers (ELBs)** or using **NAT gateways**.

11. Perform Regular Security Audits and Penetration Testing

Regularly auditing your AWS account for security risks and conducting **penetration testing** can help identify vulnerabilities before attackers can exploit them.

- **Audit tools and practices**:
    - **AWS Trusted Advisor** provides recommendations for improving your account's security posture.
    - Use the **AWS Security Hub** to centralize security findings across multiple AWS accounts

and services.

- Regularly test for common vulnerabilities using automated tools or by hiring external security professionals.

12. Enable Encryption for Data at Rest and in Transit

Encrypting your data ensures that unauthorized users cannot access sensitive information.

- **Encryption best practices**:
    - Enable **encryption** for Amazon S3 buckets, Amazon EBS volumes, and RDS instances to ensure that data is protected at rest.
    - Use **SSL/TLS** for encrypting data in transit (e.g., between your application and AWS services).
    - Leverage **AWS KMS (Key Management Service)** to manage encryption keys securely.

13. Implement Billing and Cost Management Alerts

Unusual billing activity may indicate a potential security breach, such as unauthorized usage or unanticipated spikes in resource consumption.

- **How to manage billing alerts**:
    - Set up **AWS Budgets** to monitor costs and usage, and configure **billing alerts** to notify you if spending exceeds a defined threshold.

- Use **Cost Explorer** to track and analyze spending patterns over time.

Summary

By implementing these best practices, you can significantly improve the security of your AWS account and reduce the risk of unauthorized access, data loss, or potential breaches. Always stay vigilant, keep your AWS environment updated, and regularly review and refine your security policies to adapt to evolving threats.

Role-Based Access Control (RBAC) in AWS

Role-Based Access Control (RBAC) is a security model that restricts system access based on users' roles within an organization. In the context of AWS, RBAC allows administrators to manage permissions and access to resources by assigning roles to users or services, thus ensuring that individuals and systems only have access to the resources they need to perform their job functions. AWS leverages IAM (Identity and Access Management) to implement RBAC, which can be customized to enforce the least privilege principle.

Key Components of RBAC in AWS

1. **Users**: In AWS, users represent individual identities (human or programmatic) who need access to AWS resources. They are created under IAM, and permissions are granted based on the roles assigned to them.

2. **Roles**: A role is an AWS identity that has specific permissions. Unlike users, roles do not have long-term credentials (e.g., passwords or access keys) associated with them. Instead, roles are assumed by trusted entities (users, services, or applications) that need temporary access to resources. Roles define the **permissions policies** attached to them.

3. **Groups**: Groups are collections of users with similar roles and responsibilities. By placing users into groups, you can assign permissions to the entire group, which simplifies management, especially when many users require similar access rights.

4. **Permissions**: Permissions define what actions a user, group, or role can perform on specific resources. Permissions are typically granted via policies that define actions (e.g., s3:PutObject) and

resources (e.g., arn:aws:s3:::my-bucket/*).

5. **Policies**: Policies are documents that define permissions in a JSON format. They specify the actions (e.g., s3:GetObject), resources (e.g., arn:aws:s3:::my-bucket), and conditions (e.g., IP address restrictions) under which a user or role can perform certain operations.

RBAC in AWS: Key Concepts

1. IAM Policies and Permissions

- Policies are attached to roles, users, or groups to define access rights.
- **Managed Policies**: AWS provides predefined policies for common use cases (e.g., AdministratorAccess, ReadOnlyAccess).
- **Inline Policies**: These are policies created and directly attached to users, groups, or roles.

Example of an IAM Policy (JSON format):

json

Code

```
{
  "Version": "2012-10-17",
  "Statement": [
```

```
    {
      "Effect": "Allow",
      "Action": "s3:GetObject",
      "Resource": "arn:aws:s3:::my-bucket/*"
    }
  ]
}
```

This policy allows the user or role to perform the GetObject action on objects in the my-bucket S3 bucket.

2. Creating and Managing Roles

Roles can be created to represent different job functions, and permissions are associated with these roles to determine what resources a user or service can access.

- **IAM Role for EC2 Instances**: For example, an EC2 instance may require access to S3 to download data. A role is created with the necessary permissions, and this role is then assigned to the EC2 instance.

- **IAM Role for Cross-Account Access**: You can also create roles to allow resources in one AWS account to access resources in another account. In this case, the role defines permissions for actions across multiple AWS accounts.

3. Using Groups for Efficient Management

- **Creating IAM Groups**: Instead of assigning permissions to individual users, IAM groups allow you to group users with similar access requirements. For instance, a group could be created for **developers** with permissions to manage EC2 and S3 but not access sensitive resources like RDS or DynamoDB.

- **Best Practice**: By assigning permissions to groups rather than users, you can easily manage access for a large number of users with similar roles.

4. Role Assumption and Temporary Security Credentials

One of the core aspects of RBAC in AWS is the ability to **assume roles**. Users, services, or applications that need specific permissions can assume a role temporarily.

- **Assuming a Role**: AWS provides the capability for a user to assume a role for temporary access using the sts:AssumeRole API call.

- **Temporary Credentials**: When a user assumes a role, AWS issues temporary credentials (Access Key ID, Secret Access Key, and Session Token) that can be used for the duration of the role session.

5. Managing Role-Based Access with AWS Organizations

AWS Organizations helps manage multiple AWS accounts within an organization. You can centrally manage RBAC by applying service control policies (SCPs) that restrict access across accounts in an organization.

- **Service Control Policies (SCPs)**: SCPs provide a centralized way to control the maximum permissions that are available to AWS accounts within an organization.
- **Organizational Units (OUs)**: By organizing accounts into OUs, you can apply policies that limit what roles can be assumed across accounts, enhancing the security and management of access control.

Best Practices for Implementing RBAC in AWS

1. **Adopt the Least Privilege Principle**: Only grant users, groups, or roles the permissions they absolutely need to perform their tasks, and no more. Review permissions regularly to ensure they are still valid.

2. **Separate Administrative and User Roles**: Create separate roles for administrators and users, and only grant administrative access to those

who need it. This reduces the risk of misuse and accidental changes.

3. **Use Managed Policies**: Leverage AWS managed policies as much as possible since they are maintained by AWS and adhere to best practices. Create custom policies only when necessary.

4. **Limit Root User Usage**: The root user should have very limited usage. Create administrative roles for day-to-day tasks and restrict root access to essential functions only.

5. **Enable MFA for High Privilege Roles**: Always enable multi-factor authentication (MFA) for roles with high-level access, including root and administrative roles, to add an extra layer of security.

6. **Regularly Review and Audit Access**: Perform periodic audits of your IAM roles, groups, users, and policies to ensure that permissions align with the current business requirements.

7. **Use AWS IAM Access Analyzer**: This tool helps identify any resources in your AWS account that are shared with external entities, ensuring that there are no unintended access permissions.

Summary

Role-Based Access Control (RBAC) in AWS is a powerful way to manage and restrict access to your resources, helping ensure that only authorized users can perform specific actions. By understanding and implementing RBAC properly, you can greatly enhance the security and manageability of your AWS environment.

CHAPTER 3: COST MANAGEMENT AND BILLING

Understanding AWS Pricing Models

AWS offers a wide range of services and pricing models to accommodate various use cases and customer requirements. Understanding AWS pricing models is crucial for optimizing costs and ensuring that you're paying for only what you use. AWS pricing is generally based on the pay-as-you-go model, but there are several other pricing options and services that offer different ways to optimize costs.

1. Pay-As-You-Go (On-Demand)

- **Overview**: The most flexible pricing model, where you pay for the AWS resources you use without any long-term commitments. You are charged based on usage, typically by the second or hour.

- **Ideal for**: Short-term, unpredictable workloads, or when you do not want to commit to a long-term contract.

- **Examples**: EC2 instances, S3 storage, Lambda functions, RDS databases.

- **Benefits**:
  - No upfront payments or long-term commitments.
  - Scalability to match fluctuating needs.
  - Pay only for the actual usage.

2. Reserved Instances (RIs)

- **Overview**: Reserved Instances offer a discount compared to on-demand pricing in exchange for a one-year or three-year commitment. You reserve specific EC2 instance types in particular regions for a long-term contract.

- **Types of Reserved Instances**:
  - **Standard Reserved Instances**: Provide the highest discount but

require a fixed commitment.
- **Convertible Reserved Instances**: Allow you to change instance types during the term, offering more flexibility.
- **Scheduled Reserved Instances**: Reserved for specific time slots on a recurring basis.

- **Ideal for**: Long-term, steady-state applications where you can predict your resource usage.
- **Benefits**:
  - Significant cost savings (up to 75%) compared to on-demand pricing.
  - Flexible payment options (All Upfront, Partial Upfront, No Upfront).
- **Considerations**: Not suitable for unpredictable workloads as they require a commitment to a specific instance type and term length.

3. Spot Instances

- **Overview**: Spot Instances allow you to bid on unused EC2 capacity. AWS provides deep discounts (up to 90%) compared to on-demand pricing, but the catch is that AWS can terminate these instances with little notice if the demand for capacity increases.

- **Ideal for**: Flexible, interruption-tolerant workloads that can tolerate sudden instance termination, such as batch processing, data analysis, or rendering tasks.
- **Benefits**:
    - Huge cost savings compared to on-demand instances.
    - Access to unused EC2 capacity.
- **Considerations**:
    - Instances can be terminated with little notice.
    - May require architectural adjustments to handle interruptions.

4. Savings Plans

- **Overview**: Savings Plans offer flexible pricing by committing to a consistent amount of usage (measured in $/hour) for one or three years. Savings Plans apply to a wide variety of AWS services, such as EC2, Lambda, and Fargate, and are more flexible than Reserved Instances in terms of instance family, region, operating system, and tenancy.
- **Types of Savings Plans**:
    - **Compute Savings Plans**: Provide the most flexibility by applying to any EC2 instance, regardless of instance type, region, or

operating system.
- **EC2 Instance Savings Plans**: Apply to specific EC2 instance families within a region, offering a higher discount but less flexibility.

- **Ideal for**: Customers who are willing to commit to consistent compute usage but require flexibility across instance types or services.
- **Benefits**:
  - Simplified pricing and commitment structure compared to Reserved Instances.
  - Discounts on a broad range of AWS services.
- **Considerations**: Requires a predictable usage pattern over a longer period.

5. Free Tier

- **Overview**: AWS offers a **Free Tier** for new customers, providing free usage of certain services up to a specified limit for the first 12 months following account creation. Some services also offer a free tier that's available indefinitely.
- **Ideal for**: Testing and learning purposes, proof of concepts, or small-scale workloads.
- **Examples**:
  - **EC2**: 750 hours per month of

t2.micro instances.
- **S3**: 5GB of standard storage.
- **Lambda**: 1 million free requests per month.
- **Benefits**:
  - Allows new users to explore AWS services without incurring costs.
  - Good for small-scale development and experimentation.
- **Considerations**: After the free usage limit is exceeded, you will be charged according to the service's regular pricing model.

6. AWS Marketplace

- **Overview**: The AWS Marketplace is an online store where customers can buy software and services that run on AWS. The pricing for services in the Marketplace is set by third-party vendors and may follow different models (e.g., subscription, per-user, or per-hour).
- **Ideal for**: Organizations looking to quickly integrate third-party software solutions, such as security tools, analytics services, and machine learning models.
- **Benefits**:

- Access to pre-configured, ready-to-use solutions from independent software vendors (ISVs).
- Flexible pricing options to suit different use cases.

- **Considerations**: Pricing is based on the specific terms of each vendor, and costs can vary.

7. AWS Cost and Usage Reports

- **Overview**: AWS provides several tools to help you monitor and control your spending. These tools allow you to track costs, set budgets, and receive alerts when your usage or spending exceeds certain thresholds.

- **Key Tools**:
    - **AWS Cost Explorer**: A tool to visualize and analyze your AWS spending patterns.
    - **AWS Budgets**: Set custom budgets and receive alerts when costs exceed predefined limits.
    - **AWS Cost and Usage Report**: Detailed CSV reports that provide insights into how AWS resources are being used and their costs.

- **Ideal for**: Cost-conscious organizations that want to monitor and optimize their AWS spending in real-time.

- **Benefits**:
    - Provides detailed insights into AWS usage and spending.
    - Helps prevent surprise billing and allows for cost optimization.

8. Pricing Calculators and Tools

AWS provides several pricing calculators to estimate the cost of various services:

- **AWS Pricing Calculator**: A web-based tool that helps you estimate the cost of using different AWS services based on your projected usage.
- **AWS Total Cost of Ownership (TCO) Calculator**: Helps businesses compare the cost of running workloads on AWS versus traditional on-premises infrastructure.

Best Practices for Optimizing AWS Costs

1. **Right-sizing Resources**: Continuously monitor and adjust the size of your instances, databases, and other resources to avoid over-provisioning.
2. **Auto Scaling**: Use Auto Scaling to automatically adjust resource levels based on demand, ensuring you only pay for what you need.
3. **Use Reserved Instances and Savings Plans**: Commit to consistent usage

of resources to take advantage of significant discounts offered by Reserved Instances and Savings Plans.

4. **Leverage Spot Instances**: Use Spot Instances for flexible, interruption-tolerant workloads to achieve maximum savings.

5. **Optimize Storage**: Use appropriate storage classes for S3 (e.g., Standard, Intelligent-Tiering, Glacier) to save costs based on access frequency.

6. **Monitor Costs Regularly**: Use AWS Cost Explorer and Budgets to monitor usage, track costs, and identify areas for improvement.

Summary

AWS offers a variety of pricing models designed to suit different needs, from flexible on-demand pricing to long-term commitments that deliver substantial discounts. By understanding these models and applying best practices for cost optimization, you can effectively manage your AWS expenses and get the best value for your usage.

Using AWS Cost Explorer and Budgets

AWS provides a suite of tools to help you monitor and control your cloud costs. Among the most powerful tools are AWS Cost Explorer and AWS Budgets, both of which allow you to gain deep insights into your spending patterns, track your usage, and set financial goals. Here's how you can leverage these tools effectively:

1. AWS Cost Explorer

AWS Cost Explorer is a powerful tool that allows you to visualize, understand, and analyze your AWS costs and usage. It provides a set of features to help you track and manage your spending, identify trends, and find opportunities to optimize costs.

Key Features of AWS Cost Explorer:

- **Cost and Usage Reports**: View detailed reports of your usage and costs, broken down by different dimensions such as services, linked accounts, regions, and tags.
- **Filtering and Grouping**: Filter and group data by different parameters (e.g., service type, linked accounts, regions, or tags) to get a granular view of your AWS

costs.

- **Cost Allocation Tags**: Use cost allocation tags to track costs for specific projects, departments, or business units.

- **Time Granularity**: Choose between daily, monthly, or custom time frames to examine your costs over different periods.

- **Cost Forecasting**: AWS Cost Explorer includes forecasting capabilities to predict future costs based on historical usage and spending patterns.

How to Use AWS Cost Explorer:

1. **Accessing Cost Explorer**:
   - Log in to the **AWS Management Console**.
   - Navigate to the **Billing and Cost Management Dashboard**.
   - Select **Cost Explorer** from the left-hand menu.

2. **Creating Reports**:
   - **Create a Custom Report**: Choose the type of report you want to generate, such as a usage report or a cost report, and define filters such as linked accounts, time range, or services.
   - **Analyze Data**: Use different

views to visualize costs (e.g., pie charts, line graphs) to understand your spending patterns. Group by services, linked accounts, or other dimensions to pinpoint where your costs are coming from.

3. **Identifying Trends and Anomalies**:
    - Track cost fluctuations over time and identify anomalies that might indicate inefficient usage or unexpected cost spikes.

4. **Cost Allocation Tags**:
    - Use tags to group your resources and services by project, team, or department. This can help you track costs more effectively and allocate budgets accordingly.

5. **Setting Filters**:
    - You can filter cost data based on specific criteria such as account, service, or region, to focus on particular aspects of your AWS usage.

6. **Cost Forecasting**:
    - Cost Explorer can predict future costs based on past usage. This allows you to anticipate potential increases or decreases

in spending.

2. AWS Budgets

AWS Budgets is a tool that allows you to set custom cost and usage budgets and track how well you are adhering to those budgets. With AWS Budgets, you can receive alerts when your usage or spending exceeds or is forecasted to exceed your budgeted amount.

Key Features of AWS Budgets:

- **Customizable Budgets**: Create budgets for cost, usage, and reservation utilization, tailored to your needs.
- **Budget Alerts**: Set up alerts to notify you when your costs or usage exceed predefined thresholds. Alerts can be sent via email or SMS.
- **Forecasting**: AWS Budgets can forecast future costs and usage based on historical trends, helping you predict if you're on track to exceed your budget.
- **Cost Allocation by Tags**: Like Cost Explorer, you can track budget spending by cost allocation tags.

How to Use AWS Budgets:

1. **Accessing AWS Budgets**:
    - Log in to the **AWS Management Console**.
    - Navigate to the **Billing and Cost**

Management Dashboard.
- Select **Budgets** from the left-hand menu.

2. **Creating a Budget**:
    - Click on **Create a budget** and choose the type of budget you want to set up:
        - **Cost budget**: Set a maximum cost limit for your usage.
        - **Usage budget**: Track how much you are using specific AWS services.
        - **Reservation budget**: Track Reserved Instance or Savings Plan usage.
    - Define the budget parameters (e.g., cost amount, time period, services to track).
    - Set up alerts to notify you when your actual spending or usage exceeds your budget threshold.

3. **Setting Alerts**:
    - AWS Budgets allows you to set up multiple types of alerts based on your budget's status:
        - **Actual alert**: Notify you when actual costs exceed a specified threshold.
        - **Forecast alert**: Notify you

when your forecasted cost exceeds a threshold.
- You can choose to receive these alerts via **email** or **SMS** to stay informed in real-time.

4. **Viewing Budget Reports**:
   - Once a budget is set up, you can view detailed reports on how your spending is tracking against your budget. This can include insights into your current cost or usage, as well as forecasts for the coming months.

5. **Budget Tracking**:
   - AWS Budgets will continuously track your usage and spending against your defined budget. The tool provides an ongoing view of how you're performing relative to your budget, so you can adjust as necessary.

6. **Managing Multiple Budgets**:
   - AWS Budgets allows you to manage multiple budgets for different accounts, projects, or business units, and helps ensure you're not exceeding allocated funds.

3. Best Practices for Managing AWS Costs with

Cost Explorer and Budgets

1. **Regularly Monitor Usage and Costs**:
   - Make a habit of reviewing your AWS spending with Cost Explorer and Budgets. This helps to identify potential inefficiencies or unexpected charges early on.

2. **Set Realistic Budgets**:
   - Ensure your budgets are realistic and based on historical data. For new projects or services, use AWS's cost forecasting tools to predict costs and set initial budgets.

3. **Implement Cost Allocation Tags**:
   - Tag your AWS resources and services by project, team, or department. This allows you to track costs by these tags and make data-driven decisions on cost optimization.

4. **Set Alerts for Budget Exceedance**:
   - Set up multiple alerts to notify you when your spending is likely to exceed the budget threshold. This will give you time to take corrective action.

5. **Leverage Cost Optimization Tools**:

- Use AWS Trusted Advisor, AWS Compute Optimizer, and other AWS cost optimization services in combination with Cost Explorer and Budgets to proactively reduce costs.

6. **Forecast and Adjust**:
    - Use the forecasting features in both tools to predict future usage and spending. Regularly adjust budgets based on these predictions to keep costs within acceptable limits.

7. **Review and Optimize Reserved Instance and Savings Plan Usage**:
    - Use AWS Budgets to track Reserved Instances and Savings Plans to ensure you're optimizing your long-term commitments and getting the most value from your investments.

Summary

AWS Cost Explorer and AWS Budgets are invaluable tools for managing and optimizing cloud costs. By visualizing your costs, setting up detailed budgets, and tracking usage patterns, you can ensure that you're not only staying within your financial goals but also identifying opportunities to reduce unnecessary expenses. Regularly monitoring your AWS usage and setting up alerts can help you prevent unexpected cost overruns, enabling you to maximize the value of your AWS investment.

Strategies to Optimize Costs on AWS

Optimizing costs on AWS requires proactive management, smart decisions about resource allocation, and the use of AWS tools designed to reduce unnecessary spending. Here are some effective strategies for managing and optimizing your AWS costs:

1. Right-Sizing Resources

Right-sizing refers to adjusting the size of your compute instances, storage, and other resources to match the actual demand of your workloads.

- **Monitor Resource Utilization**: Use AWS CloudWatch and the **AWS Trusted Advisor** to identify underutilized resources, such as EC2 instances or RDS databases. For example, an EC2 instance might be provisioned with more CPU or memory than necessary, leading to wasted resources.

- **Scale Up or Down**: Adjust instance sizes based on the performance metrics and actual usage. You can either downsize instances when they are underused or scale them up when demand increases.
- **Use Auto Scaling**: Set up **Auto Scaling** for your EC2 instances, which automatically adjusts the number of instances based on traffic patterns and utilization.

2. Leverage Spot Instances and Savings Plans

AWS offers cost-effective pricing options that can help reduce overall costs:

- **Spot Instances**: AWS **Spot Instances** allow you to take advantage of unused EC2 capacity at a significantly reduced price (up to 90% savings). Spot Instances are ideal for non-mission-critical workloads, batch processing, and large-scale compute jobs that can tolerate interruptions.
- **Savings Plans**: **Savings Plans** offer significant savings (up to 72%) in exchange for committing to a certain level of usage (e.g., compute usage) for a 1- or 3-year term. You can choose from Compute, EC2 Instance, or other service-specific savings plans to match your

usage patterns.

- **Reserved Instances (RIs)**: For workloads with consistent usage, consider **Reserved Instances**, which allow you to commit to specific instance types and receive a discount in exchange for the commitment period (1 or 3 years).

3. Use EC2 Instance Types and Families Wisely

AWS provides various **EC2 instance families**, each optimized for different types of workloads. By selecting the right instance family, you can save on performance and cost.

- **General Purpose (e.g., t3, t4g)**: Suitable for workloads that require a balance of compute, memory, and networking.
- **Compute-Optimized (e.g., c5, c6g)**: Ideal for high-performance computing and workloads requiring significant CPU.
- **Memory-Optimized (e.g., r5, r6g)**: Best for memory-intensive applications such as databases or big data analytics.
- **Consider Graviton2 Instances**: AWS **Graviton2 instances** powered by ARM architecture offer lower costs and better performance for certain workloads. They are suitable for web servers, containerized applications, and microservices.

4. Optimize Storage Costs

Storage is often a significant cost component in cloud environments. AWS provides several options for optimizing storage costs:

- **Use S3 Storage Classes**: AWS **S3** offers multiple storage classes with varying costs based on access frequency:
    - **S3 Standard**: For frequently accessed data.
    - **S3 Intelligent-Tiering**: Automatically moves data between frequent and infrequent access tiers.
    - **S3 Glacier and S3 Glacier Deep Archive**: Cost-effective storage for archival and long-term data that is rarely accessed.
- **Delete Unused Data**: Regularly audit your data storage and remove unused or obsolete data. Implement data lifccycle policies to automatically transition older data to cheaper storage tiers or delete it when no longer needed.
- **EBS Volume Optimization**: Use **EBS volume types** appropriately, and ensure you're using **EBS snapshots** to back up volumes without incurring excessive storage costs. Delete unused EBS volumes and snapshots.

5. Implement Auto Scaling and Elastic Load

Balancing

- **Auto Scaling**: Automatically adjust the number of EC2 instances based on demand, ensuring you only pay for what you use. With Auto Scaling, resources are added during peak times and reduced when demand decreases.

- **Elastic Load Balancer (ELB)**: Use ELB to distribute traffic across multiple EC2 instances efficiently. This can help prevent over-provisioning of compute resources and ensure efficient use of capacity.

6. Optimize Data Transfer Costs

Data transfer can become a hidden cost in AWS. To optimize these costs:

- **Use CloudFront**: AWS **CloudFront** is a content delivery network (CDN) that caches static content closer to end users, reducing data transfer costs from origin servers and improving performance.

- **Consider Cross-Region Data Transfer**: Avoid unnecessary cross-region data transfer, which can incur additional costs. If possible, keep data and applications in the same region.

- **Use VPC Peering and Direct Connect**: For internal data transfers, use **VPC**

peering or **AWS Direct Connect** to reduce costs associated with transferring data across the internet.

7. Monitor and Analyze Costs Regularly

- **Cost Explorer**: Use **AWS Cost Explorer** to identify trends, track spending, and pinpoint areas for potential savings. Regularly monitor and adjust based on insights.

- **AWS Budgets**: Set up **AWS Budgets** to receive alerts when your costs exceed thresholds. This ensures you can take corrective actions before exceeding your budget.

- **AWS Trusted Advisor**: This service provides recommendations for cost optimization, including idle resources, underutilized services, and suggestions for Reserved Instances or Savings Plans.

8. Use Serverless Architectures

Serverless computing services, such as **AWS Lambda**, allow you to run code without provisioning or managing servers, which can significantly reduce costs.

- **AWS Lambda**: Pay only for the compute time you use, and automatically scale based on the number of requests. This is ideal for event-driven applications or microservices.

- **Amazon API Gateway**: Pair Lambda with **API Gateway** to build scalable and cost-efficient APIs without needing dedicated EC2 instances.

- **AWS Fargate**: A serverless compute engine for containers, **Fargate** allows you to run containers without managing servers. It automatically scales based on demand, helping you reduce over-provisioning.

9. Use Elastic File System (EFS) and Elastic Block Store (EBS) Wisely

- **Elastic File System (EFS)**: Use **EFS** for scalable and cost-effective file storage. EFS automatically scales to accommodate workloads, which helps prevent over-provisioning.

- **Elastic Block Store (EBS)**: For persistent storage, optimize the use of EBS. Use the correct EBS volume type for your workloads, and delete any unused volumes to prevent unnecessary costs.

10. Review and Reassess Regularly

- **Audit Your Resources**: Regularly perform audits to check for underutilized or orphaned resources (e.g., unused Elastic IPs, unattached

EBS volumes, etc.), which can incur unnecessary charges.

- **Take Advantage of New Features**: AWS constantly releases new services and pricing models. Regularly review new cost optimization features and tools to ensure you're leveraging the latest solutions.

Summary

Cost optimization on AWS is an ongoing process that requires careful monitoring, right-sizing, and leveraging AWS pricing options such as Spot Instances, Reserved Instances, and Savings Plans. By adopting these strategies, you can ensure that your AWS infrastructure remains cost-effective while meeting the performance needs of your workloads. Regularly assess your usage and adjust your resources to avoid wastage and maintain an efficient and scalable cloud environment.

PART 2: CORE AWS SERVICES

CHAPTER 4: COMPUTE SERVICES

Amazon EC2: Launching and Managing Instances

Amazon Elastic Compute Cloud (Amazon EC2) is one of the core services provided by AWS, enabling you to run virtual machines (called "instances") in the cloud. EC2 instances are scalable, customizable, and integral for running applications and workloads on AWS. This section will guide you through the process of launching and managing EC2 instances effectively.

1. Understanding EC2 Instance Types

Before launching an EC2 instance, it's essential

to choose the right instance type based on your workload requirements. EC2 instances come in various types, categorized by compute, memory, storage, and networking capacities. Common instance types include:

- **General Purpose Instances**: e.g., t3, t4g (balanced CPU, memory, and network resources).
- **Compute-Optimized Instances**: e.g., c5, c6g (high performance for compute-intensive tasks).
- **Memory-Optimized Instances**: e.g., r5, r6g (ideal for memory-intensive applications).
- **Storage-Optimized Instances**: e.g., i3, d2 (high storage and I/O performance).
- **Accelerated Computing Instances**: e.g., p4, inf1 (GPU or FPGA optimized for machine learning and deep learning workloads).

2. Launching an EC2 Instance

Step 1: Sign in to AWS Management Console

1. Go to the AWS Management Console.
2. Navigate to **EC2** under the "Compute" section.

Step 2: Choose an Amazon Machine Image (AMI)

An **AMI** is a pre-configured template containing an operating system (OS) and optional software packages.

- Select an AMI based on your needs (e.g., **Amazon Linux 2**, **Windows Server**, or popular Linux distributions such as **Ubuntu** or **Red Hat**).

Step 3: Choose an Instance Type

1. Select the **instance type** based on your workload requirements.
2. For starters, you may opt for the **t3.micro** instance, which is eligible for the **AWS Free Tier** (if you are a new AWS customer).
3. Click **Next: Configure Instance Details**.

Step 4: Configure Instance Details

Here, you can define various parameters for your instance, such as:

- **Number of Instances**: Set the number of instances you want to launch.
- **Network**: Choose the **Virtual Private Cloud (VPC)** and subnet for the instance.
- **IAM Role**: Assign an **IAM role** if your instance requires access to AWS services.
- **Monitoring**: Enable **CloudWatch Monitoring** for performance metrics.
- **Shutdown Behavior**: Define the

instance's behavior when it's shut down (Stop/Terminate).

- **Advanced Details**: Customize additional options like user data scripts or cloud-init settings for configuration.

Click **Next: Add Storage**.

Step 5: Add Storage

1. By default, an EBS volume is created when an EC2 instance is launched. You can add more volumes if required.

2. Choose the **EBS volume type** (e.g., General Purpose SSD, Provisioned IOPS SSD, or Magnetic).

3. Adjust the **size** of the volume to fit your storage needs.

Click **Next: Add Tags**.

Step 6: Add Tags

1. Tags are useful for organizing and identifying your resources. For example, you can add a tag with the name of your instance.

2. A common tag is Name = <InstanceName>.

Click **Next: Configure Security Group**.

Step 7: Configure Security Group

1. A **Security Group** acts as a virtual

firewall to control inbound and outbound traffic to your instance.

2. You can either select an existing security group or create a new one.
    - Add inbound rules for protocols such as **SSH** (port 22) for Linux instances or **RDP** (port 3389) for Windows instances.
    - **HTTP (port 80)** and **HTTPS (port 443)** are commonly added for web servers.
3. Ensure that your security group is properly configured to allow access only to trusted IP addresses.

Click **Review and Launch**.

Step 8: Review and Launch

1. Review all your configurations and instance details.
2. Click **Launch** to proceed.
3. A **key pair** is required to securely connect to your instance. If you don't have a key pair, create a new one:
    - Select **Create a new key pair**.
    - Download the private key file (.pem), which will be used to connect to your instance via SSH.
    - Click **Launch Instances**.

3. Managing EC2 Instances

After your EC2 instance is up and running, you can manage it with various actions. Below are common tasks:

Connect to Your EC2 Instance

- **Linux Instances**: Use **SSH** to connect. Run the following command in your terminal:

bash

Code

ssh -i <path-to-your-key.pem> ec2-user@<instance-public-ip>

- **Windows Instances**: Use **Remote Desktop Protocol (RDP)**. First, retrieve the **Administrator password** by decrypting it using the key pair you downloaded during instance creation.

Stop and Start EC2 Instances

- **Stopping** an instance temporarily shuts it down but retains data on the attached volumes.
- **Starting** an instance powers it back up and restores the previous state.

Terminate EC2 Instances

- **Termination** permanently deletes an EC2 instance and releases the resources associated with it, including IP addresses and storage (unless they are attached as persistent volumes).

Modify EC2 Instances

- **Resize**: You can change the instance type at any time if your instance's resources need adjustment.
- **Change Security Group**: Attach or detach security groups based on access requirements.
- **Reboot**: Reboots the EC2 instance, which is equivalent to restarting the server.

Monitoring EC2 Instances

- Use **CloudWatch** to monitor performance metrics such as CPU utilization, disk I/O, and network traffic.
- Set up **CloudWatch Alarms** to receive notifications when specific thresholds (e.g., CPU usage) are breached.

Backup and Restore

- **Snapshots**: You can take **snapshots** of EC2 instances (EBS volumes) for backup purposes, enabling quick recovery in case of failure.
- **AMI Creation**: Create an **Amazon Machine Image (AMI)** of your instance, which can be used to launch identical copies of your instance.

4. Auto Scaling EC2 Instances

AWS **Auto Scaling** allows you to automatically adjust the number of EC2 instances based on the demand. This is useful for applications with variable traffic loads, such as websites that experience seasonal spikes.

- **Launch Configuration**: Define the configuration for your instances, including instance type, AMI, and other parameters.
- **Auto Scaling Groups**: Group instances that you want to scale together. Set rules for scaling (e.g., adding more instances when CPU usage exceeds 70%).

5. Best Practices for Managing EC2 Instances

- **Use EC2 Auto Scaling** to maintain optimal capacity while minimizing costs.
- **Tag Instances** for easier management, especially in large environments.
- **Use Elastic IPs** if you need static IP addresses for your instances.
- **Implement Monitoring and Alerts** using CloudWatch to keep track of your instance's health and performance.
- **Secure Your Instances** by restricting inbound traffic through security groups and using key pairs for SSH access.

Summary

Launching and managing EC2 instances involves understanding your workload requirements, selecting appropriate instance types, configuring security, and using AWS tools like **Auto Scaling** and **CloudWatch** to optimize performance and costs. With the ability to scale, modify, and monitor instances efficiently, EC2 provides the flexibility and power needed for a wide range of applications in the cloud.

AWS Lambda: Serverless Computing

AWS Lambda is a powerful, serverless compute service that enables you to run code without the need to manage servers. It automatically manages the compute resources required for running your code, scaling it based on demand. Lambda is a key component of the serverless computing model, where you focus on writing and deploying functions rather than managing infrastructure. This section will guide you through the basics of AWS Lambda, its benefits, how to set it up, and common use cases.

1. Understanding AWS Lambda

AWS Lambda is designed to run code in response to various triggers, such as HTTP requests, file uploads, database changes, or messages from other AWS services. The key concepts of Lambda include:

- **Function**: A small, self-contained piece of code written in a supported programming language (e.g., Python, Node.js, Java, Go).
- **Event**: A trigger that causes the Lambda function to run, such as an S3 file upload or an API Gateway request.
- **Execution Role**: An IAM role that grants Lambda the permissions it needs to interact with other AWS services on your behalf.
- **Timeout**: The maximum duration Lambda will allow the function to run (up to 15 minutes per invocation).

AWS Lambda is a stateless service, which means it does not retain data between invocations unless explicitly configured to use external storage (e.g., Amazon S3 or DynamoDB).

2. Benefits of AWS Lambda

AWS Lambda offers numerous benefits that make it ideal for certain workloads:

- **No Server Management**: With Lambda, you don't need to provision, manage, or scale servers. You only focus on the code itself.

- **Automatic Scaling**: Lambda automatically scales your function to handle a large number of requests, scaling down when demand decreases.
- **Cost Efficiency**: You pay only for the compute time your code consumes, based on the number of requests and execution duration, eliminating the need to pay for idle resources.
- **Event-Driven**: Lambda can be triggered by events from AWS services, providing flexibility for real-time processing and automation.
- **Support for Multiple Languages**: AWS Lambda supports several programming languages, including Node.js, Python, Ruby, Java, C#, Go, and custom runtimes.

3. Setting Up AWS Lambda

Setting up an AWS Lambda function is straightforward. Here are the basic steps to create your first Lambda function:

Step 1: Sign in to the AWS Management Console

1. Go to the AWS Lambda console.
2. Click on **Create Function**.

Step 2: Choose a Blueprint (Optional)

AWS Lambda offers several **blueprints** that can serve as templates for common use cases (e.g., invoking an API or processing S3 events). If you are new to Lambda, you can start with a blueprint or create a function from scratch.

Step 3: Configure Your Function

1. **Function Name**: Give your function a unique name (e.g., MyFirstLambdaFunction).

2. **Runtime**: Choose the programming language runtime (e.g., Python 3.x, Node.js 14.x, Java 11).

3. **Execution Role**: Select an IAM role that grants Lambda permissions to access other AWS services. You can either choose an existing role or create a new one with appropriate policies.

Step 4: Write Your Code

1. In the **Function code** section, write or upload the code for your Lambda function. If you're writing the code in the console, you can enter it directly or upload a zip file containing your code and dependencies.

2. For example, a simple Python function might look like this:

python

Code

```python
def lambda_handler(event, context):
    return {
        'statusCode': 200,
        'body': 'Hello from AWS Lambda!'
    }
```

Step 5: Set Your Trigger (Optional)

1. Lambda functions can be triggered by various AWS services, such as S3, DynamoDB, or API Gateway.
2. For example, you can trigger the function with an **API Gateway** to expose a RESTful API or configure it to process new objects uploaded to an **S3 bucket**.

Step 6: Test the Function

1. You can create a test event by clicking the **Test** button in the Lambda console. Provide sample input based on your event type (e.g., S3 event data, API request payload).
2. After running the function, review the output and logs to ensure it behaves as expected.

Step 7: Deploy the Function

Once your function is configured and tested, you can deploy it and configure more triggers or monitoring settings as needed.

4. Managing AWS Lambda Functions

After deploying your Lambda function, you can manage it by:

- **Monitoring Logs**: AWS Lambda integrates with **Amazon CloudWatch Logs**, allowing you to view logs for each invocation of your function, track performance metrics, and troubleshoot issues.

- **Setting Environment Variables**: You can define environment variables (e.g., API keys, configuration settings) that your Lambda function can access during execution.

- **Versioning and Aliases**: Lambda supports versioning, which allows you to publish and manage multiple versions of your function. You can also create aliases (e.g., prod, dev) to point to different versions.

5. Common Use Cases for AWS Lambda

AWS Lambda is versatile and can be used in a variety of scenarios. Here are some common use cases:

1. Real-Time File Processing

Lambda can be triggered by events such as new file uploads to an **S3 bucket**. For example, when an image or document is uploaded, Lambda can process the file (e.g., resizing images, converting file formats).

2. API Backend

Lambda can work in conjunction with **Amazon API Gateway** to create RESTful APIs. This is ideal for microservices architectures where individual Lambda functions handle specific operations (e.g., retrieving data from a database or performing calculations).

3. Data Streaming

Lambda can process streaming data from services like **Kinesis** or **DynamoDB Streams**. This is useful for real-time analytics, processing logs, or handling IoT data streams.

4. Automation and Orchestration

Lambda can be used for automation tasks, such as automatically provisioning resources, sending notifications, or scaling infrastructure based on events. For example, you can automatically terminate idle EC2 instances at night or scale up services when traffic increases.

5. Scheduled Tasks

Lambda integrates with **Amazon CloudWatch Events** to schedule functions to run at specified intervals (e.g., cron jobs). This is useful for periodic tasks like data backups, database maintenance, or cleanup operations.

6. Best Practices for AWS Lambda

Here are some best practices for working with AWS Lambda:

- **Optimize Cold Start Times**: Lambda functions experience "cold starts" when invoked for the first time or after being idle for a while. To minimize the cold start time, keep your functions small, optimize dependencies, and use the appropriate runtime.

- **Use Proper Resource Allocation**: Allocate sufficient memory to your Lambda function to avoid performance bottlenecks. Lambda scales based on memory, so adequate resource allocation improves performance.

- **Avoid Large Deployments**: Keep your Lambda functions lightweight by avoiding large deployments or unnecessary libraries in the deployment package.

- **Implement Error Handling**: Include error handling in your Lambda functions to gracefully handle failures and retry operations when needed.

- **Secure Your Functions**: Use IAM roles with the minimum necessary permissions for your Lambda function. Avoid using overly permissive roles that may lead to security risks.

Summary

AWS Lambda provides an efficient, cost-effective, and scalable solution for building serverless applications. With the ability to automatically scale and only charge for compute time used, Lambda is an excellent choice for event-driven architectures, real-time data processing, and microservices. By following best practices and understanding common use cases, you can effectively leverage Lambda to streamline your cloud-based applications and workflows.

AWS Elastic Beanstalk: Simplified Application Deployment

AWS Elastic Beanstalk is a fully managed service that simplifies the process of deploying and managing applications in the cloud. It abstracts much of the infrastructure management, enabling developers to focus on writing code and building features instead of worrying about the underlying infrastructure. Elastic Beanstalk supports a variety of programming languages, frameworks, and application platforms, making it a versatile tool for application deployment. This section will guide you through the basics of AWS Elastic Beanstalk, its features, and how to deploy applications using this service.

1. Understanding AWS Elastic Beanstalk

AWS Elastic Beanstalk is a Platform-as-a-Service (PaaS) offering that handles all the deployment and provisioning of infrastructure resources. Key features of Elastic Beanstalk include:

- **Automatic Scaling**: Elastic Beanstalk automatically adjusts the number of EC2 instances and other resources based on traffic, ensuring high availability and performance.

- **Managed Environment**: Elastic Beanstalk takes care of all the underlying resources such as EC2 instances, load balancers, databases, and more.

- **Multiple Platform Support**: Elastic Beanstalk supports several programming languages and frameworks, including Java, .NET, Node.js, Python, Ruby, PHP, Go, and Docker.

- **Easy Deployment**: You can deploy applications to Elastic Beanstalk via the AWS Management Console, AWS CLI, or directly from an integrated development environment (IDE).

- **Environment Configuration**: Elastic Beanstalk provides an easy-to-use configuration environment where you can manage your application settings, monitor health, and handle versioning.

2. Benefits of Using AWS Elastic Beanstalk

Elastic Beanstalk provides several advantages to developers and organizations:

- **Simplicity and Speed**: Elastic Beanstalk abstracts away the complexities of managing infrastructure, allowing developers to quickly deploy their applications and focus on coding.

- **Cost-Effective**: Since you only pay for the AWS resources you use, Elastic Beanstalk offers cost savings by scaling resources up and down based on demand.

- **Flexibility**: You can still configure and customize the environment to meet your application's needs, using both the AWS Management Console and AWS CLI.

- **Integrated Monitoring**: Elastic Beanstalk provides integrated monitoring tools to track application health, performance metrics, and logs.

- **Version Management**: It supports

versioning of your applications, so you can deploy new versions, roll back to previous versions, or manage multiple versions of your application.

- **Environment Isolation**: You can create multiple environments for different stages of development (e.g., development, staging, production), each with its own configuration.

3. Setting Up AWS Elastic Beanstalk

Deploying an application using AWS Elastic Beanstalk involves a few simple steps. Here's how to get started:

Step 1: Sign in to AWS Management Console

1. Go to the AWS Management Console.
2. Navigate to **Elastic Beanstalk** in the **Services** menu.

Step 2: Create a New Application

1. In the Elastic Beanstalk console, click on **Create New Application**.
2. Provide a name and description for your application.
3. Choose the platform that corresponds to your application (e.g., Node.js, Python, Java, Docker).

Step 3: Choose Environment Tier

Elastic Beanstalk offers two types of

environment tiers:

- **Web Server Environment**: Suitable for web applications with HTTP(S) traffic.
- **Worker Environment**: Ideal for background tasks, such as processing messages from SQS or jobs from an S3 bucket.

Choose the environment tier based on your application's needs.

Step 4: Upload Application Code

1. Click **Upload Your Code** to provide the application code (e.g., a ZIP file containing your app's source code).
2. Elastic Beanstalk will automatically detect the platform and configure the environment accordingly.

Step 5: Configure Environment Settings

1. Set environment variables, scaling settings, and more.
2. Configure monitoring and logging preferences, such as CloudWatch metrics and log files.

Step 6: Deploy Your Application

1. After configuring your environment, click **Create environment** to deploy your application.
2. Elastic Beanstalk will provision all the

necessary resources (EC2, load balancer, database, etc.), deploy your code, and make your application live.

4. Managing and Monitoring AWS Elastic Beanstalk Applications

After deploying your application, AWS Elastic Beanstalk provides several tools to manage and monitor the application:

1. Elastic Beanstalk Console

The **Elastic Beanstalk Management Console** provides a user-friendly interface where you can:

- View the health and performance of your application.
- Update configurations, such as environment variables and scaling options.
- Deploy new versions of your application.
- Roll back to previous application versions if needed.

2. AWS CloudWatch Integration

Elastic Beanstalk automatically integrates with **Amazon CloudWatch**, allowing you to monitor application performance, request counts, error rates, and more. You can set up alarms for critical thresholds (e.g., CPU utilization, memory usage).

3. Elastic Load Balancing

Elastic Beanstalk automatically provisions an

Elastic Load Balancer (ELB) to distribute incoming traffic across multiple EC2 instances, ensuring high availability and fault tolerance.

4. Logs and Monitoring

Elastic Beanstalk provides access to application logs, which can be accessed directly through the console or via Amazon CloudWatch Logs. You can configure detailed logging for better debugging and operational insights.

5. Updating and Rolling Back

To deploy new versions, you can upload updated code to Elastic Beanstalk, and the service will automatically handle the deployment process. If an issue arises, you can easily roll back to a previous version with a few clicks.

5. Common Use Cases for AWS Elastic Beanstalk

AWS Elastic Beanstalk is ideal for a wide range of applications, including:

1. Web Application Deployment

Elastic Beanstalk is commonly used to deploy web applications, such as content management systems (CMS), customer-facing websites, and microservices-based applications.

2. API Backend Services

If you're building APIs using frameworks like **Node.js**, **Django**, or **Spring**, Elastic Beanstalk makes it easy to deploy backend services without worrying about managing the infrastructure.

3. Multi-Tier Applications

Elastic Beanstalk can support applications that use multiple tiers (e.g., frontend, backend, and database). You can easily set up an environment with load balancing for the web tier and auto-scaling for backend services.

4. DevOps and Continuous Integration/Continuous Delivery (CI/CD)

Elastic Beanstalk integrates seamlessly with CI/CD pipelines, allowing developers to deploy code automatically whenever changes are pushed to a source code repository (e.g., GitHub, AWS CodeCommit).

6. Best Practices for AWS Elastic Beanstalk

To get the most out of AWS Elastic Beanstalk, follow these best practices:

- **Use Environment Variables**: Store configuration settings, secrets, and credentials in environment variables to keep your application secure and flexible.

- **Automate Deployments**: Integrate Elastic Beanstalk with your CI/CD pipeline to automate application deployment and streamline the development process.

- **Monitor Application Health**: Use

CloudWatch and Elastic Beanstalk's built-in health checks to ensure your application is running smoothly.

- **Scale with Demand**: Set up auto-scaling to ensure your application can handle varying traffic levels without manual intervention.

- **Use Elastic Beanstalk Extensions (EB Extensions)**: For more advanced configurations, use **EB Extensions** to customize the environment and automate tasks such as installing additional software or configuring the web server.

Summary

AWS Elastic Beanstalk provides a simplified, managed environment for deploying and managing web applications, APIs, and other services in the cloud. With its automatic scaling, integrated monitoring, and broad support for programming languages and frameworks, it offers a great solution for developers looking to focus on building applications rather than managing infrastructure. By following best practices and leveraging Elastic Beanstalk's features, you can efficiently deploy and maintain applications that scale and perform well in the cloud.

CHAPTER 5: STORAGE SERVICES

Amazon S3: Object Storage Basics and Advanced Features

Amazon Simple Storage Service (Amazon S3) is one of the most widely used services in AWS for storing and managing large amounts of data. It is an object storage service that provides high durability, availability, and scalability for storing various types of data, including media files, backups, logs, and much more. This section will explore the basics of Amazon S3, its core features, and some advanced functionalities that can help you optimize storage and manage your data effectively.

1. Understanding Amazon S3

Amazon S3 is a fully managed object storage service designed to store large amounts of unstructured data. It allows you to store and retrieve any amount of data from anywhere on the web, with minimal latency and high throughput.

- **Object Storage**: Unlike block storage (e.g., Amazon EBS) or file storage (e.g., Amazon EFS), Amazon S3 stores data as objects. Each object consists of the data itself, metadata, and a unique identifier (key). Objects are organized in **buckets**, which act as containers for the data.

- **Durability and Availability**: Amazon S3 provides 99.999999999% (11 nines) durability over a given year, meaning your data is highly reliable and safe from loss due to hardware failures or outages.

- **Scalability**: S3 can scale seamlessly to accommodate petabytes of data and millions of requests per second, making it suitable for a wide range of applications, from personal backups to enterprise-scale data management.

- **Security**: With built-in encryption, access control mechanisms, and logging,

Amazon S3 allows you to securely store and manage sensitive data.

2. Basic Concepts in Amazon S3

Buckets

- **Definition**: A bucket is a container for storing objects in S3. Each bucket has a globally unique name and can hold an unlimited amount of data.
- **Naming**: Bucket names must be unique across all AWS accounts globally. Bucket names must follow specific rules (e.g., only lowercase letters, numbers, and hyphens).

Objects

- **Definition**: An object in S3 is a piece of data stored in a bucket. It consists of:
    - **Data**: The actual content of the object (e.g., a file, image, or document).
    - **Metadata**: Custom or system-provided information about the object (e.g., creation date, owner).
    - **Key**: A unique identifier used to access the object within a bucket (similar to a file name).
- **Storage Class**: Objects in S3 can be stored in different storage classes based on access patterns (e.g., **Standard**, **Intelligent-Tiering**, **Glacier**).

S3 Keys

- Every object in S3 is uniquely identified by a **key**, which is its name within a bucket. The key is used to retrieve the object from S3. Keys can include directories (using slashes) to organize data, but S3 is fundamentally a flat storage system.

3. Core Features of Amazon S3

1. Data Security

- **Encryption**: S3 provides encryption at rest and in transit. You can choose to enable server-side encryption (SSE) using **SSE-S3**, **SSE-KMS**, or **SSE-C** for encrypting objects at rest. You can also enable **SSL/TLS** for data in transit.

- **Access Control**: S3 uses **AWS Identity and Access Management (IAM)** policies, **bucket policies**, and **Access Control Lists (ACLs)** to define access permissions to buckets and objects.

- **Versioning**: S3 supports versioning, allowing you to keep multiple versions of an object in the same bucket. This is useful for maintaining data history and enabling data recovery.

2. Storage Classes

- Amazon S3 provides different **storage**

classes to optimize costs based on access frequency:

- **S3 Standard**: High durability and availability for frequently accessed data.
- **S3 Intelligent-Tiering**: Automatically moves data between two access tiers (frequent and infrequent) to optimize cost.
- **S3 Standard-IA (Infrequent Access)**: Low-cost storage for infrequently accessed data.
- **S3 Glacier**: Archival storage for data that is rarely accessed, with retrieval times ranging from minutes to hours.
- **S3 Glacier Deep Archive**: Lowest-cost storage for long-term archiving, with retrieval times up to 12 hours.

3. Lifecycle Management

- S3 offers **lifecycle policies** that allow you to automatically transition objects between storage classes or delete objects after a specified period of time. This helps you manage costs and optimize data storage by automatically moving rarely accessed data to cheaper storage classes.

4. Data Access

- **Pre-signed URLs**: S3 allows you to generate temporary URLs for secure access to private objects. These URLs can be used for sharing objects with users without requiring them to have AWS credentials.
- **S3 Select**: Enables you to retrieve a subset of data from an object (e.g., CSV, JSON) using SQL queries, reducing the amount of data transferred and improving application performance.

5. Event Notifications

- Amazon S3 can trigger notifications to other AWS services (e.g., Lambda, SNS, SQS) based on object actions like uploads, deletions, or modifications. This allows you to automate workflows and integrate S3 with other services.

4. Advanced Features of Amazon S3

1. Cross-Region Replication (CRR)

- **CRR** enables automatic, asynchronous replication of objects across S3 buckets in different AWS regions. This provides geographic redundancy, improves data availability, and supports disaster recovery scenarios.

2. S3 Transfer Acceleration

- **Transfer Acceleration** improves the

upload and download speeds of objects to and from S3 by utilizing Amazon CloudFront's globally distributed edge locations. This is useful for large files or applications that require faster data transfers across the globe.

3. S3 Batch Operations

- **Batch Operations** allow you to perform bulk operations on millions or billions of objects in your S3 buckets. You can copy, tag, restore, or delete objects in large volumes using a simple API call or through the S3 console.

4. S3 Object Locking

- **S3 Object Locking** helps protect objects from being deleted or overwritten for a specified retention period. This feature is useful for compliance with regulations like the SEC Rule 17a-4(f) and other legal retention requirements.

5. S3 Replication and Versioning

- S3 supports **versioning** to retain previous versions of objects. Combined with **cross-region replication (CRR)**, versioning allows for maintaining historical records of data across regions and protecting against accidental deletions.

5. Best Practices for Using Amazon S3

- **Use Versioning**: Enable versioning to safeguard against accidental overwrites or deletions of critical data.

- **Optimize Storage Costs**: Take advantage of storage classes like **S3 Glacier** for archival data or **S3 Intelligent-Tiering** for automatically optimizing costs based on usage patterns.

- **Implement Proper Access Control**: Use IAM policies, bucket policies, and ACLs to ensure only authorized users and applications have access to your data. Always follow the principle of least privilege.

- **Enable Logging**: Use **S3 access logs** and integrate with CloudWatch to monitor and analyze access patterns to your S3 data.

- **Backup and Replication**: Use **Cross-Region Replication** (CRR) or **Cross-Availability Zone replication** to create backups of critical data and improve availability.

6. Use Cases for Amazon S3

- **Data Storage and Backup**: S3 is widely used for backup and archival storage, whether for media files, application data, or log files.

- **Big Data Analytics**: Store large volumes of unstructured data such as log files, social media data, and machine-generated data for analytics purposes.

- **Web Hosting**: Store and serve static web content such as images, videos, and HTML files.

- **Data Lake**: S3 serves as a central repository for storing all your data (structured, semi-structured, and unstructured) for analytics, machine learning, and business intelligence.

Summary

Amazon S3 is an incredibly powerful and flexible object storage service that allows you to store, manage, and protect your data in the cloud. Whether you need to store large datasets for analytics, back up critical files, or serve web content, S3 provides the durability, scalability, and security you need. By leveraging its advanced features like lifecycle management, transfer acceleration, and cross-region replication, you can optimize both cost and performance for your applications.

Amazon EBS and EFS: Block and File Storage Solutions

Amazon Web Services (AWS) offers a variety of storage options to suit different use cases. Two of the most commonly used storage services are Amazon Elastic Block Store (EBS) and Amazon Elastic File System (EFS). These services provide different storage models to meet diverse requirements, with Amazon EBS being a block storage solution and Amazon EFS being a file storage solution. This section will explore the key features, differences, and use cases of Amazon EBS and Amazon EFS.

1. Amazon Elastic Block Store (EBS)

Amazon EBS provides persistent block storage volumes that can be attached to Amazon EC2 instances. EBS is designed for applications that require a file system or a database. It is ideal for workloads that require low-latency access to data and where data needs to be persistently stored, even after an instance is stopped or terminated.

Key Features of Amazon EBS

- **Persistent Storage**: EBS volumes are persistent, meaning the data remains intact even if the EC2 instance is stopped or terminated.

- **Block-Level Storage**: EBS provides block-level storage, allowing you to format and mount it as a file system within your EC2 instances.

- **Performance Options**: EBS offers multiple volume types with different performance characteristics:
    - **General Purpose SSD (gp3)**: Balanced price and performance, ideal for most workloads.
    - **Provisioned IOPS SSD (io2)**: High-performance SSD for workloads requiring fast access to large amounts of data.
    - **Throughput Optimized HDD (st1)**: Low-cost storage for frequently accessed, throughput-intensive workloads.
    - **Cold HDD (sc1)**: Lowest-cost storage for infrequently accessed workloads.

- **Scalability**: EBS volumes can be resized to meet growing storage requirements. You can increase the volume size or change volume types without disrupting your workloads.

- **Snapshots**: EBS allows you to take point-in-time snapshots of volumes for backup, recovery, or cloning purposes. These snapshots are stored in Amazon S3.

- **Encryption**: EBS supports encryption for both data at rest and data in transit, using AWS-managed or customer-managed keys (KMS).
- **Performance Consistency**: EBS is designed for high performance and low-latency applications, making it suitable for databases, transactional systems, and other I/O-intensive workloads.

When to Use Amazon EBS

- **Databases**: EBS is well-suited for use with relational databases (e.g., MySQL, PostgreSQL) or NoSQL databases (e.g., MongoDB, Cassandra) that require low-latency access to data.
- **Enterprise Applications**: Applications such as SAP or Microsoft Exchange benefit from the persistent, low-latency storage provided by EBS.
- **Big Data and Analytics**: EBS can handle large-scale, high-throughput workloads like Hadoop or Spark.
- **File Systems**: EBS can be used to create file systems that need low-latency access and durability, such as when deploying applications that need to read/write large amounts of data in real time.

2. Amazon Elastic File System (EFS)

Amazon EFS provides a fully managed, scalable file storage service that can be mounted concurrently across multiple EC2 instances. EFS is designed to support applications that require shared file storage accessible by multiple instances simultaneously. It is an ideal solution for applications that require a traditional file system interface and the ability to scale elastically.

Key Features of Amazon EFS

- **Fully Managed**: EFS is fully managed, so AWS handles the administrative overhead of provisioning, scaling, and managing the file system.

- **File-Level Storage**: EFS provides a file storage interface, allowing you to store and organize data in directories and files, much like traditional file systems.

- **Scalability**: EFS automatically scales as your data grows. It can scale from gigabytes to petabytes without manual intervention. The system can grow and shrink as needed, making it cost-effective.

- **Shared Access**: EFS allows multiple EC2 instances to mount the same file system, making it suitable for applications that need shared access to files across instances.

- **Performance Modes**:
  - **General Purpose Mode**: Designed for latency-sensitive applications that require low-latency access to data.
  - **Max I/O Mode**: Optimized for highly parallel, large-scale workloads, such as big data applications.
- **Durability and Availability**: EFS is designed for high availability and durability. It stores data redundantly across multiple availability zones within a region.
- **Encryption**: EFS supports encryption both at rest and in transit, providing secure storage for sensitive data.
- **Integration with AWS Services**: EFS integrates with other AWS services, such as AWS Lambda, for serverless applications, and AWS CloudWatch for monitoring.

When to Use Amazon EFS

- **Shared File Storage**: EFS is ideal for applications that require a shared file system that can be accessed by multiple instances simultaneously, such as content management systems, big data analytics, or media processing.
- **Web Servers**: EFS is commonly used for

web applications that need a shared file system across multiple web servers (e.g., for storing website assets like images or logs).

- **Lift-and-Shift Applications**: EFS can be used to migrate on-premises file storage to the cloud for applications that rely on file-based data access.

- **DevOps and CI/CD**: EFS can be used in DevOps workflows where multiple instances need access to shared codebases or build files.

- **Home Directories**: EFS is suitable for storing user home directories and profiles that need to be accessed by multiple users across a fleet of EC2 instances.

3. Key Differences Between Amazon EBS and EFS

Feature	Amazon EBS	Amazon EFS
Storage Type	Block storage	File storage
Data Access	Attached to a single EC2 instance	Shared access by multiple EC2 instances simultaneously
Use Case	High-performance, low-latency storage for single-instance applications	Shared file system for multi-instance applications
Scalability	Manually resizeable, with a limit on maximum size	Automatically scales based on usage
Performance	Provides different	Supports General Purpose

	volume types for performance (SSD/ HDD)	and Max I/O performance modes
Data Structure	Data stored as blocks (individual files need to be managed)	Data stored in directories and files
Persistence	Persistent storage tied to EC2 instances	Persistent and scalable storage across instances
Snapshots	Supports snapshots for backup and cloning	No built-in snapshot feature, but can use backup tools
Pricing	Based on the provisioned size and I/O operations	Based on the storage used, with additional costs for throughput and data transfer

4. Best Practices for Using Amazon EBS and EFS

For Amazon EBS

- **Choose the Right Volume Type**: Select the appropriate EBS volume type (e.g., **gp3** for balanced workloads, **io2** for high-performance workloads) based on your application's performance needs.

- **Use Snapshots for Backup**: Regularly create EBS snapshots to ensure that your data is backed up and recoverable in case of failure.

- **Optimize for Cost**: Choose the volume size and type based on actual storage needs, and delete unused volumes to reduce costs.

- **Use Encryption**: Always enable EBS encryption to secure sensitive data at rest.

For Amazon EFS

- **Optimize for Performance**: Choose the correct performance mode (General Purpose or Max I/O) based on the expected workload.

- **Leverage Lifecycle Policies**: Use EFS lifecycle policies to automatically transition infrequently accessed data to a cheaper storage class (EFS One Zone-IA).

- **Enable Encryption**: Ensure that your EFS file system is encrypted both in transit and at rest, especially if storing sensitive data.

- **Monitor and Scale**: Use CloudWatch to monitor EFS usage and performance, and configure alarms for optimal performance.

Summary

Amazon EBS and EFS provide two distinct storage models for AWS users. EBS is ideal for block-level storage for EC2 instances, offering low-latency, high-performance storage for databases and transactional applications. EFS, on the other hand, is perfect for applications that require shared file access, making it ideal for web servers, content management systems, and big data workloads. By understanding their features and differences, you can choose the right storage solution based on your application's specific requirements.

Archiving Data with Amazon Glacier

Amazon Glacier, now known as Amazon S3 Glacier, is a low-cost, long-term archival storage service designed for data that is infrequently accessed but needs to be retained for compliance, historical, or backup purposes. It offers secure, durable, and low-cost storage for data that is not required to be accessed frequently, making it a cost-effective solution for archiving large amounts of data.

This section will cover the features, benefits, and best practices for using Amazon S3 Glacier to archive data.

1. Introduction to Amazon S3 Glacier

Amazon S3 Glacier provides a highly durable, low-cost storage solution for archiving data. It is part of the **Amazon S3** (Simple Storage Service) family, meaning it integrates seamlessly with S3's ecosystem, making it easy for users to manage and archive their data while ensuring long-term preservation.

Key Features of Amazon S3 Glacier

- **Low-Cost Storage**: S3 Glacier is designed to be one of the most cost-effective storage solutions for long-term archival storage, with pricing based on storage usage and retrieval requests.

- **Durability**: S3 Glacier is designed for 99.999999999% (11 9's) durability, meaning your archived data is highly protected against loss.

- **Secure Storage**: All data stored in Glacier is automatically encrypted at rest by default, and additional options are available for securing data in transit.

- **Compliance and Retention**: Glacier can be used to comply with data retention regulations, such as HIPAA, GDPR, and others, making it suitable for legal and regulatory requirements.

- **Retrieval Options**: S3 Glacier offers several retrieval options depending on how quickly you need access to your archived data:
    - **Expedited Retrievals**: Retrieve data within 1-5 minutes for urgent needs.
    - **Standard Retrievals**: Retrieve data in 3-5 hours for less time-sensitive needs.

- **Bulk Retrievals**: Retrieve large amounts of data within 5-12 hours, at the lowest cost per GB retrieved.

Storage Classes in S3 Glacier

- **S3 Glacier**: The standard archival storage option with retrieval times ranging from hours to minutes.
- **S3 Glacier Deep Archive**: The lowest-cost archival storage class, ideal for data that is rarely accessed and can withstand retrieval times of 12 hours or more.

2. Use Cases for Amazon S3 Glacier

Amazon S3 Glacier is designed for various use cases where large amounts of infrequently accessed data need to be stored and retained for the long term.

Common Use Cases for S3 Glacier

- **Compliance and Legal Archiving**: Organizations often need to store data for long periods for regulatory and compliance reasons. S3 Glacier provides a secure and compliant solution for retaining data such as tax records, legal documents, and financial reports.
- **Backup and Disaster Recovery**: Glacier is an ideal solution for long-term backup storage. It can be used as part of a disaster recovery plan where archived

data can be quickly restored if necessary.

- **Media Archiving**: Media organizations can use Glacier to archive video, images, and audio files that need to be kept for long periods but are not accessed frequently.

- **Scientific Data Storage**: Scientific researchers can use S3 Glacier to store large datasets from experiments and research that need to be preserved for future analysis, but are not accessed regularly.

- **Medical Records**: Healthcare organizations use Glacier to store medical records, imaging data, and other health-related information in a secure and compliant manner, allowing long-term retention with low costs.

3. Benefits of Using Amazon S3 Glacier

1. Cost-Effective

- S3 Glacier offers one of the most affordable storage solutions for large volumes of data that is rarely accessed, with a low cost per GB stored.

- The cost is further reduced with the Glacier Deep Archive option, which is the lowest-cost storage class available in AWS.

2. High Durability and Reliability

- Data stored in S3 Glacier is automatically replicated across multiple availability zones, providing high durability and protecting against data loss.
- Glacier's durability ensures that your archived data is safe from hardware failures and natural disasters.

3. Flexibility in Retrieval

- With different retrieval options (Expedited, Standard, and Bulk), S3 Glacier provides flexibility in how quickly you can access archived data. Whether you need data urgently or can wait, Glacier offers solutions to meet various timeframes and cost considerations.

4. Integration with AWS Ecosystem

- As part of the S3 family, Glacier integrates well with other AWS services, such as AWS Lambda for event-driven processing, AWS CloudTrail for monitoring, and Amazon S3 lifecycle policies for automating data transitions between storage classes.

5. Security and Compliance

- Glacier provides built-in encryption for

data at rest and in transit. You can also use AWS Identity and Access Management (IAM) policies to control access to archived data.

- S3 Glacier supports compliance with various regulatory standards, including HIPAA, SOC 1, 2, and 3, and GDPR.

4. Best Practices for Archiving Data with S3 Glacier

1. Organize Data with Lifecycle Policies

- Use **S3 Lifecycle policies** to automatically transition data to Glacier when it becomes less frequently accessed. For example, after 30 days of data being in S3 Standard, you can configure a policy to move it to Glacier for cost-effective long-term storage.

- Implement **S3 Intelligent-Tiering** for data that may change access patterns, as it automatically moves objects between frequent and infrequent access tiers based on usage patterns.

2. Plan for Retrieval Times

- When archiving data, consider the retrieval times needed. If you need data access frequently, Amazon S3 Standard or S3 Intelligent-Tiering might be a better option. Use S3 Glacier for data that can remain archived for longer periods with slower retrieval needs.

- Use **Expedited retrievals** for data that requires near-immediate access, but consider the additional costs involved compared to Standard or Bulk retrievals.

3. Encrypt Data

- Always encrypt sensitive data before archiving it to Glacier, even though S3 Glacier encrypts data at rest by default. Using AWS Key Management Service (KMS), you can manage encryption keys to ensure complete control over who can access the data.

4. Monitor and Audit with CloudWatch

- Use **Amazon CloudWatch** to track retrievals and monitor access patterns. CloudWatch can be set up to send notifications when the access to Glacier exceeds certain thresholds, allowing you to optimize retrievals and manage costs.

5. Use Glacier Deep Archive for Rarely Accessed Data

- For data that is unlikely to be retrieved for years (e.g., old media files, historical data, or long-term backups), use **S3 Glacier Deep Archive**. This option provides a significant cost savings while ensuring that the data is still accessible if needed.

5. Pricing and Costs

The pricing for Amazon S3 Glacier is based on:

- **Storage costs**: The amount of data stored in Glacier, with lower prices for larger volumes of data.
- **Retrieval costs**: Charges apply for retrieving data, and they depend on the retrieval type (Expedited, Standard, or Bulk).
- **PUT and GET requests**: You are charged for the number of requests you make for storing and retrieving data.
- **Data transfer costs**: Data transferred from Glacier to other AWS services may incur additional costs depending on the transfer volume.

Summary

Amazon S3 Glacier is an ideal solution for long-term data archiving, offering low-cost storage with high durability and secure access options. By using S3 Glacier, organizations can retain large volumes of data that need to be archived for compliance, disaster recovery, or other purposes while minimizing storage costs. With flexible retrieval options and seamless integration with other AWS services, Glacier helps businesses meet their data retention and access requirements efficiently.

By following best practices for data organization, retrieval, and security, you can ensure that your archived data is managed effectively and cost-efficiently.

CHAPTER 6: DATABASE SERVICES

Amazon RDS: Relational Database Services

Amazon Relational Database Service (Amazon RDS) is a fully managed database service that makes it easier to set up, operate, and scale relational databases in the cloud. It provides resizable capacity, automated backups, software patch management, and enhanced security, helping developers and database administrators manage relational databases more efficiently.

In this section, we'll explore the key features, benefits, use cases, and best practices for using Amazon RDS.

1. Introduction to Amazon RDS

Amazon RDS supports several popular relational database engines, including:

- **MySQL**
- **PostgreSQL**
- **MariaDB**
- **Oracle Database**
- **Microsoft SQL Server**

RDS automates time-consuming tasks such as hardware provisioning, database setup, patching, and backups, enabling you to focus on application development rather than database administration.

Key Features of Amazon RDS

- **Multi-AZ Deployments**: Amazon RDS supports multi-availability zone (Multi-AZ) deployments for high availability and automatic failover. This ensures that your database remains available even in the event of an infrastructure failure.

- **Automated Backups**: RDS automatically backs up your database and retains backup copies for a user-defined retention period. You can also create manual snapshots for point-in-time restores.

- **Scalability**: You can scale the database instance's compute and storage capacity with just a few clicks, making it suitable for dynamic workloads that require on-demand resource scaling.
- **Security**: RDS integrates with AWS Identity and Access Management (IAM) for access control and enables encryption at rest and in transit using AWS Key Management Service (KMS).
- **Monitoring and Metrics**: Amazon RDS provides integrated monitoring through **Amazon CloudWatch** for key database metrics, such as CPU utilization, storage, and I/O activity.
- **Maintenance and Patching**: Amazon RDS automatically applies patches and software updates to the database engine, ensuring that your database is up-to-date with the latest security fixes and performance improvements.

2. Benefits of Amazon RDS

1. Managed Service

- Amazon RDS reduces the administrative burden associated with database management, such as hardware setup, patching, and scaling. This allows you to focus more on building your application rather than managing the underlying infrastructure.

2. High Availability and Reliability

- With **Multi-AZ deployments**, RDS ensures that your database is highly available and fault-tolerant. In case of an outage, Amazon RDS automatically fails over to a standby instance, ensuring business continuity.

3. Scalability

- You can scale your RDS instances vertically by modifying the instance type to add more CPU, RAM, or I/O capacity, or horizontally by using **Read Replicas** to offload read-heavy operations.
- **Storage autoscaling** is available, allowing your database to scale storage automatically as needed without manual intervention.

4. Cost Efficiency

- Amazon RDS offers a pay-as-you-go pricing model with **on-demand instances** and **reserved instances** that can save costs for predictable workloads.
- You can also use **Aurora Serverless** to run databases that automatically start up, shut down, and scale based on application demand, providing a

cost-effective option for infrequent or unpredictable workloads.

5. Security

- RDS integrates with AWS security services such as **AWS IAM**, **VPC**, and **KMS** to ensure that your data is secure both in transit and at rest.
- You can use **VPC peering** to control which networks have access to your database, ensuring that only trusted applications and users can access the database.

3. Use Cases for Amazon RDS

1. Web and Mobile Applications

- Amazon RDS is widely used for running relational databases that back websites, web apps, and mobile applications. With built-in high availability, backups, and scaling, RDS is well-suited for dynamic applications with changing traffic patterns.

2. E-commerce Platforms

- E-commerce websites that need a robust relational database to store product data, customer orders, and inventory management can benefit from Amazon RDS, especially for workloads that require high availability and reliable performance during peak shopping seasons.

3. Content Management Systems (CMS)

- RDS is an excellent choice for hosting CMS platforms such as WordPress, Drupal, or Joomla, which rely on relational databases to store content, user information, and site settings.

4. Business Applications

- For applications such as Customer Relationship Management (CRM) or Enterprise Resource Planning (ERP) systems that require structured data storage, RDS provides a reliable and scalable backend database.

5. Data Warehousing and Analytics

- For workloads that require complex queries and reporting, RDS can serve as a backend relational database, or it can be integrated with AWS **Redshift** for more advanced data warehousing and analytics.

4. Amazon RDS Database Engines

Amazon RDS supports the following database engines, each with its own features and benefits:

1. MySQL

- One of the most popular open-source

relational databases. Ideal for web apps, e-commerce, and SaaS platforms.

2. PostgreSQL

- An open-source database that supports advanced features such as custom functions, JSON, and geospatial data. PostgreSQL is a great choice for developers needing advanced querying capabilities.

3. MariaDB

- A fork of MySQL that is community-driven and often used as a drop-in replacement for MySQL.

4. Oracle Database

- A fully managed relational database for enterprises that require a high-performance, highly available, and secure database solution. Often used for complex enterprise applications.

5. Microsoft SQL Server

- A relational database solution designed for enterprise applications that integrate with Microsoft software ecosystems, providing support for complex enterprise data needs.

6. Amazon Aurora

- Amazon Aurora is a fully managed

relational database compatible with MySQL and PostgreSQL that offers better performance and availability compared to traditional MySQL/PostgreSQL databases. Aurora automatically scales storage as needed, up to 64 TB.

5. Best Practices for Using Amazon RDS

1. Enable Multi-AZ for High Availability

- Use **Multi-AZ deployments** for critical applications that require high availability and disaster recovery. This ensures automatic failover to a standby database instance if the primary instance fails.

2. Implement Automated Backups

- Enable **automated backups** to protect your data from accidental deletion or corruption. Amazon RDS provides automated daily backups, transaction logs, and point-in-time recovery.

3. Use Read Replicas for Scalability

- To improve the read performance of your database, you can create **read replicas** to offload read-heavy traffic and ensure better database responsiveness. Replicas can be created in different availability zones to further enhance availability.

4. Monitor with CloudWatch

- Use **Amazon CloudWatch** to monitor performance metrics such as CPU utilization, storage, and I/O activity. CloudWatch can also trigger alarms for any performance issues, enabling proactive management of your database.

5. Secure Your Database

- Enable encryption at rest and in transit to protect sensitive data. Use **AWS Key Management Service (KMS)** to manage encryption keys.

- Restrict access to your database using **VPC security groups** and **IAM roles** to limit who can access the database.

6. Optimize Cost with Reserved Instances

- If your application has predictable workloads, you can save costs by purchasing **Reserved Instances** for a one- or three-year term. Reserved Instances offer significant discounts compared to on-demand pricing.

6. Pricing and Cost Management

Amazon RDS pricing is based on several factors:

- **Instance Type**: The compute capacity of the database instance (e.g., db.m5.large, db.r5.xlarge).

- **Storage**: The amount of storage allocated to the database.
- **Data Transfer**: The amount of data transferred in and out of the database.
- **Backup Storage**: The storage used for backups beyond the automated backup retention period.
- **License Model**: RDS offers both **License Included** and **Bring Your Own License (BYOL)** models for certain database engines, such as Oracle and SQL Server.

Summary

Amazon RDS simplifies the management of relational databases in the cloud by automating administrative tasks such as provisioning, patching, and backups. Its integration with other AWS services, support for multiple database engines, and scalability options make it an ideal solution for a wide range of applications, from small websites to large enterprise systems.

By following best practices for high availability, security, and cost optimization, you can leverage Amazon RDS to provide a reliable, scalable, and secure database solution for your applications.

DynamoDB: NoSQL Database

Amazon DynamoDB is a fully managed NoSQL database service provided by AWS, designed for high performance and scalability. It is primarily used for applications that require low-latency data access and are often characterized by large amounts of unstructured or semi-structured data. DynamoDB supports both key-value and document data models, making it suitable for a wide range of use cases, from mobile apps to real-time analytics.

In this section, we will explore the key features, benefits, use cases, and best practices for using Amazon DynamoDB.

1. Introduction to DynamoDB

Amazon DynamoDB is a serverless, highly scalable NoSQL database that allows users to store and retrieve any amount of data with predictable low-latency performance. It is fully managed, meaning AWS handles tasks such as provisioning infrastructure, patching, and scaling. DynamoDB is designed to deliver consistent performance at scale and is suitable for workloads that require high availability and low latency.

Key Features of DynamoDB:

- **Fully Managed**: DynamoDB is fully managed, so you do not need to worry about hardware, maintenance, or infrastructure scaling.

- **Scalable**: DynamoDB automatically scales to handle increases in traffic and data size. You can set up capacity modes to adjust how DynamoDB allocates throughput.

- **Low Latency**: DynamoDB is designed to deliver single-digit millisecond response times, making it ideal for real-time applications.

- **High Availability**: DynamoDB is replicated across multiple availability zones in an AWS region, ensuring high availability and fault tolerance.

- **Flexible Data Models**: DynamoDB supports both key-value and document data models, offering flexibility in how you structure and query your data.

- **Built-in Security**: DynamoDB integrates with AWS Identity and Access Management (IAM) for access control, AWS KMS for encryption, and VPC for secure network configurations.

2. Benefits of Amazon DynamoDB
1. High Performance and Scalability

- DynamoDB provides seamless scalability to handle massive amounts of data and requests per second. It can scale automatically to meet the needs of high-throughput applications while maintaining low-latency performance.

- The service supports **provisioned capacity** and **on-demand capacity modes**, allowing you to choose between predictable capacity with set throughput or an auto-scaling model for unpredictable workloads.

2. Fully Managed Service

- DynamoDB is a fully managed service, eliminating the need to manually manage servers, scaling, or patching. It automates administrative tasks, letting you focus on your application logic and features.

3. Flexible Data Model

- DynamoDB is a key-value store that allows you to store and retrieve data in both simple key-value and more complex document formats. It supports JSON documents, making it suitable for applications that require rich, flexible data structures.

4. Real-Time Access

- DynamoDB is optimized for real-time applications with consistent low-latency access to data. It is ideal for use cases like gaming, IoT, mobile apps, and more.

5. Fully Integrated with AWS Ecosystem

- DynamoDB integrates seamlessly with other AWS services such as **AWS Lambda** for serverless computing, **Amazon S3** for storage, **AWS Glue** for data processing, and **Amazon Redshift** for analytics.

6. Security and Compliance

- DynamoDB provides built-in encryption at rest using AWS Key Management Service (KMS) and integrates with AWS IAM for secure access control. It also meets several regulatory compliance standards, including PCI-DSS, HIPAA, and GDPR.

3. Key Concepts in DynamoDB

1. Tables and Items

- **Tables**: In DynamoDB, data is organized into tables. Each table has a primary key that uniquely identifies each item. A table can have one or more attributes, which are essentially data fields.
- **Items**: Items are individual records in a

table. An item consists of one or more attributes, and each attribute is a key-value pair.

2. Primary Keys

- **Partition Key**: A simple primary key consisting of one attribute. The partition key value is hashed to determine the partition where the item is stored.
- **Composite Key**: A composite primary key consists of two attributes: a partition key and a sort key. This allows for more complex querying and sorting.

3. Secondary Indexes

- DynamoDB allows you to create secondary indexes (Global Secondary Indexes and Local Secondary Indexes) to query data in ways that do not directly involve the primary key.
- **Global Secondary Index (GSI)**: A GSI allows you to query data based on attributes that are not part of the primary key.
- **Local Secondary Index (LSI)**: An LSI allows you to query data based on the partition key and a different sort key than the primary key.

4. Provisioned vs. On-Demand Capacity Modes

- **Provisioned Capacity**: You define the desired read and write throughput for your table, and DynamoDB will allocate resources accordingly.

- **On-Demand Capacity**: DynamoDB automatically adjusts its throughput capacity based on traffic patterns. It is ideal for unpredictable workloads with varying traffic.

5. Streams and Change Data Capture

- **DynamoDB Streams** capture changes made to the data in your tables. These changes can be used for real-time analytics, triggering AWS Lambda functions, or integrating with other systems.

4. Use Cases for DynamoDB

1. Real-Time Applications

- DynamoDB is well-suited for real-time applications that require low-latency access to data, such as:
    - **Gaming**: Store game scores, user progress, and player data with high-speed access.
    - **IoT**: Collect data from millions of IoT devices and process it in real time.
    - **Mobile Apps**: Provide fast, scalable backend data storage

for mobile apps, ensuring low-latency response times.

2. E-Commerce Websites

- DynamoDB can be used to store and retrieve product catalogs, inventory, user sessions, and customer orders, providing quick access to data during peak traffic periods.

3. Serverless Architectures

- DynamoDB works well with serverless computing, where AWS Lambda functions process data from DynamoDB tables in response to user events. It can be used to build serverless APIs and data-driven applications.

4. Personalization and Recommendations

- Store user activity and preferences to offer personalized experiences and recommendations. DynamoDB's low-latency performance is ideal for serving dynamic content to users in real time.

5. Mobile and Web Session Management

- DynamoDB can be used to store session data for web and mobile applications, ensuring users' session information is quickly accessible, scalable, and secure.

5. Best Practices for Using DynamoDB

1. Efficient Table Design

- Carefully plan your **primary key** design to ensure it fits your application's access patterns. Avoid hot partitions by distributing access evenly across the table.
- Use **composite keys** and **secondary indexes** to support multiple query patterns without duplicating data.

2. Provisioning Capacity Based on Use

- Choose **on-demand capacity** for unpredictable workloads and **provisioned capacity** for predictable workloads where you can estimate read and write throughput.

3. Monitor Performance with CloudWatch

- Use **Amazon CloudWatch** to monitor your DynamoDB tables for metrics such as read/write capacity usage, throttled requests, and latency. Set up alarms to notify you of any performance degradation or throttling.

4. Use DynamoDB Streams for Real-Time Data Processing

- Use **DynamoDB Streams** to track changes to your data and trigger actions, such as updating search indexes, processing transactions, or synchronizing data across different services.

5. Optimize Costs with Auto Scaling

- Enable **auto-scaling** for tables and indexes to automatically adjust read and write throughput in response to changing traffic patterns, ensuring that you only pay for the resources you need.

6. Pricing and Cost Management

DynamoDB pricing is based on several factors:

- **Provisioned Capacity**: You pay for the read and write capacity units you provision for your tables.

- **On-Demand Capacity**: You pay for the data read and written to DynamoDB based on actual requests.

- **Storage**: You are billed for the amount of data stored in your DynamoDB tables.

- **Data Transfer**: Costs are incurred when transferring data out of DynamoDB to other AWS services or external networks.

- **DynamoDB Streams**: You are billed based on the amount of data written to the stream.

To manage costs effectively, optimize table design, use auto-scaling, and select the appropriate capacity mode based on your workload.

Summary

Amazon DynamoDB provides a powerful, fully managed NoSQL database solution for applications that need to handle large volumes of data with low-latency access. Its flexibility, scalability, and integration with the AWS ecosystem make it suitable for a wide range of use cases, from mobile apps to real-time analytics. By following best practices for table design, capacity management, and monitoring, you can leverage DynamoDB to build fast, scalable, and cost-efficient applications.

Amazon Redshift: Data Warehousing Solutions

Amazon Redshift is a fully managed, petabyte-scale data warehousing service in the cloud. It is designed for high-performance analytics and provides a fast, easy-to-use platform for analyzing large datasets using SQL-based queries. With Amazon Redshift, users can perform complex queries and analyses on massive datasets at high speeds, making it ideal for businesses that need to process and analyze large volumes of structured data.

In this section, we will cover the key features,

benefits, architecture, use cases, and best practices for using Amazon Redshift as your data warehousing solution.

1. Introduction to Amazon Redshift

Amazon Redshift is a fully managed data warehouse that enables fast querying and analytics of large datasets. It is built on top of PostgreSQL and optimized for performance and scalability in a cloud environment. Redshift uses a massively parallel processing (MPP) architecture, which allows it to distribute the processing of data across many nodes for faster query performance.

Key Features of Amazon Redshift:

- **Massively Parallel Processing (MPP)**: Redshift distributes queries across multiple nodes, enabling it to handle large datasets and complex queries efficiently.

- **Columnar Storage**: Redshift stores data in a columnar format, which allows for faster scans, improved compression, and more efficient analytics compared to traditional row-based storage.

- **Data Compression**: Data is compressed to reduce storage requirements and speed up query performance by minimizing the amount of data read.

- **Integration with AWS Ecosystem**: Redshift integrates with other AWS services like **Amazon S3**, **AWS Glue**, **Amazon QuickSight**, and **AWS Lambda**, providing a complete solution for data processing and analytics.
- **Scalable Storage and Compute**: You can scale both storage and compute independently to meet the needs of your workload. This flexibility allows you to optimize performance and cost.
- **Security**: Amazon Redshift provides encryption at rest and in transit, along with integration with AWS IAM for access control, ensuring your data is secure.
- **SQL Interface**: Redshift supports standard SQL, making it easy for users familiar with SQL to query and analyze data without needing to learn new query languages.

2. Benefits of Amazon Redshift

1. High Performance

- Redshift's MPP architecture and columnar storage ensure that queries can be processed quickly, even for complex or large-scale analytics workloads.

- Redshift can perform queries across petabytes of data in seconds or minutes, making it a powerful tool for real-time business intelligence (BI) and data analysis.

2. Cost-Effective

- With Redshift, you only pay for what you use, and pricing is based on the amount of storage and compute capacity used. You can start with small clusters and scale as your data grows.
- Redshift's columnar storage and data compression reduce the amount of data that needs to be stored and read, lowering storage and query costs.

3. Fully Managed Service

- Redshift is a fully managed service, meaning AWS handles infrastructure, setup, scaling, patching, and backups. This lets businesses focus on analyzing data instead of managing a complex database environment.
- Automated backups and continuous data protection ensure that your data is secure and recoverable in case of failure.

4. Scalability

- Redshift can scale from gigabytes to petabytes of data, allowing you to start small and grow your data warehouse as your needs increase. You can also resize your Redshift clusters and adjust storage and compute independently based on your workload requirements.

5. Integration with BI Tools

- Redshift integrates with many popular BI tools, such as **Tableau**, **Power BI**, and **Amazon QuickSight**, enabling seamless data visualization and reporting. You can connect directly to Redshift to create insightful dashboards and reports.

6. Secure Data Handling

- Redshift supports **encryption at rest and in transit**, and integrates with **AWS Key Management Service (KMS)** for key management. Additionally, it supports **virtual private cloud (VPC)** and **AWS Identity and Access Management (IAM)** for controlling access to data and resources.

3. Key Components of Amazon Redshift

1. Redshift Clusters

- A Redshift cluster consists of one or more **compute nodes**. The **leader node** is responsible for managing queries, distributing workloads to compute nodes, and aggregating results.

- Each compute node has its own **local storage** and is responsible for a subset of the overall dataset. Nodes work together to process large datasets efficiently using MPP.

2. Redshift Nodes

- **Leader Node**: The leader node manages query coordination and aggregates results from the compute nodes. It does not store user data.

- **Compute Nodes**: These nodes store data and perform the majority of the computational tasks. Each node in a Redshift cluster processes a portion of the overall data and performs distributed query processing.

- **Dense Compute Nodes**: High-performance nodes designed for fast query processing.

- **Dense Storage Nodes**: Provide larger storage capacity, suitable for long-term storage of large datasets.

3. Data Distribution and Sorting

- **Data Distribution**: Data in Redshift is distributed across compute nodes to improve parallel processing. You can specify how data is distributed using one of the following methods:
    - **Key Distribution**: Data is

distributed based on a column's value, ensuring rows with the same key are on the same node.
- **Even Distribution**: Data is distributed evenly across nodes, ensuring balanced storage and query performance.
- **All Distribution**: All data is replicated across all nodes, useful for small lookup tables.

- **Data Sorting**: Redshift uses **sort keys** to determine the order in which data is stored on disk. This allows for fast scanning and filtering of large datasets.

4. Redshift Spectrum

- Redshift Spectrum extends Redshift's capabilities to directly query data stored in Amazon S3 without the need to load it into the data warehouse. It enables you to perform complex queries on both structured and unstructured data residing in S3, making it easier to integrate Redshift with big data workflows.

4. Use Cases for Amazon Redshift

1. Business Intelligence and Analytics

- Redshift is widely used in business intelligence (BI) for aggregating and analyzing large datasets. Its high performance makes it suitable for real-time reporting, dashboarding, and ad-hoc query processing.

2. Data Lakes and Big Data Analytics

- Redshift can be part of a data lake architecture, where it integrates with S3 to store raw data and then use **Redshift Spectrum** to query that data directly. This enables you to run complex queries across structured and unstructured data in a data lake.

3. Customer Insights and Personalization

- Redshift can store and process customer data, enabling businesses to analyze customer behavior and preferences. Insights can be used for personalization and targeted marketing.

4. Fraud Detection and Risk Management

- Redshift's fast query processing makes it ideal for real-time fraud detection and risk management in industries like finance and e-commerce. It can process large volumes of transaction data to identify patterns indicative of fraudulent activity.

5. Data Warehousing for Cloud-Native Applications

- Redshift is commonly used in cloud-native applications that require high-speed data analysis. It integrates seamlessly with AWS services and is optimized for performance on the AWS cloud.

5. Best Practices for Using Amazon Redshift

1. Schema Design

- Choose your **distribution keys** and **sort keys** wisely. Proper schema design helps optimize query performance by minimizing the amount of data scanned.
- Use **normalized** schemas for transactional data and **denormalized** schemas for analytics workloads to improve query performance.

2. Optimize Query Performance

- Use **compression encodings** to reduce the amount of data scanned during queries and lower storage costs.
- Run **VACUUM** and **ANALYZE** commands regularly to maintain performance by reorganizing data and updating statistics.
- Leverage **result caching** to improve query performance for frequently executed queries.

3. Data Security

- Use **encryption** to protect sensitive data.

Encrypt data at rest using **AWS KMS** and secure data in transit with **SSL**.

- Implement **fine-grained access control** using **AWS IAM** to ensure that only authorized users can access specific data.

4. Cost Management

- Use **Redshift Spectrum** to avoid storing large amounts of data within Redshift itself and minimize costs.
- Opt for **reserved instances** for long-term workloads to save on compute costs.
- Monitor your **Redshift performance** using **AWS CloudWatch** and adjust your cluster size based on workload requirements.

Summary

Amazon Redshift offers a powerful, scalable, and cost-effective data warehousing solution that allows businesses to perform complex analytics and gain valuable insights from large datasets. Its high performance, ease of use, and seamless integration with the AWS ecosystem make it a popular choice for organizations looking to scale their data analysis capabilities in the cloud. By following best practices for schema design, query optimization, and cost management, you can maximize the benefits of using Redshift for your data warehousing and analytics needs.

CHAPTER 7: NETWORKING AND CONTENT DELIVERY

Amazon VPC: Building Your Virtual Network

Amazon Virtual Private Cloud (Amazon VPC) enables users to create isolated and secure virtual networks within the AWS cloud. It provides complete control over your network architecture, including configuring IP address ranges, subnets, route tables, and network gateways. VPC is a foundational service for running resources like EC2 instances, databases, and other services in a secure and scalable environment.

In this section, we will explore how to build and manage a Virtual Private Cloud, the components that make up a VPC, best practices, and key use cases.

1. Introduction to Amazon VPC

Amazon VPC allows you to create a private, isolated network within AWS, where you can launch AWS resources such as EC2 instances, RDS databases, and other services securely. With VPC, you can define your own IP address range, subnets, and route tables, giving you full control over your network's configuration.

Key Features of Amazon VPC:

- **Isolation**: Create a logically isolated network in the cloud. Each VPC is isolated from other VPCs, ensuring no overlap or communication unless explicitly configured.

- **Customizable Network Configuration**: Control the IP address range, subnets, route tables, and network gateways. You can also set up private IP addressing and public-facing services.

- **Security**: Implement security groups and network ACLs (Access Control Lists) for granular control over inbound and outbound traffic at the instance and subnet levels.

- **Peering and VPN Connectivity**: VPC allows you to connect with other VPCs (using VPC peering) or with your on-premises network (via VPN or Direct Connect), enabling hybrid cloud solutions.

- **Private and Public Subnets**: Easily create both public and private subnets within your VPC for different types of workloads, like web servers or application databases.

2. Key Components of Amazon VPC

Amazon VPC is built from several key components that together form your virtual network architecture. Here are the main components:

1. VPC

- A VPC is your isolated network within AWS. When you create a VPC, you define an IP address range using **CIDR (Classless Inter-Domain Routing)** notation (e.g., 10.0.0.0/16).

2. Subnets

- Subnets divide your VPC's network into smaller, more manageable sections. Each subnet resides within a specific **Availability Zone** (AZ) and can either be:
    - **Public Subnets**: Subnets with a route to the internet (via an

Internet Gateway).

- **Private Subnets**: Subnets that do not have a direct route to the internet, used for backend services like databases.

3. Route Tables

- Route tables are used to control the routing of traffic within your VPC and between subnets. Each subnet is associated with a route table, and you can define routes to direct traffic to the internet, to other subnets, or to on-premises networks.
    - **Main Route Table**: Every VPC has a default route table called the **Main Route Table**. Custom route tables can also be created for more specific traffic control.

4. Internet Gateway (IGW)

- An Internet Gateway is required to allow communication between instances in a public subnet and the internet. It is attached to the VPC and provides a target for route table entries to direct internet-bound traffic.

5. NAT Gateway/Instance

- A **NAT Gateway** or **NAT instance** allows instances in private subnets to access the internet for software updates and other outbound traffic without exposing them to incoming internet traffic.

6. Security Groups

- Security groups are virtual firewalls that control inbound and outbound traffic for resources (e.g., EC2 instances) in a VPC. They operate at the instance level and allow you to define which traffic is permitted to/from your resources.

7. Network ACLs

- Network ACLs (Access Control Lists) provide an additional layer of security and work at the subnet level. They allow you to set rules for both inbound and outbound traffic at the subnet boundary.

8. VPC Peering

- VPC peering allows you to connect multiple VPCs, either within the same region or across regions, to enable communication between resources in different VPCs.

9. VPN Connections

- A **VPN Connection** can be established between your VPC and your on-premises network, providing secure, encrypted communication between your AWS environment and your corporate data center.

10. Direct Connect

- **AWS Direct Connect** provides a dedicated network connection from your on-premises data center to AWS, offering lower latency and more reliable performance compared to VPN connections.

3. Setting Up Your VPC

1. Creating a VPC

To create a VPC, follow these basic steps:

1. **Choose a CIDR block**: Define the IP address range for your VPC.
2. **Create subnets**: Decide on how you want to split your VPC into subnets (public, private) and assign them to different AZs.
3. **Set up route tables**: Ensure proper routing of traffic between your subnets and other resources.
4. **Add an internet gateway** (for public subnets): Attach an IGW to enable internet connectivity for resources in your public subnets.
5. **Configure security**: Set up security groups and network ACLs to secure your resources and traffic.

2. Creating Subnets

- When creating subnets, choose the

CIDR blocks to allocate to each subnet. Typically, you want to split your network into:
- **Public Subnets** for web servers, load balancers, or other services that need to be accessible from the internet.
- **Private Subnets** for internal services like databases or application servers that should not be directly accessed from the internet.

3. Configuring Route Tables

- Set up route tables to define how traffic is routed in and out of your VPC. For example:
  - **Public Subnet Route Table**: Routes to the internet through the IGW.
  - **Private Subnet Route Table**: Routes traffic through a **NAT Gateway** or private VPN connection to the internet.

4. Configuring Security Groups and Network ACLs

- **Security Groups** are stateful, meaning if you allow inbound traffic, the corresponding outbound traffic is automatically allowed.
- **Network ACLs** are stateless and allow you to set both inbound and outbound

traffic rules at the subnet level.

4. Best Practices for Using Amazon VPC

1. Isolate Subnets for Security

- Use private subnets for sensitive data or backend applications that should not be exposed to the internet. Place your databases, application servers, and other critical resources in private subnets.

2. Use Network ACLs and Security Groups Together

- While security groups offer instance-level security, use network ACLs for subnet-level security. Both layers provide additional control over your traffic flow.

3. Employ Multiple Availability Zones

- Distribute your resources across multiple Availability Zones for higher availability and fault tolerance. This ensures that if one AZ goes down, your applications continue to run in another AZ.

4. Enable Flow Logs for Monitoring

- Enable **VPC Flow Logs** to monitor the traffic going in and out of your VPC. This helps you with security audits, troubleshooting, and monitoring network performance.

5. Use Peering and VPN for Hybrid Cloud

- Use **VPC Peering** or **VPN Connections** to securely connect your AWS environment with your on-premises network or other VPCs, allowing hybrid architectures.

6. Leverage Direct Connect for Consistent Performance

- If you require dedicated, high-performance connectivity between your on-premises data center and AWS, use **AWS Direct Connect** to bypass the internet and reduce latency.

5. Use Cases for Amazon VPC

1. Hosting Web Applications

- VPC allows you to host scalable, secure web applications. You can set up load balancers in public subnets and deploy web servers and databases in private subnets, ensuring security and isolation.

2. Hybrid Cloud Architectures

- For businesses with on-premises infrastructure, VPC can serve as the foundation for a hybrid cloud, connecting on-premises resources to cloud-based services through VPN or Direct Connect.

3. Running Multi-Tier Applications

- Use VPC to create separate layers for your application architecture, such as a web layer, application layer, and database layer. This enhances both security and scalability.

4. Data Protection and Compliance

- VPC offers complete control over your network security. You can isolate sensitive data and ensure compliance with industry regulations by using private subnets, security groups, and encryption.

Summary

Amazon VPC is a critical service for building secure, scalable, and isolated networks within AWS. It enables businesses to take full advantage of the cloud's flexibility while maintaining control over their network configuration and security. By understanding the components of Amazon VPC, best practices for setup, and common use cases, you can design robust cloud architectures that meet your needs for performance, security, and scalability.

Elastic Load Balancing (ELB) and Auto Scaling

Elastic Load Balancing (ELB) and Auto Scaling are two powerful AWS services that help ensure high availability, fault tolerance, and scalability for applications running in the cloud. Together, they allow your applications to automatically adjust to varying levels of traffic while maintaining performance and minimizing downtime. In this section, we'll explore how ELB and Auto Scaling work, their key features, and best practices for implementation.

1. Introduction to Elastic Load Balancing (ELB)

Elastic Load Balancing automatically distributes incoming application traffic across multiple targets, such as EC2 instances, containers, and IP addresses, to ensure that no single resource is overwhelmed with traffic. ELB provides several types of load balancers suited for different types of applications, offering flexibility and reliability.

Types of Elastic Load Balancers:

1. **Application Load Balancer (ALB):**
    - **Best for HTTP and HTTPS traffic**: ALB operates at the application layer (Layer 7 of the OSI model) and routes traffic

based on advanced request-routing mechanisms such as host-based or path-based routing.

- **Ideal for Microservices**: ALB is designed for modern, microservices-based architectures, including containerized applications running on ECS, EKS, or Kubernetes.
- **Key Features**:
  - Content-based routing (path, host, query string, headers)
  - WebSocket support
  - HTTP/2 support
  - SSL termination

2. **Network Load Balancer (NLB)**:
   - **Best for TCP/UDP traffic**: NLB operates at the transport layer (Layer 4) and is optimized for high-performance traffic handling, such as TCP and UDP traffic.
   - **Ideal for Low-Latency Applications**: It is designed to handle millions of requests per second while maintaining high throughput and low latency.

- **Key Features**:
  - Static IP support
  - SSL termination
  - Supports WebSocket connections
  - Suitable for applications that require extreme performance and low latency

3. **Classic Load Balancer (CLB)**:
   - **Legacy load balancer**: CLB operates at both Layer 4 and Layer 7 and is typically used for applications built using EC2-Classic network.
   - **Best for legacy applications**: While it is still supported, AWS recommends using ALB or NLB for new applications due to the additional features they provide.

How ELB Works:

- **Distributes Traffic**: ELB automatically distributes incoming traffic across multiple targets in one or more Availability Zones to ensure that no single target is overloaded, thus improving fault tolerance.
- **Health Checks**: ELB performs health checks on your targets (e.g., EC2

instances). If a target becomes unhealthy, traffic is routed to healthy instances until the unhealthy instance recovers.

- **Scaling and Performance**: As the volume of incoming traffic increases, ELB can distribute traffic across an increasing number of healthy instances, ensuring that your application maintains high performance.

2. Introduction to Auto Scaling

Auto Scaling allows you to automatically adjust the number of EC2 instances or other resources in your environment based on demand. It ensures that you have the right number of instances running at any given time to handle traffic efficiently, thus optimizing both performance and cost.

Key Features of Auto Scaling:

1. **Automatic Scaling**:
    - Automatically scale your EC2 instances up or down based on real-time traffic demand or custom metrics (e.g., CPU usage, memory, request count).
    - Auto Scaling helps maintain optimal performance and avoids over-provisioning or under-provisioning of resources.

2. **Scaling Policies**:
   - **Dynamic Scaling**: Based on the demand, the number of instances in an Auto Scaling group increases or decreases automatically.
   - **Scheduled Scaling**: Scale resources based on predictable traffic patterns (e.g., scale up during business hours, scale down at night).
3. **Health Checks**:
   - Auto Scaling automatically replaces unhealthy instances with new healthy ones. This ensures that your application remains highly available, even when individual instances experience issues.
4. **Integration with ELB**:
   - Auto Scaling can work together with ELB to automatically add or remove EC2 instances from the load balancer's pool of targets. When Auto Scaling adds new instances, ELB begins routing traffic to them. When instances are terminated, ELB stops sending traffic to those instances.

How Auto Scaling Works:

- **Launch Configuration**: Auto Scaling uses a launch configuration (or launch template) to define the configuration of the instances it will launch, such as instance type, AMI, key pair, and security groups.

- **Auto Scaling Group (ASG)**: The Auto Scaling group defines the number of EC2 instances to run and the scaling policies (minimum, maximum, and desired instances).

- **Scaling Triggers**: You can configure Auto Scaling to trigger scaling actions based on CloudWatch alarms (e.g., scale out when CPU usage exceeds a threshold).

3. Integrating ELB with Auto Scaling

By integrating ELB with Auto Scaling, you can build a highly scalable and resilient application that can automatically adjust to varying levels of traffic. Here's how ELB and Auto Scaling work together:

1. **Initial Setup**:
    - When you create an Auto Scaling group, you specify an ELB as the load balancer for your instances.
    - As Auto Scaling launches

or terminates instances, it automatically registers or deregisters the instances with the ELB, ensuring that traffic is evenly distributed.

2. **Scaling Up**:
   - When traffic increases and your Auto Scaling policies trigger a scaling-up event, new EC2 instances are launched. ELB immediately begins routing traffic to the newly launched instances.
   - If needed, Auto Scaling can add more instances to handle the increased load while ELB ensures the distribution of traffic.

3. **Scaling Down**:
   - When traffic decreases, Auto Scaling automatically terminates instances to reduce costs. As instances are terminated, ELB stops sending traffic to the instances before they are fully terminated.
   - The load balancer continues to route traffic to the remaining healthy instances, ensuring that the application remains

available during the scaling-down process.

4. **Fault Tolerance**:
    - ELB continuously checks the health of your EC2 instances. If an instance becomes unhealthy, ELB routes traffic to the healthy instances.
    - If an EC2 instance becomes unhealthy and Auto Scaling replaces it with a new one, the new instance is automatically registered with ELB, ensuring no disruption in service.

4. Best Practices for Using ELB and Auto Scaling

1. Use Auto Scaling with Multiple Availability Zones:

- Distribute your resources across multiple Availability Zones (AZs) to improve fault tolerance. ELB will automatically distribute traffic across healthy instances in multiple AZs.

2. Set Up Health Checks:

- Ensure that both ELB and Auto Scaling perform health checks. ELB checks the health of individual instances, while Auto Scaling checks the health of the entire instance group.

- Customize health check settings based on your application's response times and failure conditions.

3. Optimize Scaling Policies:

- Set scaling policies that reflect your application's actual needs. Use CloudWatch metrics like CPU usage, request count, or custom metrics to trigger scaling actions.
- Avoid scaling too aggressively. Use cooldown periods to prevent unnecessary scaling events.

4. Monitor with CloudWatch:

- Use CloudWatch to monitor your ELB and Auto Scaling performance. Set up CloudWatch Alarms to receive notifications when your load balancer or Auto Scaling group is scaling.
- Analyze metrics like request count, response times, and error rates to fine-tune your scaling policies.

5. Use Sticky Sessions for Session-Based Applications:

- If your application relies on session data stored on specific instances, use **sticky sessions** in ELB. This ensures that subsequent requests from the same client are routed to the same instance.

5. Use Cases for ELB and Auto Scaling

1. Web Applications:

- Scale your web applications based on incoming traffic. ELB distributes traffic, while Auto Scaling adjusts the number of instances as needed.

2. Real-Time Applications:

- For real-time applications such as gaming or financial trading platforms, ELB and Auto Scaling provide automatic scaling to handle fluctuating loads, ensuring high availability and minimal latency.

3. Batch Processing:

- For batch-processing jobs, Auto Scaling can launch instances based on the size of the dataset. ELB can distribute tasks efficiently to those instances.

4. Microservices:

- In microservices architectures, ALB can route traffic to different services based on path or host, and Auto Scaling can manage each service's scaling independently.

Summary

Elastic Load Balancing (ELB) and Auto Scaling are powerful tools that enable automatic traffic distribution and dynamic resource scaling in AWS. Together, they ensure high availability, fault tolerance, and the ability to handle varying workloads efficiently. By integrating ELB with Auto Scaling, you can build resilient, scalable, and cost-effective applications that can automatically adjust to traffic changes, all while maintaining performance and minimizing downtime.

Amazon CloudFront: Content Delivery Network (CDN)

Amazon CloudFront is AWS's Content Delivery Network (CDN) service, designed to accelerate the delivery of your content (such as websites, videos, APIs, and other resources) to users worldwide. By distributing content across a network of edge locations, CloudFront ensures low-latency, high-speed delivery, improving the performance of your applications and providing a seamless user experience.

In this section, we'll dive into the key concepts, features, and use cases of Amazon CloudFront and explore how it can be leveraged to optimize content delivery for your applications.

1. Introduction to Amazon CloudFront

CloudFront is a globally distributed CDN that caches and serves content from a network of edge locations located around the world. When users request content, CloudFront automatically routes the request to the nearest edge location, ensuring faster load times and reduced latency.

How CloudFront Works:

- **Edge Locations**: CloudFront uses a vast network of edge locations that are geographically closer to end users. These locations cache copies of your content and serve them directly to users, minimizing the distance the data must travel.

- **Origin Server**: CloudFront fetches the content from the origin server (e.g., Amazon S3, EC2, or your own custom server) if it's not available in the cache, ensuring that users receive the most up-to-date content.

- **Caching**: Once content is served to users, it's cached at the edge location for a specified duration, known as the TTL (Time-to-Live). This reduces the load on the origin server and speeds up subsequent requests for the same content.

2. Key Features of Amazon CloudFront

1. Global Distribution of Content:

- **Edge Locations**: CloudFront has a wide network of edge locations in many countries across the globe, which ensures that content is delivered with minimal latency to users, regardless of their geographical location.
- **Regional Edge Caches**: CloudFront uses regional edge caches to further reduce latency and improve performance by caching frequently requested content that doesn't fit in the edge location cache.

2. Dynamic and Static Content Delivery:

- **Static Content**: CloudFront excels at delivering static assets such as images, JavaScript, CSS, and videos by caching them at the edge locations for faster delivery.
- **Dynamic Content**: CloudFront can also accelerate dynamic content (e.g., API responses, database queries) by routing requests to the nearest origin server and utilizing caching techniques where applicable.

3. Security Features:

- **Encryption**: CloudFront supports SSL/

TLS encryption, allowing you to deliver content securely over HTTPS, and enabling SSL termination at the edge locations.

- **Access Control**: You can configure CloudFront with AWS Identity and Access Management (IAM) and use signed URLs or cookies to control access to your content.

- **DDoS Protection**: CloudFront integrates with AWS Shield, offering protection against Distributed Denial of Service (DDoS) attacks to ensure content availability even during malicious traffic spikes.

- **Field-Level Encryption**: Protect sensitive data at the edge with CloudFront's field-level encryption capabilities.

4. Seamless Integration with AWS Services:

- **Amazon S3**: CloudFront works seamlessly with Amazon S3 to deliver content stored in S3 buckets to end users. You can use CloudFront to distribute static assets like images and videos, reducing the load on your S3 bucket and improving performance.

- **Elastic Load Balancing (ELB)**: For dynamic content, CloudFront integrates with ELB to distribute traffic across your EC2 instances, ensuring better performance and fault tolerance.

- **AWS Lambda@Edge**: With Lambda@Edge, you can run serverless functions at CloudFront edge locations, allowing you to customize content delivery, modify requests and responses, and more.
- **Amazon Route 53**: CloudFront works in tandem with Amazon Route 53, AWS's DNS service, to route users to the optimal CloudFront edge location.

5. Content Optimization:

- **Compression**: CloudFront can automatically compress text-based content (e.g., HTML, CSS, JavaScript) to reduce bandwidth usage and speed up page load times.
- **Custom Error Pages**: CloudFront allows you to define custom error pages that provide a better user experience in the event of errors, such as 404 (Not Found) or 500 (Internal Server Error).
- **Content Versioning**: CloudFront supports content versioning, allowing you to create new versions of assets (e.g., images, stylesheets) while maintaining cache control to ensure users get the

latest versions when required.

3. How Amazon CloudFront Improves Performance

CloudFront significantly reduces latency and improves the user experience by caching content closer to users and using techniques such as:

1. **Low Latency**: By caching content in edge locations, CloudFront minimizes the number of hops the request has to make, reducing latency and ensuring faster load times.

2. **High Availability and Fault Tolerance**: CloudFront automatically routes requests to healthy edge locations, ensuring that content is available even if one or more locations experience issues.

3. **Scalable Content Delivery**: CloudFront can handle spikes in traffic, making it ideal for applications that experience fluctuating traffic levels. It can scale up during periods of high demand and scale down when traffic decreases, optimizing performance and cost.

4. CloudFront Cache Behavior and Configuration

CloudFront offers flexibility in caching content, allowing you to configure the cache behavior based on your needs:

1. Cache TTL (Time-to-Live):

- You can set the cache expiration time for each cached object. A longer TTL reduces the number of requests to the origin server, improving performance. However, it may also result in serving outdated content, so it's essential to strike a balance.
- Cache TTL can be configured at the object level or by using custom cache behaviors for different paths (e.g., longer TTL for images, shorter TTL for API responses).

2. Cache Invalidation:

- CloudFront offers the ability to invalidate cached objects when content is updated on the origin server, ensuring users always receive the latest version.
- You can invalidate specific objects by URL or use patterns, allowing precise control over which content is refreshed.

3. Query String Parameters:

- CloudFront can cache content based on query string parameters, allowing for different cached versions of the same resource depending on the parameters in the URL.
- For example, caching different versions

of an image based on size or color parameters in the query string.

5. Pricing of Amazon CloudFront

CloudFront's pricing is based on several factors, including:

- **Data Transfer Out**: The cost of delivering content from CloudFront to end users (charged per GB).
- **Requests**: The number of requests made for content, including HTTP/HTTPS requests and data retrieval requests.
- **Data Transfer Between Regions**: If you transfer content between AWS regions or from CloudFront to an AWS origin server, additional charges may apply.
- **Invalidations**: The cost of invalidating objects from CloudFront's cache is generally free for the first 1,000 invalidation requests per month, with charges applying to additional requests.

6. Use Cases for Amazon CloudFront

CloudFront is ideal for a wide range of content delivery use cases:

1. Website Acceleration:

- Improve the load times of static and dynamic content (e.g., images, CSS, JavaScript) for global users. By caching these resources in edge locations, CloudFront can reduce load times and provide a better user experience.

2. Video Streaming:

- CloudFront is optimized for delivering large video files in formats such as HLS (HTTP Live Streaming) and DASH (Dynamic Adaptive Streaming over HTTP). It supports adaptive bitrate streaming, ensuring a smooth playback experience regardless of network conditions.

3. Software Distribution:

- Use CloudFront to distribute software updates and patches to users worldwide. By caching these updates at edge locations, you can reduce the strain on your origin server and ensure faster delivery.

4. API Acceleration:

- If you're using APIs to serve content or provide services, CloudFront can cache API responses and accelerate the delivery of content to users. It also integrates seamlessly with AWS Lambda@Edge, allowing you to modify API requests and responses at the edge.

5. E-commerce:

- E-commerce platforms often need to deliver a large amount of dynamic and static content. CloudFront ensures that product images, catalog pages, and transaction data are delivered quickly, even during high-traffic periods like sales events.

Summary

Amazon CloudFront is a powerful, scalable, and secure CDN solution that optimizes the delivery of content to users around the world. By leveraging its global network of edge locations, CloudFront ensures low-latency access to static and dynamic content, accelerates API performance, and integrates seamlessly with other AWS services to provide a comprehensive, high-performance solution for your content delivery needs.

Whether you're delivering static assets, streaming media, or accelerating API requests, CloudFront provides the tools and capabilities to meet your needs while improving application performance, reducing costs, and enhancing the user experience.

PART 3: ADVANCED AWS SOLUTIONS

CHAPTER 8: SECURITY AND COMPLIANCE

AWS Shared Responsibility Model

The AWS Shared Responsibility Model is a critical concept for understanding the division of security and compliance responsibilities between AWS and its customers. In this model, AWS takes responsibility for securing the cloud infrastructure, while customers are responsible for securing their data, applications, and resources deployed within AWS services.

By clarifying the responsibilities of both AWS and customers, the Shared Responsibility Model helps ensure a clear understanding of security roles, which in turn reduces risks and strengthens security posture.

1. Overview of the Shared Responsibility Model

The Shared Responsibility Model divides security responsibilities into two broad categories:

- **AWS's Responsibilities (Security of the Cloud)**: AWS is responsible for protecting the cloud infrastructure, including hardware, software, networking, and facilities that run AWS services.
- **Customer's Responsibilities (Security in the Cloud)**: Customers are responsible for securing their own applications, data, operating systems, networks, and configurations within AWS services.

This separation ensures that AWS customers have control over their resources in the cloud, while AWS ensures the foundational security of the services.

2. AWS's Responsibilities (Security of the Cloud)

AWS is responsible for securing the underlying infrastructure that supports cloud services. This includes:

1. Physical Security

- **Data Centers**: AWS ensures physical security at their data centers, including

24/7 surveillance, restricted access to authorized personnel, and the use of advanced security systems to protect physical assets.

- **Hardware**: AWS is responsible for the security of all hardware used in their data centers, including servers, storage devices, and network equipment.

2. Network Security

- **Infrastructure Protection**: AWS is responsible for securing the network and networking components, such as routers, firewalls, and load balancers, that enable connectivity within the AWS cloud infrastructure.

- **DDoS Protection**: AWS provides Distributed Denial of Service (DDoS) protection through AWS Shield to protect applications hosted in AWS from malicious attacks.

3. Hypervisor and Virtualization Layer Security

- **Virtual Machine Isolation**: AWS ensures that its hypervisor (software layer that manages virtual machines) is secure and isolates virtual machines from one another, preventing unauthorized access.

- **Infrastructure Management**: AWS manages the virtualized resources that underpin customer workloads, including storage, computing, and networking services.

4. Software and Service Security

- **Service Maintenance**: AWS is responsible for patching and maintaining the operating system and underlying services that run AWS-managed services such as EC2, S3, RDS, etc.
- **Service Availability**: AWS guarantees the uptime and availability of the services it provides, including availability guarantees as specified in Service Level Agreements (SLAs).

3. Customer's Responsibilities (Security in the Cloud)

While AWS takes care of the underlying infrastructure, customers are responsible for securing their applications, data, and configurations within AWS services. Customer responsibilities include:

1. Data Protection

- **Data Encryption**: Customers are responsible for encrypting their data both in transit and at rest. AWS provides tools such as AWS Key Management Service (KMS) and encryption options in services like S3 and EBS, but it is up to customers to enable and manage encryption.

- **Data Integrity**: Customers must ensure the integrity of their data through appropriate access controls, monitoring, and logging.

2. Identity and Access Management (IAM)

- **User Access Control**: Customers are responsible for configuring AWS Identity and Access Management (IAM) to manage user access to their resources. This includes creating IAM users, groups, and roles, setting permissions, and enabling multi-factor authentication (MFA).

- **Permission Management**: Customers must ensure that the principle of least privilege is followed by granting only the minimum necessary permissions to users and services.

3. Operating System and Application Security

- **OS Patching**: Customers are responsible for patching and securing the operating systems that they deploy on EC2 instances, including keeping the OS up-to-date with security patches.

- **Application Security**: Customers must secure the applications they build and deploy on AWS. This includes conducting regular security audits, vulnerability assessments, and ensuring that code is free from known security issues.

4. Networking and Firewalls

- **VPC Configuration**: Customers are responsible for configuring and managing their Virtual Private Cloud (VPC), including the setup of subnets, routing tables, internet gateways, and network access controls.

- **Security Groups and NACLs**: Customers must configure security groups (firewall rules) and Network Access Control Lists (NACLs) to control inbound and outbound traffic to and from their instances.

5. Monitoring and Logging

- **CloudTrail and CloudWatch**: Customers are responsible for configuring logging and monitoring services such as AWS CloudTrail (for auditing API calls) and Amazon CloudWatch (for monitoring performance and security metrics).

- **Alerts and Notifications**: Customers need to set up alerts and notifications for suspicious activity or changes to their resources in AWS.

6. Backup and Disaster Recovery

- **Data Backup**: Customers are responsible for ensuring that their data is properly backed up and that they have a disaster recovery strategy in place.
- **Redundancy and Availability**: While AWS offers highly available services, customers must architect their applications for fault tolerance and high availability by using multiple availability zones or regions where necessary.

4. Key Areas of Responsibility

To better understand the shared responsibilities, let's look at how they map to specific AWS services and use cases:

Security Aspect	AWS Responsibility	Customer Responsibility
Physical Security	Data center security, access control, physical equipment management	N/A
Network Security	Protection of AWS network infrastructure and services	VPC configuration, security groups, NACLs
Data Security	Infrastructure-level data protection (e.g., disk encryption)	Data encryption (in transit and at rest), data integrity
Access Control	Management of AWS access and permissions at the infrastructure level	Configuring IAM roles, policies, and access management
Operating System Security	Security of AWS-managed operating systems and environments	Patching and securing the operating systems on EC2 instances

Application Security	Security of AWS-managed services and environments	Securing the applications deployed in AWS
Monitoring	Providing tools for monitoring and logging	Configuring and using CloudWatch and CloudTrail
Compliance	Compliance certifications for AWS infrastructure	Ensuring compliance for data, applications, and resources

5. Shared Responsibility Model for Specific AWS Services

While the general framework of the Shared Responsibility Model remains the same across all AWS services, there are specific nuances depending on the service. Let's examine how the model applies to a few core AWS services:

Amazon EC2 (Compute Service)

- **AWS's Responsibility**: Securing the physical hardware, hypervisor, and network.
- **Customer's Responsibility**: Managing the operating system, applications, firewalls, IAM permissions, and ensuring EC2 instances are properly patched.

Amazon S3 (Storage Service)

- **AWS's Responsibility**: Ensuring the security of the underlying infrastructure, hardware, and the S3 service.
- **Customer's Responsibility**: Configuring

access controls, managing bucket policies, and encrypting data.

AWS Lambda (Serverless Service)

- **AWS's Responsibility**: Managing the infrastructure and runtime environment of Lambda functions.
- **Customer's Responsibility**: Writing secure Lambda functions, managing function permissions, and ensuring secure input/output data processing.

Amazon RDS (Database Service)

- **AWS's Responsibility**: Securing the database infrastructure and the underlying hardware.
- **Customer's Responsibility**: Managing database access, user permissions, encryption, backups, and updates.

6. Compliance and Auditing

The AWS Shared Responsibility Model also ties into AWS's compliance offerings. AWS provides customers with access to compliance reports, certifications, and tools to help meet regulatory requirements.

- **AWS Compliance Programs**: AWS complies with various regulatory frameworks, including GDPR, HIPAA, PCI DSS, SOC 1, SOC 2, and ISO 27001. Customers must ensure that their use of AWS services complies with these frameworks, particularly when handling sensitive or regulated data.

- **Customer Audits**: Customers are responsible for conducting audits of their applications, configurations, and operations within AWS to ensure they meet their specific security and compliance standards.

Summary

The AWS Shared Responsibility Model is crucial for understanding the division of security duties between AWS and its customers. AWS secures the underlying cloud infrastructure, while customers are responsible for securing their data, applications, and configurations. By clearly delineating these responsibilities, AWS enables customers to leverage its cloud services securely while maintaining control over their workloads and data.

Understanding and adhering to this model ensures that security risks are managed appropriately, helping customers deploy secure and compliant solutions on AWS.

AWS Key Management Service (KMS)

AWS Key Management Service (KMS) is a fully managed service that makes it easy to create and control the encryption keys used to encrypt your data in the cloud. KMS is designed to simplify the process of managing encryption keys and ensures that your sensitive data remains secure. It integrates with various AWS services and supports both symmetric and asymmetric encryption. KMS also provides centralized management, access control, auditing, and integration with other AWS services to meet your security and compliance requirements.

1. Overview of AWS KMS

AWS KMS provides the following core features:

- **Centralized Key Management**: Create, store, and manage encryption keys used across AWS services and applications.

- **Encryption and Decryption**: Use KMS to encrypt data with a simple API call and decrypt it when needed.

- **Access Control**: Define who can access and manage keys using IAM policies and KMS-specific policies.

- **Audit and Compliance**: Track usage and

access to keys with AWS CloudTrail logs to ensure compliance.

- **Key Rotation**: Automate key rotation for regular security practices.
- **Integration with AWS Services**: KMS works seamlessly with a wide range of AWS services like Amazon S3, Amazon EBS, Amazon RDS, and more to provide transparent encryption.

2. Core Concepts in AWS KMS

1. Customer Master Keys (CMKs)

- **Definition**: CMKs are the primary encryption keys used in AWS KMS. They can be either symmetric or asymmetric, depending on the use case.
- **Types of CMKs**:
  - **Symmetric CMKs**: The same key is used for both encryption and decryption. These are ideal for most use cases, such as encrypting data in Amazon S3 or Amazon EBS.
  - **Asymmetric CMKs**: These use a key pair, one for encryption and another for decryption. Asymmetric keys are used for tasks such as digital signatures or public key encryption.

2. Key Policies

- **Definition**: Key policies are used to define permissions and control who can use or manage the keys. These policies are essential for governing access to CMKs and help ensure that only authorized users or applications can perform encryption or decryption operations.

3. Grants

- **Definition**: Grants are temporary permissions associated with a specific user or application to use a key. Grants can be used to allow other services to use a key for encryption/decryption without modifying the key policy.

4. Key Rotation

- **Definition**: AWS KMS supports automatic rotation of symmetric CMKs at a defined interval (typically every year). Regular key rotation helps maintain security by minimizing the risk of key compromise over time.

5. Encryption Context

- **Definition**: An optional feature that provides additional metadata during encryption and decryption, allowing for context-aware access control.

3. Features and Capabilities of AWS KMS

1. Simplified Encryption

- **Encryption as a Service**: AWS KMS provides a simple API that can be used to encrypt and decrypt data programmatically across AWS services. This eliminates the complexity of managing your own encryption algorithms and key storage.
- **Integrated Encryption**: KMS integrates with AWS services like Amazon S3, Amazon RDS, Amazon EBS, and others to provide transparent encryption with minimal effort required from the user.

2. Granular Access Control

- **IAM Policies**: KMS allows fine-grained access control through AWS Identity and Access Management (IAM) policies. You can specify which IAM users or roles have access to particular keys, and what actions they can perform (e.g., encrypt, decrypt, generate data keys).
- **Key Policies**: These policies allow you to define who can manage the CMKs, and who can perform cryptographic operations on encrypted data.

3. Auditing and Compliance

- **Integration with CloudTrail**: AWS KMS integrates with AWS CloudTrail, allowing you to monitor and log every action related to key usage, including who accessed the key and what operations they performed. This is important for auditing and compliance purposes.

- **Regulatory Compliance**: AWS KMS is designed to meet various compliance standards like PCI DSS, HIPAA, FISMA, and others. It helps organizations meet regulatory requirements by providing encryption at rest, key management capabilities, and audit logging.

4. Multi-Region Support

- **Cross-Region Replication**: KMS allows you to replicate CMKs across different AWS regions, enabling the encryption of data in multiple regions and providing a consistent security model for global operations.

5. Integration with External Systems

- **CloudHSM Integration**: AWS KMS can integrate with AWS CloudHSM, an external hardware security module (HSM) service, to create and manage cryptographic keys that are stored in hardware and meet strict compliance requirements.

4. Using AWS KMS

1. Creating Keys

To use AWS KMS, you need to create Customer Master Keys (CMKs). Here's how you can create a CMK:

1. **Through the AWS Management Console**:
   - Go to the KMS service in the AWS Console.
   - Click "Create Key."
   - Choose either a symmetric or asymmetric key, depending on your needs.
   - Define key policy and permissions (who can manage and use the key).

2. **Using the AWS CLI**:
   - You can create a key by running the create-key command in the AWS CLI. Example:

bash

code

```
aws kms create-key --description "MyKey" --key-usage ENCRYPT_DECRYPT
```

2. Encrypting Data

Once you've created your CMK, you can use KMS to encrypt data by invoking the Encrypt operation. The Encrypt API call requires the CMK identifier and the data to encrypt.

For example, using the AWS SDK, you can encrypt data like this:

python

code

```
import boto3
kms = boto3.client('kms')
response = kms.encrypt(
    KeyId='arn:aws:kms:region:account-id:key/key-id',
    Plaintext='Your data to encrypt'
)
ciphertext = response['CiphertextBlob']
```

3. Decrypting Data

Decryption is just as simple. Once the data is encrypted, you can decrypt it with the Decrypt API:

python

Code

```
response = kms.decrypt(
    CiphertextBlob=ciphertext
)
plaintext = response['Plaintext']
```

4. Key Rotation

To enable automatic key rotation for a symmetric CMK, you can turn on rotation in the AWS Console or via the CLI:

bash

Code

```
aws kms enable-key-rotation --key-id key-id
```

5. Best Practices for Using AWS KMS

1. Least Privilege

- Ensure that you follow the principle of least privilege when granting access to encryption keys. Only users or roles that absolutely need to perform cryptographic operations should be granted permissions.

2. Enable Key Rotation

- Regularly rotate your CMKs to enhance security. Enable automatic key rotation for symmetric keys, and rotate keys manually if needed for asymmetric keys.

3. Monitor Key Usage

- Use AWS CloudTrail to track key usage and ensure compliance with internal security policies. Set up alarms for any unexpected activity related to key access or usage.

4. Separate Keys by Use Case

- If you have different use cases (e.g., one

for storing sensitive customer data and another for logs), create separate CMKs for each use case to improve security and control access.

5. Secure Key Management

- Treat CMKs like any other sensitive data and restrict access to them using IAM policies and key policies.

Summary

AWS KMS is a powerful service for managing encryption keys and ensuring the security of your sensitive data in the cloud. It simplifies the encryption process, provides granular access control, and integrates seamlessly with other AWS services. By following best practices such as least privilege access, key rotation, and continuous monitoring, you can effectively manage encryption keys and enhance the security of your AWS workloads.

Using AWS WAF and Shield for Protection

AWS Web Application Firewall (WAF) and AWS Shield are essential services for protecting your applications and data

from various security threats, such as DDoS attacks and malicious web traffic. These services are designed to work together, offering layered protection for your applications hosted on AWS.

1. Overview of AWS WAF and Shield

AWS WAF (Web Application Firewall)

AWS WAF is a managed service that helps protect web applications from common web exploits and vulnerabilities. It allows you to create customizable rules to block or allow HTTP and HTTPS requests based on conditions such as IP address, HTTP headers, URI strings, query parameters, and more. AWS WAF is designed to safeguard applications against common attack vectors, such as SQL injection, cross-site scripting (XSS), and other OWASP Top 10 vulnerabilities.

- **Customizable Rules**: You can define your own rules or use managed rule sets to block malicious traffic.

- **Real-Time Protection**: AWS WAF provides real-time traffic monitoring and blocking to mitigate web application attacks.

- **Integration with Other AWS Services**: AWS WAF integrates seamlessly with services like Amazon CloudFront, Application Load Balancer (ALB), and API Gateway.

AWS Shield

AWS Shield is a managed Distributed Denial-of-Service (DDoS) protection service that protects applications running on AWS from external DDoS attacks. There are two levels of AWS Shield:

- **AWS Shield Standard**: Provides protection against the most common types of DDoS attacks at no additional cost. This level protects against attacks targeting AWS infrastructure like EC2, ELB, and CloudFront.

- **AWS Shield Advanced**: Offers enhanced protection for applications against larger and more sophisticated DDoS attacks. It includes advanced detection, DDoS cost protection, real-time attack visibility, and 24/7 DDoS response team (DRT) support.

2. Key Features and Capabilities

AWS WAF

1. **Custom Web Access Control**:
    - Define custom rules to allow or block traffic based on specific conditions like IP address, HTTP method, query string, headers, URI paths, and more.
    - Protect against malicious traffic, including SQL injection and

cross-site scripting (XSS) attacks.

2. **Managed Rule Groups**:
   - Use pre-configured rule sets from AWS Managed Rules to automatically protect your application from common threats.
   - AWS Marketplace also offers third-party managed rule groups for specialized protections.

3. **Real-Time Metrics and Logging**:
   - AWS WAF provides real-time monitoring and logging via Amazon CloudWatch. You can set up alerts based on the number of blocked requests or detected threats.
   - You can also log all traffic to Amazon S3 for auditing and further analysis.

4. **Rate-Based Rules**:
   - Create rate-based rules to limit the number of requests from a particular IP address. This helps to mitigate brute-force attacks or DDoS attempts.

5. **Bot Protection**:
   - AWS WAF can identify and block automated bots by inspecting

request patterns and behaviors. This is useful for preventing bot-driven attacks like credential stuffing or web scraping.

AWS Shield

1. **DDoS Protection**:
    - AWS Shield provides automatic protection against DDoS attacks at the infrastructure level. It detects and mitigates attacks targeting your AWS resources in real-time.
    - Protection includes both volumetric and state-exhaustion attacks, which are commonly used in DDoS attempts.

2. **Layered Protection**:
    - AWS Shield is designed to protect at multiple layers of the OSI model, including:
        - **Network Layer**: Protection against large-scale attacks that aim to overwhelm your AWS infrastructure (e.g., UDP reflection attacks).
        - **Application Layer**: Protection against more targeted attacks on specific applications, including HTTP floods.

3. **AWS Shield Advanced Features**:
    - **24/7 DDoS Response Team (DRT) Access**: AWS Shield Advanced customers have access to the DDoS Response Team for immediate support during a DDoS attack.
    - **Cost Protection**: In the event of a DDoS attack, AWS Shield Advanced protects you from additional costs incurred due to increased traffic or scaling.
    - **Real-Time Attack Visibility**: AWS Shield Advanced provides detailed visibility into ongoing attacks via CloudWatch and AWS Shield Dashboard.
4. **Global DDoS Protection**:
    - AWS Shield protects all AWS services globally, including Amazon EC2, CloudFront, Route 53, ELB, and more.
    - Protection scales automatically with your AWS resources, ensuring that traffic surges due to DDoS attacks do not overwhelm your systems.

3. How AWS WAF and Shield Work Together

While AWS Shield provides essential protection

against large-scale DDoS attacks at the network and infrastructure level, AWS WAF focuses on protecting your application against more targeted, application-layer attacks (like SQL injection, cross-site scripting, and other web exploits). Using AWS WAF in conjunction with Shield gives you layered protection for your applications hosted on AWS.

Protection Layers

- **Shield Standard**: Protects against volumetric DDoS attacks at no cost. This is automatically enabled for all AWS customers.

- **AWS WAF**: Adds web application-specific protections to block malicious requests and exploits at the application layer.

- **Shield Advanced**: Provides enhanced DDoS protection for high-risk or high-traffic applications, along with real-time DDoS visibility and support.

4. Best Practices for Using AWS WAF and Shield

1. Use AWS WAF for Application-Level Protection

- **Create Custom Rules**: Customize AWS WAF to block common attack patterns specific to your application, such as SQL injection or XSS.

- **Enable Managed Rule Sets**: Use AWS Managed Rules for added protection against common web application attacks.

- **Set Up Rate-Limiting Rules**: Prevent brute-force attacks and minimize the impact of traffic spikes by setting rate-based rules.

- **Block Unwanted IPs**: Use AWS WAF to block requests from known malicious IP addresses or geo-block countries you don't need traffic from.

2. Enable AWS Shield Advanced for High-Traffic Applications

- **Activate Shield Advanced for DDoS Protection**: For applications with critical uptime requirements or high traffic, enable Shield Advanced for proactive protection against DDoS attacks.

- **Monitor Real-Time Attack Insights**: Use the AWS Shield Dashboard to get real-time insights into ongoing attacks, including attack types, sources, and traffic patterns.

- **Leverage 24/7 DRT Support**: Ensure that your application has 24/7 support from AWS DDoS experts during any ongoing attacks.

3. Integrate with Other AWS Services

- **Amazon CloudFront**: Integrate AWS WAF with Amazon CloudFront for enhanced protection against global threats while benefiting from CDN services like caching and faster content delivery.

- **Elastic Load Balancer (ELB)**: Integrate AWS WAF with ELB to protect backend applications from malicious traffic and DDoS attacks at the load balancer level.

4. Continuous Monitoring and Logging

- **Monitor Web Traffic**: Continuously monitor traffic patterns using AWS CloudWatch to identify unusual spikes or malicious activity.

- **Enable Logging**: Use AWS WAF logs to track blocked requests, analyze patterns, and improve your security rules.

- **Review Shield Metrics**: Regularly review AWS Shield metrics to detect potential DDoS threats early and take proactive action.

Summary

AWS WAF and Shield provide robust, multi-layered protection for your applications hosted on AWS. While AWS WAF focuses on protecting against application-level vulnerabilities, AWS

Shield offers comprehensive DDoS protection, ensuring that your applications are safeguarded from both small-scale and large-scale attacks. By leveraging both services together, you can ensure comprehensive protection, real-time monitoring, and continuous defense against evolving security threats.

CHAPTER 9: MONITORING AND MANAGEMENT

AWS CloudWatch: Metrics, Logs, and Alarms

Amazon CloudWatch is a monitoring and observability service in AWS that provides insights into the performance and health of your AWS resources and applications. It enables you to collect, monitor, and analyze operational data such as metrics, logs, and events in real-time. This helps you ensure the availability, reliability, and performance of your applications while optimizing resource utilization and troubleshooting issues.

CloudWatch is an essential tool for DevOps, security, and operational teams as it helps improve operational visibility and automate responses to incidents or events in your AWS environment.

1. Overview of AWS CloudWatch

AWS CloudWatch provides three key functionalities:

- **Metrics**: Collects and stores key data points about your AWS resources, such as EC2 instances, RDS databases, Lambda functions, and other services.

- **Logs**: Centralizes and monitors logs from applications, operating systems, and AWS services to gain insights into system performance and diagnose issues.

- **Alarms**: Allows you to set thresholds for metrics and trigger automated actions based on specific conditions, such as sending notifications, scaling resources, or executing Lambda functions.

These features work together to help monitor and optimize the performance of your AWS environment in real time.

2. AWS CloudWatch Metrics

CloudWatch Metrics provide detailed insights into the performance of AWS resources. These metrics are automatically collected by AWS services and can also be created by custom applications and systems.

Types of CloudWatch Metrics

1. **AWS Service Metrics**:
   - Metrics collected by AWS services such as EC2 (CPU utilization, network traffic, disk I/O), RDS (database CPU utilization, read/write latency), Lambda (invocation count, duration, error rate), and more.
   - These metrics are provided at no extra cost and are available by default for supported AWS services.

2. **Custom Metrics**:
   - You can also create your own metrics to monitor application-specific data or resources not automatically monitored by AWS.
   - Custom metrics can be pushed to CloudWatch using the **PutMetricData** API or via the CloudWatch Agent for system-level monitoring.

CloudWatch Metric Collection

- Metrics are collected in **CloudWatch namespaces**. A namespace is a container for metrics that allows you to group them based on an application or environment (e.g., "AWS/EC2" for EC2-related metrics).

- Metrics are automatically updated at regular intervals (e.g., every minute or five minutes, depending on the metric granularity).

Common Metrics

- **EC2**: CPU utilization, network traffic, disk I/O.
- **S3**: Request count, data transfer, error rates.
- **Lambda**: Invocations, duration, error count.
- **RDS**: CPU utilization, database connections, free storage space.

3. AWS CloudWatch Logs

CloudWatch Logs enables you to centralize and analyze logs from your AWS services, operating systems, and applications. It allows you to search, monitor, and archive log data, which is crucial for debugging, troubleshooting, and compliance monitoring.

Features of CloudWatch Logs

1. **Log Streams**:
   - Logs are stored in **Log Groups** and organized into **Log Streams**. A log stream typically represents a sequence of log events from a single source (e.g., an EC2 instance or Lambda function).
   - CloudWatch can collect logs from various sources, including EC2 instances, Lambda functions, CloudTrail, VPC flow logs, and custom applications.

2. **Log Retention**:
   - CloudWatch Logs supports automatic retention policies, allowing you to set the duration for which log data is kept. You can define retention periods to automatically delete logs after a set period.

3. **Log Searching and Analysis**:
   - CloudWatch Logs provides advanced querying capabilities, using **CloudWatch Logs Insights**, to filter and search log data to troubleshoot issues. Logs can be searched based on time ranges, log levels, or specific

keywords.

4. **Log Subscription**:
    - You can stream CloudWatch Logs to other AWS services, such as **Amazon S3**, **Amazon Elasticsearch Service**, or **AWS Lambda** for further analysis or processing.

Common Use Cases

- **Application Logs**: Collect logs from web servers, application servers, or database servers to track application behavior and performance.
- **Security Logs**: Use CloudWatch Logs to capture security-related events such as login attempts, API calls, and access logs from security tools.
- **System Logs**: Monitor system health and resource utilization by collecting operating system logs and custom application logs.

4. AWS CloudWatch Alarms

CloudWatch Alarms enable you to set thresholds for your metrics and trigger actions when those thresholds are breached. This is useful for automating responses to operational events, sending notifications, or taking corrective actions.

Features of CloudWatch Alarms

1. **Metric-Based Alarms**:
   - Alarms are based on CloudWatch Metrics and are triggered when the metric value breaches a defined threshold for a specified number of periods (e.g., if CPU utilization exceeds 80% for 5 minutes).
   - You can set conditions to trigger alarms for any metric, whether it's an AWS service metric or a custom metric.

2. **Actions and Notifications**:
   - When an alarm state is triggered (e.g., ALARM, OK, or INSUFFICIENT_DATA), CloudWatch can take actions such as:
     - Sending notifications via **Amazon SNS** (Simple Notification Service) to alert you or your team.
     - Triggering AWS Lambda functions to automatically resolve issues (e.g., scale an EC2 instance).
     - Auto-scaling resources to match demand by integrating with **Auto Scaling Groups**.

3. **Composite Alarms**:
    - Composite alarms allow you to combine multiple alarms into a single alarm. The composite alarm triggers when multiple conditions are met across different alarms, helping you reduce noise and focus on critical issues.

4. **State Transitions**:
    - CloudWatch alarms can be in different states:
        - **OK**: The metric is within the normal range.
        - **ALARM**: The metric breaches the specified threshold.
        - **INSUFFICIENT_DATA**: CloudWatch has not received enough data points to determine the alarm state.

5. Best Practices for Using AWS CloudWatch

1. Use CloudWatch Metrics for Real-Time Monitoring

- Regularly monitor key performance indicators (KPIs) for your AWS resources to ensure optimal performance. Set up alarms to notify you of any abnormal behavior or performance degradation.

2. Centralize and Analyze Logs

- Collect and centralize logs from all your AWS resources and applications in CloudWatch Logs for better visibility and troubleshooting. Use CloudWatch Logs Insights to run queries and identify the root cause of issues quickly.

3. Set Up Alarms for Proactive Monitoring

- Set up CloudWatch alarms on critical metrics (e.g., CPU utilization, memory usage, error rates) to receive alerts before issues become critical. This allows you to take corrective actions promptly, minimizing downtime.

4. Automate Responses Using Alarms

- Automate responses to CloudWatch alarms by triggering actions like scaling resources, invoking Lambda functions, or sending notifications. For example, scale your EC2 instances automatically based on CPU usage or error rates.

5. Optimize Log Retention and Costs

- Set appropriate retention policies to avoid unnecessary log storage costs. You can also archive old logs to Amazon S3 for long-term storage at a lower cost.

6. Integrate CloudWatch with Other AWS Services

- Use CloudWatch in combination with other AWS services like AWS Auto Scaling, Lambda, SNS, and S3 to create a fully integrated monitoring and response system.

Summary

AWS CloudWatch is a powerful monitoring and management tool that helps you keep your AWS infrastructure and applications running smoothly. By leveraging CloudWatch's metrics, logs, and alarms, you can gain deep insights into the performance of your resources, troubleshoot issues efficiently, and automate responses to events. Using CloudWatch effectively is key to maintaining operational excellence in your AWS environment.

AWS CloudTrail: Auditing and Compliance

AWS CloudTrail is a service that enables you to monitor and log activity across your AWS environment. It helps with security, auditing, compliance, and operational monitoring by recording API calls made on your AWS resources. Every action taken by users, services, and even automated processes is captured and logged by CloudTrail, which provides valuable insights into who did what, when, and from where within your AWS environment.

CloudTrail is essential for tracking user activity, ensuring compliance with regulatory requirements, identifying security incidents, and troubleshooting operational issues.

1. Overview of AWS CloudTrail

AWS CloudTrail provides a history of AWS API calls made within your account. It logs API requests to services like Amazon EC2, Amazon S3, IAM, Lambda, and others, including the identity of the requester, the actions they took, and the source IP address.

Key Features of AWS CloudTrail:

1. **API Call Logging**:
    - CloudTrail records every API call made to AWS services. This includes requests initiated through the AWS Management Console, AWS CLI, AWS SDKs, and other tools.
    - Logs include details such as request parameters, the source IP address, the requester's identity, and the response.

2. **Event History**:

- CloudTrail stores up to 90 days of event history by default. This enables you to search and analyze API activity within the past 90 days without the need for external tools.

3. **Log File Integrity**:
    - CloudTrail ensures that logs are immutable and tamper-proof by using **Amazon S3** with **encryption** and **log file validation**.
    - CloudTrail logs can be encrypted using AWS Key Management Service (KMS) for additional security.

4. **Multi-Region and Multi-Account Support**:
    - You can configure CloudTrail to log events across multiple AWS regions and even multiple AWS accounts. This provides a comprehensive view of activities across your entire AWS environment.

5. **Integration with Other AWS Services**:
    - CloudTrail integrates with services like **AWS CloudWatch** (for creating alarms), **Amazon S3**

(for log storage), **AWS Lambda** (for automated responses), and **AWS Athena** (for querying logs).

- You can also use CloudTrail with **AWS Config** to track configuration changes and ensure compliance.

2. Understanding CloudTrail Logs

CloudTrail logs consist of detailed records of the API calls made in your AWS account. These logs are stored in JSON format and contain information about each API request, including the following:

Key Components of CloudTrail Logs:

1. **Event Name**: The specific API action taken (e.g., CreateBucket, RunInstances).

2. **Event Source**: The AWS service that received the API request (e.g., ec2.amazonaws.com).

3. **User Identity**: The IAM user or role that initiated the request, or the AWS service making the call.

4. **Request Parameters**: The parameters passed to the API action, such as the EC2 instance ID or S3 bucket name.

5. **Response Elements**: Information about the result of the API request (e.g., success or failure, error messages).

6. **Timestamp**: The time when the API request was made.
7. **Source IP Address**: The IP address from which the request originated.
8. **User Agent**: The tool or interface used to make the request (e.g., AWS SDK, CLI, or Console).
9. **Event Type**: The type of event, such as AwsApiCall, AwsServiceEvent, or AwsConsoleSignIn.

CloudTrail Log Example:

json

Code

```
{
  "eventVersion": "1.05",
  "userIdentity": {
    "type": "IAMUser",
    "principalId": "AWSAccountID",
    "arn": "arn:aws:iam::AWSAccountID:user/username",
    "accountId": "AWSAccountID",
    "userName": "username"
  },
  "eventTime": "2024-01-01T12:00:00Z",
  "eventSource": "ec2.amazonaws.com",
```

```
"eventName": "RunInstances",
"awsRegion": "us-west-2",
"sourceIPAddress": "192.168.1.1",
"userAgent": "aws-cli/2.0.0",
"requestParameters": {
  "instanceType": "t2.micro",
  "imageId": "ami-12345678",
  "maxCount": 1,
  "minCount": 1
},
"responseElements": {
  "instancesSet": {
    "item": [
      {
        "instanceId": "i-1234567890abcdef0"
      }
    ]
  }
}
}
```

3. Configuring and Managing CloudTrail

AWS CloudTrail is easy to set up and configure for logging and monitoring activities in your account.

Key Configuration Steps:

1. **Creating a Trail**:
    - A trail is a configuration that enables CloudTrail to log events for your AWS account. When creating a trail, you can choose:
        - **Multi-Region Logging**: Enable logging for all regions or for specific regions.
        - **S3 Bucket for Log Storage**: Specify an S3 bucket to store your logs.
        - **Log File Encryption**: Enable encryption using KMS for log file security.
        - **Log File Integrity Validation**: Enable log file validation to ensure that log files are not tampered with.

2. **Managing Log Storage**:
    - You can store CloudTrail logs in Amazon S3, which allows you to retain logs for long-term archival and compliance purposes. CloudTrail logs can be managed using Amazon S3 lifecycle policies to automatically delete or archive logs after a specified period.

3. **CloudTrail Insights**:
    - CloudTrail Insights automatically detects unusual activity in your AWS account by analyzing API activity patterns. It can alert you to potential security threats, such as spikes in resource provisioning or sudden increases in specific API requests.

4. **Enabling CloudTrail Across Multiple Accounts**:
    - CloudTrail can be configured for multiple accounts in an AWS Organization to centralize logs in a single S3 bucket. This helps streamline auditing and compliance efforts for large environments.

4. Use Cases for AWS CloudTrail

1. **Security Auditing and Monitoring**:
    - CloudTrail helps detect unauthorized or malicious activity by logging all API calls. You can use CloudTrail logs to identify security incidents like privilege escalation, unauthorized resource access, or unusual API activity.

2. **Compliance and Governance**:

- CloudTrail logs provide a comprehensive audit trail of all actions in your AWS account, which is critical for meeting regulatory requirements like GDPR, HIPAA, SOC 2, PCI-DSS, and more. You can use CloudTrail to demonstrate compliance with access controls, data retention policies, and resource management.

3. **Operational Monitoring**:
    - CloudTrail allows you to monitor user actions, resource changes, and system configurations. You can track who made changes to resources, what changes were made, and when they occurred. This is particularly useful for troubleshooting operational issues or verifying system configurations.

4. **Incident Response and Forensics**:
    - When a security incident or operational failure occurs, CloudTrail can be used to trace the actions that led up to the event. This helps with investigating the cause and identifying any potential

security gaps.

5. **Cost Management and Billing**:
    - By tracking API calls that result in resource creation or modification, CloudTrail can help you monitor resource usage and cost trends. You can correlate API activity with billing data to gain better visibility into spending.

5. Best Practices for Using AWS CloudTrail

1. **Enable Multi-Region Trails**:
    - Enable CloudTrail logging across all AWS regions to ensure that no activity is missed. This is especially important if your organization uses resources across multiple regions.

2. **Store Logs in Secure S3 Buckets**:
    - Ensure that CloudTrail logs are stored in a dedicated, secure Amazon S3 bucket. Implement access control policies (e.g., IAM roles and bucket policies) to restrict access to the logs.

3. **Enable Log File Integrity Validation**:
    - Enable **log file integrity validation** to ensure the integrity of your CloudTrail logs

and detect any tampering or unauthorized changes.

4. **Use CloudTrail Insights**:
   - Enable CloudTrail Insights to automatically detect unusual or unexpected activity patterns, helping you quickly identify potential threats or misconfigurations.

5. **Archive and Retain Logs for Compliance**:
   - Store CloudTrail logs for the required retention period to comply with regulatory standards. You can set up **lifecycle policies** in Amazon S3 to manage the logs and archive them for long-term retention.

6. **Integrate with AWS Security Tools**:
   - Use CloudTrail in conjunction with other AWS security services, such as **AWS Security Hub**, **AWS GuardDuty**, and **AWS Config**, to create a more comprehensive security monitoring and incident response system.

Summary

AWS CloudTrail is an invaluable service for

auditing, monitoring, and ensuring compliance in your AWS environment. By capturing a comprehensive history of API calls, CloudTrail enables better security, operational visibility, and regulatory compliance. With its deep integration across AWS services, CloudTrail is essential for organizations looking to maintain a secure and well-governed AWS environment.

AWS Config: Resource Management

AWS Config is a service that provides a detailed view of the configuration of AWS resources in your account. It allows you to assess, audit, and evaluate the configurations of your AWS resources, track configuration changes over time, and ensure compliance with internal policies or regulatory standards. AWS Config is a vital tool for resource management, as it enables organizations to maintain a consistent and compliant cloud environment.

1. Overview of AWS Config

AWS Config continuously monitors and records your AWS resource configurations, including their relationships to each other. It stores configuration history and allows you to track how your resources change over time. This information is essential for understanding the relationships between resources, ensuring compliance, and identifying the cause of configuration-related issues.

Key Features of AWS Config:

1. **Resource Configuration Tracking**:
   - AWS Config records changes in your AWS resource configurations, including their current state and history. It helps maintain a record of what your resources looked like at any given point in time.

2. **Configuration Snapshot**:
   - You can take a snapshot of your resource configurations, which is useful for compliance audits or troubleshooting configuration issues.

3. **Configuration History**:
   - AWS Config stores a history of configuration changes, allowing you to review past resource configurations and changes.

4. **Compliance Checking**:
   - AWS Config helps ensure that your resources comply with

internal policies or industry standards by enabling you to define and evaluate rules that describe your desired configuration state.

5. **Resource Relationships**:
    - It visualizes the relationships between your resources, helping you understand how they interact. This is especially useful when troubleshooting issues or identifying the impact of changes on other resources.

6. **AWS Config Rules**:
    - You can create AWS Config Rules to automatically evaluate whether your resources comply with specific configuration requirements, such as ensuring that security groups are appropriately configured or that instances are not running with unrestricted access.

2. How AWS Config Works

AWS Config works by recording configuration snapshots of your resources and continuously monitoring their configurations to detect changes. When a change occurs, AWS Config creates a new configuration record. It can then notify you of the change or perform compliance checks against predefined rules.

AWS Config Components:

1. **AWS Config Recorder**:
   - The Config Recorder continuously records the configuration changes of AWS resources in your account. You can enable the recorder for specific regions and for the resources you want to track.

2. **AWS Config Rules**:
   - These are predefined or custom rules that evaluate the configurations of your AWS resources. They can be used to enforce compliance with best practices or regulatory standards.

3. **AWS Config History**:
   - Configuration history refers to a series of configuration snapshots stored by AWS Config. You can query this history to review the state of your resources at any point in time.

4. **Configuration Aggregators**:
   - Configuration Aggregators allow you to aggregate AWS Config

data from multiple accounts and regions into a single view. This is particularly useful for multi-account or multi-region environments.

3. Key Benefits of AWS Config

1. **Compliance and Auditing**:
    - AWS Config is an essential tool for compliance auditing. It provides a detailed history of your resource configurations, which can be used for auditing purposes. By comparing past and current configurations, you can verify that your resources comply with internal policies, regulatory requirements, or industry standards.

2. **Real-Time Monitoring of Resource Configurations**:
    - AWS Config continuously monitors your resources for changes, allowing you to detect configuration drift or unintended changes in real-time. This ensures that resources remain in their desired state and adhere to compliance guidelines.

3. **Improved Troubleshooting and**

Incident Response:
- AWS Config enables you to track resource configurations and changes over time, which helps in troubleshooting incidents and understanding how issues arose. By examining the configuration history, you can pinpoint changes that might have caused an issue.

4. **Automated Remediation**:
   - With AWS Config, you can automate remediation actions based on the evaluation of configuration rules. For example, if a security group is misconfigured, AWS Config can automatically correct it or notify the relevant team to take corrective action.

5. **Visibility into Resource Relationships**:
   - AWS Config maps out the relationships between resources, which is critical when understanding the impact of changes. For instance, if you modify an EC2 instance, AWS Config shows how it affects related resources such as security groups or network

interfaces.

4. AWS Config Rules and Compliance

One of the most powerful features of AWS Config is the ability to set up rules that automatically evaluate resource configurations and ensure compliance with your standards. These rules can be managed directly in the AWS Management Console, or you can create custom rules using AWS Lambda functions.

Types of AWS Config Rules:

1. **Managed Rules**:
    - AWS provides a set of predefined, out-of-the-box rules that you can enable with just a few clicks. These rules cover a broad range of best practices, such as ensuring that resources are encrypted, that security groups are properly configured, or that certain types of instances are disabled.

2. **Custom Rules**:
    - Custom rules can be created using AWS Lambda functions. This allows you to tailor compliance checks to your specific use case or organizational policies. For instance, you can create a rule

to check that all EC2 instances are tagged according to your company's tagging policy.

3. **Rule Evaluations**:
    - AWS Config continuously evaluates resources based on the rules you set up. You can set rules to run automatically when a configuration change occurs, ensuring that compliance is continuously monitored.

4. **Remediation of Non-Compliant Resources**:
    - AWS Config can trigger automatic remediation actions when a resource is found to be non-compliant with your defined rules. For example, if an EC2 instance is found without the required encryption, AWS Config can trigger an AWS Lambda function to enable encryption on the instance.

5. Visualizing Resource Configurations

AWS Config enables the visualization of the relationships between resources and changes over time. This helps you better understand how your resources interact and how configuration changes impact the environment.

Resource Relationship Visualization:

1. Configuration Timeline:
- You can view a timeline of configuration changes to see how a resource's configuration has evolved over time. This helps when identifying the root cause of issues that arise from misconfigurations.

2. Resource Relationship Graph:
- AWS Config provides a visual graph that shows how resources are interconnected. For instance, you can visualize how an EC2 instance is connected to an Elastic IP, security group, or IAM role.

6. Best Practices for Using AWS Config

1. Enable AWS Config for All Regions:
- It's best to enable AWS Config for all regions where your AWS resources are deployed. This ensures that you are capturing the configuration of every resource across your entire AWS environment.

2. Use Managed Rules:
- Start by using AWS Config's managed rules to get

quick insights into common best practices and compliance requirements. These rules are preconfigured and help ensure that your resources are following security and operational best practices.

3. **Integrate with AWS CloudTrail**:
    - To enhance your auditing capabilities, integrate AWS Config with AWS CloudTrail. This allows you to get a full picture of resource configurations as well as API call activities.

4. **Automate Remediation**:
    - Set up automated remediation for non-compliant resources to reduce the manual effort involved in compliance monitoring and to maintain a consistent configuration across your environment.

5. **Use Configuration Aggregators**:
    - If you operate in a multi-account or multi-region setup, use AWS Config Aggregators to centralize your configuration data and simplify compliance checks and auditing.

Summary

AWS Config is a powerful service for resource management in the AWS cloud. It provides visibility into your AWS resources' configurations, ensures compliance with standards, and enables proactive management of your cloud environment. By tracking configuration changes, enforcing best practices with AWS Config Rules, and visualizing resource relationships, AWS Config helps maintain an efficient, secure, and compliant AWS environment. It is an essential tool for organizations that aim to streamline operations, improve security, and ensure compliance in the cloud.

CHAPTER 10: DEVOPS AND AUTOMATION

AWS CodePipeline, CodeBuild, and CodeDeploy

AWS offers a suite of tools designed to automate and streamline the continuous integration and continuous delivery (CI/CD) process for application development. These tools—AWS CodePipeline, CodeBuild, and CodeDeploy—are all integral components of AWS's DevOps offering, designed to help teams automate their software release workflows, manage and deploy code, and ensure faster and more reliable software delivery.

1. Overview of AWS CodePipeline

AWS CodePipeline is a fully managed continuous delivery (CD) service that automates the steps required to release software. CodePipeline enables you to model, visualize, and automate the flow of your software code from source to deployment, integrating various stages of your development lifecycle.

Key Features of AWS CodePipeline:

- **Automated CI/CD Pipelines**: CodePipeline automates the software release process by creating a pipeline that includes stages such as building, testing, and deploying.

- **Integration with Other AWS Services**: CodePipeline integrates with AWS services like CodeBuild, CodeDeploy, AWS Lambda, Amazon ECS, and third-party tools such as GitHub, Jenkins, and others.

- **Customizable Stages**: You can customize your pipeline with actions such as building the application, running tests, or deploying it to staging or production environments.

- **Real-Time Feedback**: It provides feedback on the status of each stage and alerts the team if there are failures, making it easier to pinpoint where issues arise.

Pipeline Stages in CodePipeline:

1. **Source**: The starting point of the pipeline, where the source code is pulled from a version control system (e.g., GitHub, AWS CodeCommit, Bitbucket).

2. **Build**: The code is compiled and built using AWS CodeBuild or other build tools.

3. **Test**: Automated tests are run to verify that the software behaves as expected.

4. **Deploy**: The application is deployed to staging or production environments using AWS CodeDeploy or other deployment mechanisms.

5. **Approval**: Optional manual approval stage before the deployment proceeds to production.

6. **Monitor**: After deployment, monitoring tools like AWS CloudWatch can track the performance of the application.

2. Overview of AWS CodeBuild

AWS CodeBuild is a fully managed build service that compiles source code, runs tests, and produces software packages ready for deployment. CodeBuild eliminates the need for managing build servers and provides scalability for handling multiple build jobs concurrently.

Key Features of AWS CodeBuild:

- **Fully Managed Build Service**: CodeBuild handles the entire build process, from compiling source code to running tests, and packaging it for deployment.
- **Custom Build Environments**: CodeBuild offers predefined environments for popular programming languages like Java, Python, Node.js, and others. You can also create custom build environments with Docker images.
- **Scalability**: CodeBuild automatically scales to handle the number of concurrent builds, helping reduce build times and costs.
- **Integration with CodePipeline**: CodeBuild integrates seamlessly with AWS CodePipeline to automate the build process as part of a CI/CD pipeline.
- **Build Logs**: CodeBuild generates detailed logs that allow you to troubleshoot build errors and optimize your build process.

How CodeBuild Works:

1. **Source**: CodeBuild retrieves the source code from a repository such as GitHub, AWS CodeCommit, or S3.
2. **Build**: CodeBuild compiles the source code, runs tests, and produces build artifacts such as executables or libraries.

3. **Output**: The built artifacts are stored in Amazon S3, which can be used in later stages of a pipeline or for deployment.

3. Overview of AWS CodeDeploy

AWS CodeDeploy is a fully managed deployment service that automates the process of deploying applications to Amazon EC2 instances, AWS Lambda functions, or on-premises servers. CodeDeploy supports rolling updates, blue/green deployments, and can manage deployments to both serverless and traditional infrastructure.

Key Features of AWS CodeDeploy:

- **Automated Deployments**: CodeDeploy automates the process of deploying code to your target infrastructure. It handles tasks such as installing updates, configuring settings, and running deployment scripts.

- **Deployment Strategies**: CodeDeploy supports various deployment strategies:
    - **In-Place Deployments**: Updates are made to the application on existing infrastructure.
    - **Blue/Green Deployments**: A new version of the application is deployed to a separate environment (green), while the current version continues to run in the original environment (blue). Traffic is switched to

the green environment once it's verified.

- **Integration with CodePipeline**: CodeDeploy is often used as the deployment stage in a CI/CD pipeline, ensuring that applications are automatically deployed after being built and tested.

- **Rollback Capabilities**: If a deployment fails, CodeDeploy can automatically roll back to the previous version to minimize downtime and errors.

- **Support for Multiple Environments**: You can deploy to Amazon EC2 instances, Lambda functions, or on-premises servers, making it versatile for different architectures.

Deployment Options in CodeDeploy:

1. **Amazon EC2 Instances**: You can deploy your applications to Amazon EC2 instances, ensuring that all the necessary software configurations are in place.

2. **AWS Lambda Functions**: CodeDeploy can automate the deployment of code to serverless Lambda functions.

3. **On-Premises Servers**: For hybrid environments, CodeDeploy can deploy applications to your on-premises

servers.

4. Integrating CodePipeline, CodeBuild, and CodeDeploy

Together, AWS CodePipeline, CodeBuild, and CodeDeploy form a powerful CI/CD pipeline for automating the build, test, and deployment process. Here's how they work together in a typical DevOps workflow:

1. **Source Stage**: CodePipeline retrieves the source code from your version control system (e.g., GitHub, AWS CodeCommit).

2. **Build Stage**: CodePipeline triggers CodeBuild to compile the code, run unit tests, and create build artifacts (e.g., executable files, libraries).

3. **Test Stage**: Optionally, CodeBuild can run automated tests, ensuring the code works as expected before it is deployed.

4. **Deploy Stage**: CodePipeline triggers CodeDeploy to automatically deploy the application to EC2 instances, Lambda functions, or on-premises servers.

5. **Approval and Monitoring**: After the deployment, manual approval or monitoring stages in CodePipeline can be used to ensure the deployment is successful before pushing to production.

5. Best Practices for Using CodePipeline,

CodeBuild, and CodeDeploy

- **Use Version Control**: Integrate your pipeline with version control systems like AWS CodeCommit or GitHub to manage your source code and track changes.

- **Automate Testing**: Incorporate automated testing in the build stage with CodeBuild to ensure that new code is functional and does not break existing functionality.

- **Monitor Deployment Success**: Use AWS CloudWatch and CloudTrail to monitor the success or failure of deployments and generate alerts if there are any issues.

- **Ensure Rollback Plans**: Set up rollback mechanisms in CodeDeploy to ensure that your application can be restored in case of deployment failure.

- **Optimize Build Environments**: Use custom Docker images for CodeBuild to create build environments that fit your project's specific needs and dependencies.

Summary

AWS CodePipeline, CodeBuild, and CodeDeploy are powerful tools that simplify the process of automating software development and deployment. Together, they enable developers to build, test, and deploy applications faster and more reliably, while minimizing manual intervention. Whether you are deploying code to EC2 instances, Lambda, or on-premises servers, these tools integrate seamlessly into a DevOps workflow, ensuring that you can deliver high-quality applications with greater speed and efficiency. By leveraging AWS's CI/CD tools, organizations can accelerate their software release cycles and reduce the complexity of managing deployments.

Infrastructure as Code with AWS CloudFormation

AWS CloudFormation is a powerful service that enables you to define and provision AWS infrastructure using a declarative template. This approach, known as Infrastructure as Code (IaC), allows developers and systems administrators to automate the process of setting up and managing AWS resources, ensuring consistency, repeatability, and scalability.

1. What is AWS CloudFormation?

AWS CloudFormation is a service that helps you model and set up your Amazon Web Services (AWS) resources so that they can be automatically provisioned and managed through code. By defining infrastructure in a template, you can deploy and manage resources as a stack. These stacks can be updated, replicated, and scaled with ease, ensuring efficient and automated management of cloud infrastructure.

Key Features of AWS CloudFormation:

- **Declarative Language**: CloudFormation uses JSON or YAML to define infrastructure, where you declare the desired resources and configurations.

- **Stack Management**: CloudFormation organizes resources into stacks, which can be easily managed, updated, or deleted as a single unit.

- **Cross-Region and Cross-Account Deployment**: You can deploy CloudFormation templates across different AWS regions and accounts, facilitating scalability and multi-region infrastructure setups.

- **Automated Provisioning and Updates**: Resources can be provisioned, configured, and updated automatically by applying templates, eliminating manual processes.

- **Version Control**: CloudFormation templates can be stored in version-controlled repositories, enabling tracking of changes and rollback to previous configurations.

2. CloudFormation Template Structure

CloudFormation templates define the infrastructure components in a declarative way. They consist of several key sections that describe different parts of your AWS resources.

Basic Components of a CloudFormation Template:

1. **Metadata**: Optional section that provides additional information about the template.

2. **Parameters**: Allows users to pass input values when creating or updating a stack, enabling template reusability and flexibility.

3. **Resources**: The most important section, where the actual AWS resources (such as EC2 instances, S3 buckets, and RDS databases) are defined.

4. **Outputs**: Defines output values that can be used by other stacks or services. For example, you might output the public IP of an EC2 instance or the URL of a load

balancer.

5. **Mappings**: Allows you to create conditional mappings, such as environment-specific configurations (e.g., different configurations for development and production environments).

6. **Conditions**: Used to specify whether certain resources or properties should be created based on specific conditions (e.g., only creating a resource if it's in the production environment).

7. **Resources**: Defines AWS resources like EC2 instances, S3 buckets, Lambda functions, etc., that will be provisioned as part of the stack.

Example of a Simple CloudFormation Template (YAML):

yaml

Code

```yaml
AWSTemplateFormatVersion: '2010-09-09'
Parameters:
  InstanceType:
    Type: String
    Default: t2.micro
Resources:
```

```yaml
MyEC2Instance:
  Type: AWS::EC2::Instance
  Properties:
    InstanceType: !Ref InstanceType
    ImageId: ami-0c55b159cbfafe1f0
Outputs:
  InstanceId:
    Description: "Instance ID"
    Value: !Ref MyEC2Instance
```

3. Benefits of Using AWS CloudFormation

- **Consistency and Repeatability**: Since the infrastructure is defined in code, CloudFormation ensures that resources are created and configured exactly as specified every time. This reduces the risk of human error and ensures consistency across environments.

- **Version Control and Collaboration**: CloudFormation templates can be stored in version control systems, allowing teams to collaborate on infrastructure changes and track modifications over time.

- **Automation**: CloudFormation automates the provisioning, configuration, and management of AWS resources, significantly reducing manual efforts and errors.

- **Scalability**: CloudFormation makes it easy to scale your infrastructure by using parameters, loops, and macros to define and provision scalable resources.
- **Cost Management**: CloudFormation can help optimize infrastructure by enabling the deletion of resources that are no longer needed or by simplifying cost calculations via templated deployments.

4. How CloudFormation Works

The process of using AWS CloudFormation involves several steps:

1. **Write a Template**: You define your infrastructure requirements in a CloudFormation template using YAML or JSON.
2. **Create a Stack**: Using the template, you create a CloudFormation stack, which is a collection of AWS resources that CloudFormation manages as a single unit.
3. **Provision Resources**: CloudFormation provisions the resources defined in the template. It automatically handles the ordering of resource creation based on dependencies.
4. **Update Stacks**: You can update stacks

by modifying the template and applying the changes. CloudFormation will ensure resources are updated or replaced as needed.

5. **Stack Deletion**: When you no longer need the resources, you can delete the stack, and CloudFormation will remove all the associated resources.

5. CloudFormation Stack Types

AWS CloudFormation supports different types of stacks for various use cases:

- **Single-Region Stacks**: These stacks are created and managed within a single AWS region, typically for applications that reside in one region.
- **Cross-Region Stacks**: CloudFormation enables you to deploy stacks across multiple regions, which is useful for high availability and disaster recovery strategies.
- **Nested Stacks**: These are stacks that reference other CloudFormation templates, which helps modularize your infrastructure by creating smaller, reusable templates.

6. Advanced CloudFormation Concepts

- **CloudFormation StackSets**: StackSets allow you to deploy a CloudFormation template to multiple AWS accounts and regions in one operation. This is useful for organizations that want to manage large, multi-region infrastructure.

- **Macros**: AWS CloudFormation macros let you extend CloudFormation's capabilities by enabling you to write custom logic in the template. Macros can be used to dynamically generate portions of a template or modify the structure of the stack during creation or updates.

- **Change Sets**: Before applying changes to a stack, CloudFormation can generate a change set, which outlines the differences between the current stack and the proposed update. This helps ensure that the changes are well-understood and minimize surprises.

7. **Best Practices for Using AWS CloudFormation**

- **Use Version Control**: Always store your CloudFormation templates in a version control system to track changes and collaborate effectively.

- **Test Your Templates**: Use AWS CloudFormation Designer or AWS CloudFormation Linter to visually design and validate templates before deploying them.

- **Modularize Templates**: Break large, complex templates into smaller, reusable ones. Use nested stacks for better organization and maintainability.

- **Use Parameters and Outputs**: Leverage parameters to create reusable templates and outputs to share values between stacks.

- **Validate Templates**: Use the aws cloudformation validate-template command to validate your templates before deploying them.

8. Common Use Cases for CloudFormation

- **Infrastructure Automation**: CloudFormation automates the provisioning of complete infrastructure stacks, such as web applications with load balancers, EC2 instances, databases, and networking components.

- **Environment Replication**: You can use CloudFormation templates to replicate infrastructure environments, such as staging, testing, and production, ensuring consistency across different environments.

- **Multi-Tier Applications**: CloudFormation is ideal for deploying multi-tier applications that involve complex networking, security, and resource management across different AWS services.

- **Disaster Recovery and Backup**: CloudFormation can help you quickly recreate environments in another region or account in case of failures, supporting business continuity strategies.

Summary

AWS CloudFormation provides a powerful way to manage infrastructure using code, offering automation, scalability, and version control. By defining infrastructure as code, teams can ensure consistency, reduce errors, and accelerate the deployment and management of AWS resources. Whether for single-region applications, multi-region deployments, or complex multi-tier systems, CloudFormation simplifies infrastructure management and enables organizations to scale their AWS environments efficiently.

Using AWS CLI and SDK for Automation

AWS provides two powerful tools for automating and managing AWS services: the AWS Command Line Interface (CLI) and the AWS Software Development Kit (SDK). Both allow users to interact with AWS resources programmatically, automate tasks, and integrate AWS services into custom applications. While the AWS CLI is designed for terminal-based command execution, the SDK provides libraries for building and interacting with AWS resources within various programming languages.

1. AWS CLI Overview

The **AWS Command Line Interface (CLI)** is a unified tool that allows you to control multiple AWS services using commands in your terminal or command prompt. With the AWS CLI, you can automate routine tasks such as creating EC2 instances, uploading files to S3, and managing AWS resources without having to manually log into the AWS Management Console.

Key Features of AWS CLI:

- **Unified Command Set**: The CLI allows you to manage AWS services such as EC2, S3, IAM, Lambda, and more from a single interface.

- **Scripting and Automation**: It enables automation through shell scripts, which can be scheduled to run on a regular basis for routine operations.
- **Cross-Platform**: The AWS CLI is available for Windows, macOS, and Linux, providing consistent functionality across platforms.
- **Support for Profiles**: The CLI can manage multiple AWS profiles, making it easy to switch between different accounts or regions.

Installation of AWS CLI:

- You can install the AWS CLI by downloading the installer from the AWS website or using package managers like pip for Python or brew for macOS.

For example, to install AWS CLI on macOS using brew:

bash

Code

brew install awscli

Configuring the AWS CLI:

Once installed, you need to configure the CLI with your AWS credentials, region, and output format:

bash

Code

aws configure

It will prompt you for:

- **AWS Access Key ID**
- **AWS Secret Access Key**
- **Default region name**
- **Default output format**

Example AWS CLI Command:

To list all S3 buckets:

bash

Code

aws s3 ls

2. AWS SDK Overview

The **AWS Software Development Kit (SDK)** is a set of libraries and tools for various programming languages that allow you to interact programmatically with AWS services. The SDK abstracts many complexities of API calls, allowing developers to focus on building applications rather than managing low-level details of HTTP requests.

Supported Programming Languages:

- **Python (Boto3)**
- **Java**
- **JavaScript (Node.js)**

- **Ruby**
- **.NET (C#)**
- **Go**
- **PHP**
- **Swift**
- **Others**

Key Features of AWS SDK:

- **Rich API Coverage**: Provides comprehensive APIs to manage nearly all AWS services, from EC2 and S3 to advanced services like AWS Machine Learning and AWS IoT.
- **Async and Sync Methods**: SDKs support both synchronous and asynchronous methods for handling requests and responses.
- **Authentication and Security**: The SDK manages secure access using AWS IAM roles, policies, and API credentials.
- **High-Level Abstractions**: It simplifies complex tasks like managing sessions, handling retries, and paginating through results.

3. Automating with AWS CLI

Automating tasks with the AWS CLI typically involves creating shell scripts or batch files that execute multiple commands in a sequence.

Below are a few examples of tasks you can automate using the AWS CLI:

Example 1: Automating EC2 Instance Creation

bash

Code

```bash
#!/bin/bash
# This script creates an EC2 instance using AWS CLI

# Specify the instance type, AMI ID, and key name
INSTANCE_TYPE="t2.micro"
AMI_ID="ami-0c55b159cbfafe1f0"
KEY_NAME="my-key-pair"

# Launch the EC2 instance
aws ec2 run-instances --image-id $AMI_ID --instance-type $INSTANCE_TYPE --key-name $KEY_NAME --count 1
```

Example 2: Backing Up Files to S3

bash

Code

```bash
#!/bin/bash
# This script uploads a directory to S3
```

```bash
# Define the local directory and S3 bucket
LOCAL_DIR="/path/to/local/files"
S3_BUCKET="s3://my-backup-bucket"

# Sync the local directory with the S3 bucket
aws s3 sync $LOCAL_DIR $S3_BUCKET
```

Example 3: Automating Auto Scaling Group Update

bash

Code

```bash
#!/bin/bash
# This script updates the Auto Scaling Group to use a new AMI

# Define Auto Scaling Group name and new AMI ID
ASG_NAME="my-auto-scaling-group"
NEW_AMI_ID="ami-0c55b159cbfafe1f0"

# Update the Auto Scaling Group to use the new AMI
aws autoscaling update-auto-scaling-group --auto-scaling-group-name $ASG_NAME --launch-configuration-name $NEW_AMI_ID
```

4. Automating with AWS SDK

The AWS SDK makes it easy to automate tasks programmatically within applications. Below are examples of using the SDK in Python (Boto3) and Node.js (AWS SDK for JavaScript).

Example 1: Automating EC2 Instance Launch with Python (Boto3)

python

Code

```python
import boto3

# Create an EC2 client
ec2 = boto3.client('ec2')

# Define instance parameters
instance_params = {
    'ImageId': 'ami-0c55b159cbfafe1f0',
    'InstanceType': 't2.micro',
    'MinCount': 1,
    'MaxCount': 1,
    'KeyName': 'my-key-pair'
}

# Launch the instance
ec2.run_instances(**instance_params)
```

Example 2: Uploading Files to S3 with Python

(Boto3)

python

Code

```python
import boto3

# Create an S3 client
s3 = boto3.client('s3')

# Define the file and bucket
file_path = 'path/to/local/file.txt'
bucket_name = 'my-backup-bucket'

# Upload the file to S3
s3.upload_file(file_path, bucket_name, 'file.txt')
```

Example 3: Automating DynamoDB Table Operations with Node.js

javascript

Code

```javascript
const AWS = require('aws-sdk');

// Create DynamoDB document client
const dynamodb = new AWS.DynamoDB.DocumentClient();

// Define parameters for a new item
```

```javascript
const params = {
    TableName: 'MyTable',
    Item: {
        'ID': '123',
        'Name': 'John Doe'
    }
};


// Put item into DynamoDB
dynamodb.put(params, function(err, data) {
    if (err) {
        console.log('Error: ', err);
    } else {
        console.log('Success: ', data);
    }
});
```

5. Best Practices for Automation with AWS CLI and SDK

- **Use IAM Roles and Policies**: Ensure that you are using the principle of least privilege by assigning appropriate IAM roles and policies for the automation tasks.

- **Error Handling**: Always include error handling and logging in your scripts and code to ensure that failures are caught and can be acted upon.

- **Use Environment Variables**: For security reasons, avoid hardcoding sensitive information (e.g., AWS Access Keys) in your scripts or code. Use environment variables or AWS Secrets Manager.

- **Testing**: Test your automation scripts and code in non-production environments before deploying them in production to avoid unintended consequences.

- **Version Control**: Store automation scripts and code in version control systems (like Git) to keep track of changes and facilitate collaboration.

Summary

The **AWS CLI** and **SDK** are indispensable tools for automating tasks and managing AWS resources. The AWS CLI is perfect for those who prefer command-line operations and scripting, while the SDK is ideal for integrating AWS services into custom applications. Together, they provide a powerful automation solution, enabling you to optimize workflows, increase productivity, and reduce manual efforts across AWS services. Whether you're launching instances, managing data, or configuring networking, using the AWS

CLI and SDK ensures that your tasks are automated and scalable.

CHAPTER 11: BIG DATA AND ANALYTICS

Amazon EMR: Hadoop Ecosystem on AWS

Amazon Elastic MapReduce (EMR) is a fully managed big data processing service that allows users to run big data frameworks such as Apache Hadoop, Apache Spark, Apache HBase, and other related open-source frameworks at scale. It simplifies the process of deploying and managing clusters for big data processing on AWS. EMR provides a powerful solution for processing large datasets, enabling users to analyze and store big data efficiently, at a fraction of the cost compared to traditional on-premises systems.

1. What is Amazon EMR?

Amazon EMR is a cloud-native platform that enables you to easily run big data applications and frameworks, including Hadoop and Spark, on AWS infrastructure. EMR clusters can scale up or down depending on the computational resources required, providing flexibility and cost savings. The service allows you to process vast amounts of data in parallel, making it ideal for batch processing, data transformation, machine learning, and more.

Key Features of Amazon EMR:

- **Fully Managed**: EMR eliminates the need for you to manually configure and manage Hadoop clusters. AWS handles cluster provisioning, scaling, and maintenance.

- **Scalable**: Automatically scale up or down depending on your workload requirements, making it cost-effective.

- **Preconfigured Frameworks**: Amazon EMR comes with preconfigured versions of Hadoop, Spark, HBase, and other frameworks, reducing setup time.

- **Integration with AWS Services**: Seamlessly integrates with services like Amazon S3 for storage, Amazon RDS for relational databases, and Amazon DynamoDB for NoSQL data.

- **Security**: Provides built-in security features like IAM roles, encryption at rest and in transit, and Kerberos authentication.

2. How Does Amazon EMR Work?

EMR allows you to run distributed computing tasks across a collection of Amazon EC2 instances that are grouped together in an **EMR cluster**. These clusters are responsible for processing the data and managing the resources. The key components of an EMR cluster include:

- **Master Node**: Coordinates the distribution of work across the cluster and stores metadata.
- **Core Nodes**: Run the tasks that store data in Amazon S3 and HDFS (Hadoop Distributed File System).
- **Task Nodes**: Perform the data processing tasks but do not store data.

Users can run jobs on EMR using common frameworks like Apache Hadoop and Apache Spark. After the tasks are completed, the results can be stored in Amazon S3, Amazon DynamoDB, or other storage solutions.

3. Supported Frameworks on Amazon EMR

Amazon EMR supports a wide range of big data frameworks, including but not limited to:

- **Apache Hadoop**: A distributed storage

and processing framework used for big data applications.

- **Apache Spark**: A unified analytics engine for big data processing, known for its speed and flexibility.
- **Apache Hive**: A data warehouse built on top of Hadoop for querying and managing large datasets.
- **Apache HBase**: A distributed NoSQL database that runs on top of Hadoop.
- **Apache Flink**: A stream processing framework for real-time analytics.
- **Presto**: A distributed SQL query engine for big data analytics.

4. Key Use Cases for Amazon EMR

Amazon EMR is ideal for a variety of big data processing and analytics workloads, including:

- **Data Warehousing**: Running queries on large datasets using frameworks like Apache Hive or Presto.
- **Data Transformation and ETL**: Using Spark or Hadoop MapReduce to perform batch processing or ETL (extract, transform, load) operations on data stored in Amazon S3 or other storage systems.
- **Machine Learning**: Using Spark MLlib or other machine learning frameworks for

training models on large datasets.

- **Real-Time Data Processing**: Using Apache Flink or Spark Streaming for real-time data analysis.
- **Log Analysis**: Processing log data generated by servers, applications, or web services for analytics.
- **Clickstream Analysis**: Analyzing web traffic data to gain insights into user behavior.
- **Financial and Risk Modeling**: Running complex calculations and simulations on large datasets for financial analysis or risk modeling.

5. Launching and Managing an EMR Cluster

Steps to Launch an EMR Cluster:

1. **Access the AWS Management Console**: Navigate to the **Amazon EMR** section.
2. **Create a Cluster**:
   - Select the required version of Hadoop or Spark.
   - Choose the number of instances and instance types (Master, Core, Task nodes).
   - Specify other settings like the IAM roles, networking, and security configurations.

3. **Choose Data Storage**: Select Amazon S3 or HDFS for data storage.
4. **Launch the Cluster**: Review the configuration and launch the cluster.

After the cluster is launched, users can submit jobs using the AWS Management Console, AWS CLI, or APIs.

Using the EMR Console for Job Submission:

- Once the cluster is running, jobs can be submitted to the cluster via the **EMR Console** or by using command-line tools like spark-submit (for Spark jobs) or hadoop jar (for Hadoop jobs).
- You can also use the **AWS SDK** to programmatically submit jobs.

6. Monitoring and Scaling Amazon EMR

Amazon EMR provides built-in tools for monitoring the performance of your clusters:

- **Amazon CloudWatch**: Monitor cluster metrics such as CPU usage, memory usage, and disk space.
- **Ganglia**: A monitoring tool integrated into EMR for detailed performance analysis of the cluster.
- **Amazon CloudTrail**: Track and log API calls made on your EMR clusters for auditing and compliance purposes.

Scaling an EMR cluster is easy, allowing you to add or remove nodes as required based on workload. **Auto Scaling** can also be configured to automatically scale the cluster based on pre-defined thresholds.

7. Cost Management for Amazon EMR

Amazon EMR offers a **pay-as-you-go pricing model**, meaning you only pay for the EC2 instances you use and the storage consumed by the data. Costs are primarily driven by the type and number of instances used in your EMR cluster and the duration the cluster is running.

- **Spot Instances**: You can save on costs by using **Spot Instances** for non-critical tasks. Spot instances allow you to bid for unused EC2 capacity at a significantly lower cost.
- **Reserved Instances**: For more predictable workloads, you can reserve EC2 instances for a longer term at a discounted rate.

Example Pricing Components:

- **EC2 Instance Costs**: Based on instance type, region, and running time.
- **EMR Pricing**: Charged on a per-second basis based on the instance types and clusters.
- **Storage Costs**: Associated with using

Amazon S3, HDFS, or other data storage services.

8. Best Practices for Using Amazon EMR

- **Use Spot Instances** for cost savings: Spot instances are a cost-effective option for batch processing or non-critical jobs.

- **Optimize Storage**: Store data in **Amazon S3** to avoid the limitations and overhead of HDFS.

- **Leverage Auto Scaling**: Set up auto-scaling to dynamically adjust cluster resources according to demand.

- **Monitor Cluster Performance**: Use Amazon CloudWatch and Ganglia to monitor the performance and health of your EMR clusters.

- **Security**: Use **AWS IAM roles** to restrict access, and enable **encryption** for data at rest and in transit.

Summary

Amazon EMR is a versatile and scalable solution for running big data applications on AWS. By leveraging its integration with various big data frameworks, EMR allows organizations to efficiently process and analyze large datasets. Whether you are building a data lake, performing real-time analytics, or running machine learning models, Amazon

EMR provides the tools and flexibility to meet your needs while saving on infrastructure management overhead. With features like auto-scaling, security integration, and cost-saving options like Spot Instances, EMR ensures that you can process big data at scale while optimizing your resources.

AWS Glue: ETL Service

AWS Glue is a fully managed Extract, Transform, Load (ETL) service that enables you to easily prepare and load your data for analytics. It helps you move data between your data sources, transform it according to your needs, and load it into data storage or data warehouses for further analysis. AWS Glue automates much of the data processing, providing a serverless architecture that scales automatically based on your workload, so you only pay for the resources you consume.

1. What is AWS Glue?

AWS Glue is a serverless ETL service that facilitates the process of preparing, cleaning, and transforming data for analytics. It can crawl data from a variety of sources, transform it into a consistent format, and load it into a data lake, data warehouse, or other storage solutions. AWS Glue integrates seamlessly with other AWS services such as **Amazon S3**, **Amazon Redshift**, **Amazon RDS**, and **Amazon DynamoDB**, making it an integral part of the AWS data ecosystem.

Key Features of AWS Glue:

- **Serverless**: No infrastructure to manage, automatically scales based on demand.
- **Data Catalog**: Centralized metadata repository for all your data assets.
- **ETL Jobs**: Supports the creation of ETL jobs to extract, transform, and load data.
- **Data Crawlers**: Automatically discover and catalog data across a wide range of data sources.
- **Integration with AWS Services**: Works seamlessly with S3, Redshift, RDS, and other AWS data services.
- **Scalable**: Handles large-scale data processing efficiently, from small datasets to petabytes of data.
- **Comprehensive Transformations**: Provides built-in transformations like join, filter, aggregation, and others.

2. Key Components of AWS Glue

AWS Glue is composed of several core

components, each serving a specific purpose in the data transformation and loading process.

AWS Glue Data Catalog

The **AWS Glue Data Catalog** is a centralized repository that stores metadata about your data. It acts as an index for all the data stored in various sources across AWS. The catalog enables you to easily discover and query data and serves as the metadata store for ETL operations.

- **Tables**: Contains metadata definitions about the datasets.
- **Databases**: Logical containers for organizing tables within the catalog.
- **Partitions**: Helps organize data in large tables based on common column values for optimized querying.

AWS Glue Crawlers

A **Crawler** is an automated service that scans your data sources, extracts metadata, and creates or updates tables in the AWS Glue Data Catalog. Crawlers can be set to run on a schedule, enabling the catalog to stay up-to-date with new or updated data. Crawlers are used to automatically discover schema and partition information.

AWS Glue ETL Jobs

An **ETL job** defines the specific actions that need to be performed on the data: extraction, transformation, and loading. You can create ETL jobs using **AWS Glue Studio** (a visual interface) or **Apache Spark** scripts (for more complex transformations). ETL jobs can be executed on-demand or on a schedule.

AWS Glue Jobs and Scripts

AWS Glue can generate Python or Scala scripts for the ETL jobs, allowing you to customize the transformation logic. Glue automatically handles tasks like parallel execution, job retries, and job monitoring.

3. How AWS Glue Works

The general workflow for using AWS Glue involves three key steps:

Step 1: Data Discovery with Glue Crawlers

- **Crawling Data Sources**: The Glue crawler automatically discovers your data in various AWS data stores (S3, RDS, DynamoDB, etc.), extracts metadata, and stores this information in the Glue Data Catalog.
- **Schema Detection**: The crawler infers the schema (structure) of your data and stores it in the catalog. It can also detect changes in schema over time.

Step 2: Data Transformation with Glue ETL Jobs

- **Defining ETL Jobs**: After crawling the data, you can define an ETL job that specifies how data should be processed. You can create jobs to clean, filter, enrich, or transform data.

- **Building Transformations**: AWS Glue provides built-in transformations that allow you to manipulate data, such as applying filters, joins, aggregations, and custom Python or Scala code.

- **Executing ETL Jobs**: Once the job is defined, it can be executed either on-demand or on a schedule. AWS Glue will automatically handle scaling and resource allocation.

Step 3: Loading Data into Target Systems

- **Loading Transformed Data**: After the transformation is complete, the data is loaded into your target systems. These targets can be **Amazon S3** (for data lakes), **Amazon Redshift** (for data warehousing), **Amazon RDS**, **DynamoDB**, or any other compatible destination.

4. Key Benefits of Using AWS Glue

- **Serverless Architecture**: No infrastructure to manage or provision. AWS Glue automatically scales based on the data processing needs.

- **Cost-Effective**: You only pay for the

resources you use, such as the compute time used by ETL jobs and crawlers.

- **Automated Data Discovery**: Crawlers automatically detect and catalog data sources, reducing manual intervention and accelerating data preparation.
- **Fast and Scalable**: AWS Glue is built on top of Apache Spark, providing the scalability and performance needed to handle large datasets.
- **Integration with AWS Data Ecosystem**: Tight integration with other AWS services such as Amazon S3, Redshift, RDS, and Athena, providing a seamless experience across your data pipeline.
- **Easy-to-Use**: AWS Glue provides a visual interface (Glue Studio) for building and managing ETL workflows, making it accessible to both technical and non-technical users.
- **Custom Transformations**: Advanced users can write custom transformations in Python or Scala for more complex data processing needs.

5. Use Cases for AWS Glue

AWS Glue is suitable for a wide range of use cases, including:

- **Data Lakes**: Automatically ingest and

process raw data into a structured format for analytics in data lakes on Amazon S3.

- **Data Warehousing**: Extract, transform, and load (ETL) data into **Amazon Redshift** for analytics.
- **Real-time Data Processing**: Combine AWS Glue with services like **Amazon Kinesis** for near real-time ETL processing.
- **Data Migration**: Migrate data from on-premises systems or other cloud platforms to AWS services using Glue ETL jobs.
- **Data Integration**: Combine data from various sources (such as relational databases, log files, and web services) and transform it into a unified format for analysis.
- **Log Analysis**: Aggregate logs from multiple sources, transform them into a structured format, and store them for analysis.

6. Monitoring and Debugging AWS Glue Jobs

AWS Glue provides several tools for monitoring and debugging ETL jobs:

- **AWS Glue Console**: Monitor job runs, view logs, and debug any issues with

ETL jobs directly from the Glue console.

- **Amazon CloudWatch**: Integrated with AWS Glue to provide detailed logs and metrics for job execution, performance, and errors.
- **AWS Glue Job Metrics**: Track metrics such as job duration, input/output data volume, and success or failure status.

7. Pricing for AWS Glue

AWS Glue pricing is based on the resources consumed during ETL jobs and data crawlers. Key pricing components include:

- **ETL Jobs**: Charged based on the amount of processing time used by the job, measured in **Data Processing Units (DPU)**. You are billed for the time the job runs.
- **Crawlers**: Charged based on the time taken by the crawler to process the data and catalog it in the Glue Data Catalog.
- **Data Catalog**: Storage costs apply based on the amount of metadata stored in the Glue Data Catalog.

8. Best Practices for Using AWS Glue

- **Efficient Job Design**: Break down large ETL jobs into smaller, more manageable tasks to improve performance and scalability.

- **Use Partitioning**: When processing large datasets, use partitioning to improve read and write efficiency and reduce costs.

- **Monitor Jobs**: Regularly monitor the performance of your ETL jobs and optimize them to reduce processing time and cost.

- **Leverage Auto-scaling**: Use the auto-scaling capabilities of AWS Glue to ensure that your ETL jobs run efficiently without over-provisioning resources.

- **Enable Encryption**: Ensure that your data is encrypted both in transit and at rest to maintain security.

Summary

AWS Glue is a powerful, serverless ETL service that simplifies the process of preparing and transforming data for analytics. By automating many of the manual processes involved in ETL, Glue saves time, reduces complexity, and helps organizations scale their data workflows with ease. With tight integration into the AWS ecosystem, Glue is ideal for use cases ranging from data lakes and data warehousing to real-time processing and data migration.

Amazon QuickSight:

Data Visualization

Amazon QuickSight is a scalable, fast, and cloud-powered business intelligence (BI) service designed to enable data analysis and visualization. It allows users to quickly create interactive dashboards, reports, and visualizations, making it easier for organizations to analyze and share insights from their data. QuickSight integrates seamlessly with a variety of AWS data sources, including Amazon S3, Amazon RDS, Redshift, and other AWS services, as well as third-party data sources, to help users unlock the value of their data.

1. What is Amazon QuickSight?

Amazon QuickSight is a fully managed BI service that makes it easy to create and publish interactive dashboards, analyze data, and share insights with others. Unlike traditional BI tools, QuickSight is designed for fast, scalable, and serverless operations, enabling organizations to easily analyze large volumes of data without worrying about infrastructure management. It provides a rich set of data visualization options that can help non-technical users as well as data professionals to quickly interpret data trends and insights.

Key Features of Amazon QuickSight:

- **Scalable**: Scales automatically to accommodate more users and larger data sets without needing manual intervention.
- **Fast and Interactive**: Provides fast rendering of data visualizations, even with large datasets, and allows for real-time interactive analysis.
- **Pay-per-Use**: Flexible pricing where you pay only for what you use, based on the number of users and queries.
- **Integration with AWS Services**: Integrates with Amazon S3, Redshift, RDS, Athena, and other AWS data sources.
- **Data Prep and ETL**: Includes built-in features for preparing, cleaning, and transforming data before analysis.
- **Machine Learning Insights**: Provides ML-powered insights such as anomaly detection, forecasting, and the ability to automatically generate recommendations.

2. Core Components of Amazon QuickSight

Datasets

Datasets are the primary components in QuickSight, where raw data from various sources is imported, cleaned, and transformed for analysis. QuickSight can connect to multiple data sources, both from AWS and external sources, and load them into datasets.

- **Data Sources**: QuickSight can pull data from services like **Amazon S3**, **Redshift**, **RDS**, **Athena**, and **third-party databases**.
- **SPICE** (Super-fast, Parallel, In-memory Calculation Engine): A memory-optimized engine that stores data for fast, in-memory analysis.

Analysis

An analysis is a workspace within QuickSight where users can interact with datasets, create visualizations, apply filters, and build reports and dashboards. It enables users to explore and analyze data interactively.

- **Visualizations**: Create charts, graphs, and tables to represent data insights visually. QuickSight supports various types of visualizations such as bar charts, pie charts, line graphs, scatter plots, heatmaps, and geographical maps.
- **Filters and Controls**: Allows users to filter and refine the data visualized in the analysis.
- **Calculated Fields**: Users can create new

fields based on existing ones using built-in formulas or custom expressions for more advanced analysis.

Dashboards

Once analysis is complete, users can publish their work as **dashboards**. Dashboards are fully interactive, providing a visual display of key metrics and data visualizations that can be shared across teams or embedded in other applications.

- **Sharing and Embedding**: Dashboards can be shared with users via email or a URL, and can also be embedded in websites and applications.
- **User Access**: Users can control who can view or modify dashboards through user roles and permissions.

3. How Amazon QuickSight Works

The workflow for using Amazon QuickSight typically follows these steps:

Step 1: Connect to Data Sources

- **Data Integration**: Connect QuickSight to various data sources, including AWS data services (e.g., Redshift, S3, Athena) or third-party databases (e.g., SQL, Salesforce, etc.).
- **Data Preparation**: Import data into QuickSight and use its tools to clean,

transform, and prepare data for analysis. You can also set up automatic data refreshes.

Step 2: Create Analysis

- **Data Exploration**: Once your data is imported, you can explore and visualize it. QuickSight provides a drag-and-drop interface to help users create visualizations without needing to write complex code.

- **Build Visuals**: Choose from a wide variety of chart types to represent your data. Customize these visualizations with filters, colors, and formatting to highlight key insights.

Step 3: Publish and Share Dashboards

- **Publish Dashboards**: Once your analysis is ready, publish it as an interactive dashboard. Dashboards can include multiple visualizations to provide a comprehensive view of your data.

- **Sharing and Collaboration**: Share dashboards with stakeholders or team members, and allow them to interact with the data directly.

4. Key Benefits of Using Amazon QuickSight

- **Ease of Use**: QuickSight's user-friendly interface makes it accessible to both non-technical users and experienced data analysts.

- **Scalability**: Can handle large data volumes and scale automatically to accommodate more users and data without any manual intervention.

- **Serverless**: No infrastructure management is required. QuickSight is fully managed and runs entirely on the cloud.

- **Cost Efficiency**: Pay only for what you use, based on the number of users and queries. The SPICE engine further optimizes costs by reducing the amount of data that needs to be processed for each query.

- **Integration with AWS Ecosystem**: QuickSight integrates with a wide array of AWS services, making it easy to analyze data from multiple AWS sources.

- **Machine Learning Insights**: Built-in machine learning capabilities provide predictive analytics, anomaly detection, and auto-generated insights, even for users with no data science background.

5. Types of Visualizations in Amazon QuickSight

Amazon QuickSight offers a wide range of

visualization options to represent your data clearly and effectively:

- **Bar Charts**: Display quantities or values for comparison between different categories.
- **Line and Area Charts**: Used for trend analysis over time.
- **Pie and Donut Charts**: Display the percentage contribution of parts to a whole.
- **Scatter Plots**: Show the relationship between two continuous variables.
- **Heatmaps**: Visualize data in matrix form, showing relationships between two categorical variables.
- **Geospatial Visualizations**: Display data on geographical maps, useful for location-based analysis.
- **Tables**: Present raw data in a tabular format, which can be customized with sorting, conditional formatting, and more.

6. Machine Learning Insights in Amazon QuickSight

Amazon QuickSight offers built-in machine learning (ML) capabilities that empower users to gain deeper insights from their data. These include:

- **Anomaly Detection**: QuickSight automatically detects anomalies in your data and highlights them in your visualizations, helping you spot unexpected trends or outliers.
- **Forecasting**: Predict future trends based on historical data. QuickSight uses ML models to generate time-series forecasts, helping users make data-driven predictions.
- **Auto-Insights**: The "Auto-Insight" feature automatically surfaces hidden insights and patterns in your data, without requiring users to have advanced analytics skills.

7. Pricing for Amazon QuickSight

Amazon QuickSight offers a flexible pricing model that is based on usage and the type of user:

- **Standard Edition**: Suitable for individuals or small teams. Priced based on monthly per-user charges.
- **Enterprise Edition**: Designed for organizations with larger teams and more advanced BI needs. Offers features such as row-level security, SSO integration, and additional scalability options.

The pricing is also based on:

- **SPICE Capacity**: The amount of data stored in the SPICE engine for fast, in-memory analysis.

- **Data Refreshes**: Charges for automatic or scheduled data refreshes.

- **Active Users**: Costs vary based on the number of active users viewing and interacting with dashboards.

8. Best Practices for Using Amazon QuickSight

- **Organize Your Data**: Structure your datasets and organize them logically in QuickSight to make analysis easier.

- **Use SPICE for Faster Queries**: Load data into the SPICE engine for faster query performance and lower costs.

- **Utilize Filters**: Make use of filters and controls to provide users with dynamic and interactive dashboards.

- **Optimize Visualizations**: Choose the right type of visualization to best convey the insights from your data, and ensure clarity and simplicity.

- **Leverage ML Insights**: Take advantage of the machine learning features to enhance your analysis, detect anomalies, and forecast trends.

- **Regularly Update Data**: Schedule automatic data refreshes to keep your dashboards up to date with the latest information.

Summary

Amazon QuickSight is a powerful and flexible BI tool that allows users to easily analyze, visualize, and share insights from their data. Its integration with AWS services, scalability, and pay-per-use pricing model make it a great choice for organizations of all sizes. Whether you're an individual user or part of a larger team, QuickSight provides the tools you need to make data-driven decisions and gain valuable business insights.

PART 4: SPECIALIZED AWS SERVICES

CHAPTER 12: MACHINE LEARNING AND AI

Amazon SageMaker: Building Machine Learning Models

Amazon SageMaker is a fully managed service that provides every tool required to build, train, and deploy machine learning (ML) models at scale. It simplifies the machine learning workflow by automating and optimizing many of the complex tasks involved in developing ML models. SageMaker offers a wide range of features and capabilities to help data scientists, developers, and business analysts build and deploy machine learning models efficiently without needing to manage infrastructure.

1. What is Amazon SageMaker?

Amazon SageMaker is a cloud-based machine learning platform that helps users quickly develop, train, and deploy ML models. It integrates a variety of services, tools, and algorithms to support end-to-end machine learning workflows, from data preprocessing and model training to model deployment and monitoring.

Key Features of Amazon SageMaker:

- **Pre-built Algorithms**: Offers a library of pre-built machine learning algorithms that are optimized for performance and scalability.

- **Managed Training**: Automates model training with distributed infrastructure for large-scale data processing.

- **Model Hosting**: Simplifies the process of deploying trained models into production with automatic scaling and managed hosting.

- **End-to-End Pipeline**: Supports the entire machine learning lifecycle, from data preparation to model training, evaluation, and deployment.

- **Automatic Model Tuning**: Uses hyperparameter optimization to automatically fine-tune model performance.
- **Integration with AWS Services**: Seamlessly integrates with AWS data services like Amazon S3, Redshift, and DynamoDB, among others.

2. Components of Amazon SageMaker

Amazon SageMaker provides several core components that make it easier for users to build, train, and deploy machine learning models:

1. SageMaker Studio

SageMaker Studio is an integrated development environment (IDE) that provides a unified, web-based interface for the entire machine learning lifecycle. It allows users to prepare data, build models, track experiments, and deploy models all in one place. SageMaker Studio offers visual tools, notebooks, and debugging tools that streamline ML development.

2. SageMaker Notebooks

SageMaker provides fully managed Jupyter notebooks for data exploration, preprocessing, and experimentation. These notebooks are designed for ease of use, allowing data scientists to write and execute code quickly, analyze data, and visualize results.

3. SageMaker Ground Truth

Ground Truth is a data labeling service that helps build highly accurate training datasets for machine learning. It leverages human labeling and machine learning to create labeled datasets more efficiently, saving time and costs.

4. SageMaker Training

SageMaker makes model training easy by providing fully managed, scalable compute resources. It automatically provisions the infrastructure required for training, supports distributed training, and integrates with popular ML frameworks like TensorFlow, PyTorch, and MXNet.

5. SageMaker Experiments

Experiments allow users to organize, track, and compare machine learning model experiments. It helps keep track of different training runs and parameters, making it easier to manage the iterative process of model development.

6. SageMaker Autopilot

Autopilot automatically trains and tunes machine learning models without requiring users to have deep ML expertise. By uploading data to SageMaker, users can generate fully trained and optimized models with minimal manual intervention.

7. SageMaker Debugger

SageMaker Debugger monitors training jobs in real-time to detect and resolve issues like overfitting or poor convergence during the model training process. It provides detailed metrics, insights, and visualizations for debugging and improving model performance.

8. SageMaker Model Monitor

SageMaker Model Monitor allows users to track and monitor deployed models in production, detecting performance drift or bias and triggering alerts to ensure models continue to perform optimally over time.

9. SageMaker Pipelines

SageMaker Pipelines is a continuous integration/continuous delivery (CI/CD) service that automates the creation, deployment, and management of machine learning workflows. It supports versioning and tracking of models, data, and code.

3. The Machine Learning Workflow in SageMaker

Amazon SageMaker streamlines the machine learning process with a fully managed, end-to-end workflow. Below are the key steps in the machine learning lifecycle using SageMaker:

Step 1: Data Collection and Preprocessing

- **Data Sources**: Amazon SageMaker

integrates with AWS services like S3, Redshift, and DynamoDB to pull data for training and testing.

- **Preprocessing**: Data scientists can clean and preprocess data directly in SageMaker Studio or use SageMaker Processing to run batch data processing jobs at scale. This includes tasks such as data normalization, feature engineering, and handling missing values.

Step 2: Model Building and Experimentation

- **Notebook Integration**: Data scientists use SageMaker Notebooks to write and test machine learning code. SageMaker provides a rich set of algorithms and pre-built libraries, such as TensorFlow, PyTorch, and Scikit-learn.

- **Model Training**: SageMaker allows for distributed training, enabling users to train models on large datasets using GPUs, TPUs, or CPU clusters, depending on the model's requirements. SageMaker also supports **automatic model tuning** using **Hyperparameter Optimization (HPO)**, which tunes the model's hyperparameters to improve accuracy.

- **Model Evaluation**: After training, SageMaker allows users to evaluate the model's performance on test datasets using built-in metrics.

Step 3: Model Deployment

- **Managed Deployment**: Once a model is trained and evaluated, SageMaker offers a simple way to deploy the model to production using fully managed infrastructure.
- **Auto Scaling**: Deployed models can automatically scale based on incoming traffic, ensuring the model can handle production workloads.
- **Endpoints**: SageMaker creates an endpoint for real-time predictions and supports batch processing for large-scale predictions.

Step 4: Model Monitoring and Optimization

- **Monitoring**: SageMaker Model Monitor tracks deployed models' performance over time, identifying potential issues like data drift or model degradation.
- **Debugging**: SageMaker Debugger helps track and improve training performance by providing detailed logs, metrics, and visualizations to identify problems during the model training process.

4. Pre-built Algorithms in Amazon SageMaker

SageMaker offers a wide selection of pre-built machine learning algorithms optimized for performance and scalability. These algorithms include:

- **Linear Learner**: A linear model for regression and classification problems.
- **XGBoost**: A popular gradient boosting algorithm for classification and regression tasks.
- **K-Means**: A clustering algorithm used for unsupervised learning tasks.
- **BlazingText**: A fast text processing algorithm for natural language processing (NLP) tasks.
- **DeepAR**: A time-series forecasting model.
- **Object Detection**: Used for detecting objects in images using deep learning.

These algorithms are optimized for performance, scalability, and cost-efficiency, and can be easily integrated into your SageMaker workflow.

5. Model Deployment and Hosting

Amazon SageMaker makes it easy to deploy trained models into production. Key features include:

- **Real-time Inference**: Deploy models as an endpoint for real-time predictions, which can be called via an API.

- **Batch Inference**: Perform batch predictions on large datasets by processing data in batches asynchronously.
- **Model Hosting**: SageMaker manages the underlying infrastructure, scaling the resources up or down depending on demand.
- **Multi-Model Endpoints**: Host multiple models on the same endpoint to optimize costs while managing different use cases.

6. Pricing for Amazon SageMaker

Amazon SageMaker follows a pay-as-you-go pricing model, where customers are charged for the resources they use, including compute instances, data storage, and training. The main pricing components include:

- **Data Storage**: Charges for data stored in S3 buckets and SageMaker volumes.
- **Training**: Pricing is based on the type of instances used for training, including CPU, GPU, or distributed instances.
- **Hosting**: Pricing for hosting models in production is based on the compute resources required to deploy the model and serve predictions.
- **Data Processing**: Charges for batch

processing, labeling data via Ground Truth, and using SageMaker's built-in services like Processing and Pipelines.

7. Best Practices for Using Amazon SageMaker

- **Leverage Managed Spot Training**: To reduce training costs, consider using Amazon SageMaker Managed Spot Training, which uses unused EC2 capacity to train models at a lower cost.

- **Monitor Model Performance**: Use SageMaker Model Monitor to track model performance over time and detect any data drift or degradation.

- **Use Built-in Algorithms**: Take advantage of SageMaker's pre-built algorithms and models to speed up development and reduce the need for custom model creation.

- **Use SageMaker Pipelines**: Automate and streamline your machine learning workflows by integrating SageMaker Pipelines for continuous integration and delivery (CI/CD) of ML models.

- **Scale Infrastructure**: Use the auto-scaling features of SageMaker to optimize model hosting and inference costs as traffic changes.

Summary

Amazon SageMaker provides a comprehensive suite of tools and services for building, training, and deploying machine learning models. Its fully managed infrastructure, pre-built algorithms, and end-to-end workflow simplify the machine learning process, enabling users to focus on model development and business insights rather than managing infrastructure. Whether you're a beginner or an experienced data scientist, SageMaker offers the flexibility, scalability, and ease of use needed to deploy machine learning models at scale.

AI Services: Rekognition, Polly, and Lex

Amazon Web Services (AWS) provides a wide array of Artificial Intelligence (AI) services designed to help developers and organizations incorporate machine learning (ML) capabilities into their applications without needing deep expertise in the field. Three powerful AI services that AWS offers are Amazon Rekognition, Amazon Polly, and Amazon Lex. These services enable image and video analysis, text-to-speech conversion, and building conversational interfaces, respectively.

1. Amazon Rekognition: Image and Video Analysis

Amazon Rekognition is a deep learning-based image and video analysis service that helps developers identify objects, scenes, people, and activities in images and videos. Rekognition can also detect inappropriate content and perform facial analysis, which is useful for various applications, such as security, media, and entertainment.

Key Features of Amazon Rekognition:

- **Object and Scene Detection**: Recognize over 1,000 objects and scenes (e.g., animals, vehicles, landmarks).

- **Facial Analysis and Recognition**: Detect and analyze faces, including estimating attributes such as age, gender, emotion, and more. It can also compare faces for matching purposes.

- **Text Detection**: Extract text from images and videos (e.g., from signs, documents, or license plates).

- **Celebrity Recognition**: Identify famous people in images or video clips.

- **Content Moderation**: Automatically detect inappropriate content, such as nudity, violence, or explicit language, in images and videos.

- **Video Analysis**: Analyze video files for object tracking, movement detection, and scene changes.
- **Facial Search**: Search a collection of images for matches to a given face.

Use Cases:

- **Security and Surveillance**: Recognize suspicious activities or people in video feeds.
- **Media and Entertainment**: Automatically tag and catalog content based on objects and scenes.
- **Retail**: Enhance shopping experiences by recognizing products or providing augmented reality features.
- **Healthcare**: Analyze medical imaging to detect anomalies.

2. Amazon Polly: Text-to-Speech Service

Amazon Polly is a service that turns text into lifelike speech using advanced deep learning techniques. It provides developers with the ability to create applications that can "speak" to users in a variety of voices and languages. Polly supports multiple languages and dialects, offering a wide range of natural-sounding voices, which makes it ideal for creating interactive applications that require voice feedback.

Key Features of Amazon Polly:

- **Multiple Voices and Languages**: Supports over 60 voices in more than 30 languages, including English, Spanish, French, and Mandarin.

- **Neural Text-to-Speech (NTTS)**: Polly offers an advanced feature called Neural TTS, which produces more natural-sounding speech by modeling complex speech patterns.

- **SSML Support**: Speech Synthesis Markup Language (SSML) allows users to control aspects of speech output, including pitch, rate, and volume, and even add pauses or emphasize certain words.

- **Streaming and Offline Mode**: Polly can generate speech in real time for live applications or convert large amounts of text into speech for offline use.

- **Cost-Effective**: Polly's pricing is based on the number of characters you convert to speech, allowing you to scale your application efficiently.

- **Real-Time Speech**: Can be integrated into real-time applications such as chatbots, navigation systems, and assistive technology.

Use Cases:

- **Interactive Voice Response (IVR) Systems**: Enhance customer service applications with conversational speech capabilities.
- **Assistive Technology**: Enable accessibility for individuals with visual impairments or other disabilities by reading text aloud from websites, documents, or books.
- **E-Learning and Education**: Convert written educational content into speech for students to listen to while learning.
- **Media and Entertainment**: Create voiceovers for videos, games, or podcasts.

3. Amazon Lex: Building Conversational Interfaces

Amazon Lex is a service for building conversational interfaces into any application. It provides advanced deep learning functionalities for natural language processing (NLP) and automatic speech recognition (ASR), making it easy to create chatbots and voice-driven applications. Lex powers the popular voice assistant **Amazon Alexa** and enables developers to build highly functional chatbots that can engage users in natural, human-like conversations.

Key Features of Amazon Lex:

- **Natural Language Understanding (NLU)**: Lex can understand user input in natural language, identifying intent and extracting relevant information (known as slots).

- **Automatic Speech Recognition (ASR)**: Lex allows for voice-based interaction by converting speech to text, enabling voice commands.

- **Multilingual Support**: Supports multiple languages and can recognize user inputs in the chosen language.

- **Integrated with AWS Services**: Lex integrates easily with other AWS services, such as AWS Lambda (for backend processing), Amazon CloudWatch (for monitoring), and Amazon DynamoDB (for storing user data).

- **Text and Voice Chatbot Capabilities**: You can create both text-based and voice-based chatbots.

- **Contextual Conversations**: Lex can manage the context of the conversation, maintaining continuity across interactions and handling follow-up queries.

Use Cases:

- **Customer Support**: Create chatbots that can answer customer queries 24/7, reducing response times and operational costs.

- **Voice Assistants**: Develop voice-enabled applications for mobile devices, smart speakers, and other devices.

- **E-commerce**: Use conversational interfaces for product recommendations, order management, or personalized customer interactions.

- **Healthcare**: Enable patients to interact with healthcare systems via voice or text, scheduling appointments, refilling prescriptions, or getting information on medical conditions.

Comparing Rekognition, Polly, and Lex

Service	Main Functionality	Key Use Cases	Integration
Rekognition	Image and video analysis (objects, faces, scenes)	Security, media, retail, healthcare	Integrates with Lambda, S3, etc.
Polly	Text-to-speech (converts text into lifelike speech)	Accessibility, IVR, e-learning, media production	Integrates with Lambda, S3, etc.
Lex	Conversational interfaces (chatbots, voice)	Customer support, voice assistants, e-commerce	Integrates with Lambda, S3, DynamoDB, etc.

Summary

AWS AI services, namely **Amazon Rekognition**, **Amazon Polly**, and **Amazon Lex**, offer powerful tools for developers to build intelligent, interactive, and scalable applications. Whether you're looking to analyze images and videos, convert text to speech, or build chatbots with natural language understanding, these services provide the flexibility and performance needed to create high-quality, AI-powered solutions. Each of these services allows organizations to integrate AI into their operations with minimal machine learning expertise, making sophisticated AI capabilities accessible for businesses of all sizes.

CHAPTER 13: INTERNET OF THINGS (IOT)

AWS IoT Core: Internet of Things (IoT) Solution

AWS IoT Core is a managed cloud service provided by Amazon Web Services (AWS) that allows businesses to easily connect Internet of Things (IoT) devices to the cloud and securely process, manage, and analyze data at scale. It supports the development of IoT applications by providing a scalable and secure platform to handle the connectivity, device management, and data collection needs of IoT ecosystems.

Key Features of AWS IoT Core:

1. **Device Connectivity and Communication:**
   - **Supports MQTT and HTTP protocols**: AWS IoT Core uses lightweight protocols such as MQTT (Message Queuing Telemetry Transport) and HTTPS to ensure secure, real-time communication between devices and the cloud.
   - **Device Shadow**: The "Device Shadow" feature allows the state of IoT devices to be stored in the cloud and synchronized with the device. This enables applications to interact with devices even when they are offline.
   - **Secure Communication**: End-to-end encryption and authentication mechanisms ensure secure device-to-cloud communication. Devices are authenticated using X.509 certificates, which guarantees that only authorized devices can communicate with the cloud.

2. **Device Management:**
   - **Device Registration**: Devices can be securely registered to AWS IoT Core with unique identifiers and

credentials. This process makes it easier to track and manage devices over time.

- **Over-the-Air (OTA) Updates**: AWS IoT Core enables remote firmware and software updates for IoT devices, which ensures that devices stay up to date with the latest security patches and features.
- **Fleet Management**: Manage large fleets of IoT devices, including provisioning, tracking, and monitoring their health and status.

3. **Data Processing and Analysis:**
    - **Rules Engine**: The AWS IoT Core Rules Engine allows you to filter, transform, and route data from devices to other AWS services such as AWS Lambda, Amazon Kinesis, Amazon S3, or Amazon DynamoDB. This enables real-time data processing and analytics.
    - **Integration with AWS Analytics Services**: You can easily integrate AWS IoT Core with analytics services like AWS IoT Analytics, Amazon QuickSight,

and Amazon SageMaker for deeper data insights and machine learning (ML) model deployment.

4. **Security and Compliance:**
    - **Device Authentication and Authorization**: AWS IoT Core uses mutual TLS (Transport Layer Security) for device authentication and ensures only authorized devices can communicate with the cloud.
    - **IoT Device Defender**: AWS IoT Core integrates with **AWS IoT Device Defender**, a service that continuously audits the security of IoT devices and helps ensure they are not behaving abnormally or becoming vulnerable to threats.
    - **Fine-Grained Permissions**: Using AWS Identity and Access Management (IAM), you can define specific permissions and policies for users, devices, and applications interacting with AWS IoT Core.

5. **Scalability and Flexibility:**
    - **Scalable Infrastructure**: AWS

IoT Core can handle millions of connected devices, making it ideal for large-scale IoT applications. The service automatically scales to accommodate increasing traffic, device registrations, and data processing needs.

- **Edge Computing**: With AWS IoT Core, you can extend your IoT infrastructure to the edge by using services like **AWS IoT Greengrass**. This allows you to run machine learning models and process data locally on devices, reducing latency and reliance on the cloud.

How AWS IoT Core Works:

1. **Device Registration and Connection:** Devices are registered in AWS IoT Core, and each device is assigned unique security credentials (such as X.509 certificates). Once registered, devices can securely connect to AWS IoT Core using MQTT or HTTP protocols.

2. **Data Transmission:** Devices transmit data to AWS IoT Core, where it is securely processed. Data can include sensor readings, device status updates,

logs, or other relevant information.

3. **Rules Engine Processing:** The IoT Core Rules Engine processes incoming data, performing actions based on defined rules. For example, you could set up a rule to send an alert to AWS Lambda if a temperature sensor exceeds a threshold.

4. **Storage and Analysis:** Processed data can be sent to other AWS services, such as Amazon S3 for storage or AWS IoT Analytics for further data analysis. You can also use **Amazon QuickSight** for data visualization or **Amazon SageMaker** for predictive analytics and machine learning models.

5. **Device Management:** Devices can be monitored and updated remotely via over-the-air (OTA) updates. You can also monitor device health and manage device states using the Device Shadow feature.

Use Cases for AWS IoT Core:

1. **Smart Homes and Buildings:**
    - AWS IoT Core can be used to connect smart devices in homes and buildings, such as lights, thermostats, and security cameras. These devices can send data (e.g., energy consumption,

status updates) to the cloud, and users can control them through mobile apps or web interfaces.

2. **Industrial IoT (IIoT):**
   - In manufacturing, AWS IoT Core can connect industrial machines, sensors, and control systems to monitor machine performance, predict maintenance needs, and improve operational efficiency.
   - Predictive maintenance can be achieved by processing data from sensors to anticipate failures before they happen.

3. **Healthcare and Wearables:**
   - AWS IoT Core supports the connectivity of health devices, such as wearable fitness trackers, smart medical devices, and patient monitoring systems. This data can be analyzed in real time for health monitoring or sent to healthcare providers for further analysis.

4. **Fleet Management and Logistics:**
   - In the transportation and logistics sector, AWS IoT Core can be used to track vehicle

fleets, monitor fuel usage, location, and sensor data, and optimize routes in real time.

5. **Agriculture and Environmental Monitoring:**
   - IoT sensors in agricultural fields or environmental monitoring systems can use AWS IoT Core to collect data on soil moisture, temperature, air quality, or weather conditions. This data can help optimize farming practices or track environmental changes.

6. **Energy and Utilities:**
   - AWS IoT Core can be used to monitor and control smart meters, grid systems, and energy-efficient devices, providing insights into energy usage and enabling real-time responses to changing energy demands.

Integrating AWS IoT Core with Other AWS Services:

AWS IoT Core integrates seamlessly with a range of AWS services to extend its capabilities:

- **AWS IoT Analytics**: For advanced data processing, analysis, and visualization.

- **AWS Lambda**: To trigger serverless functions in response to IoT data events.
- **Amazon S3**: For storing raw or processed IoT data.
- **Amazon Kinesis**: For real-time data streaming and processing.
- **Amazon DynamoDB**: For storing IoT device state and other data.
- **AWS IoT Greengrass**: For edge computing and running applications locally on IoT devices.

Summary:

AWS IoT Core is a powerful and flexible platform that allows businesses to scale their IoT applications and securely connect devices to the cloud. By offering real-time data processing, device management, and integration with AWS's wide range of services, AWS IoT Core makes it easier for businesses to build, manage, and scale IoT solutions. Whether you're creating smart home devices, industrial IoT applications, or monitoring healthcare systems, AWS IoT Core provides the tools needed to build secure, reliable, and intelligent IoT ecosystems.

Managing IoT Devices and Data on AWS IoT Core

Managing Internet of Things (IoT) devices and the data they generate is central to building successful IoT applications. AWS IoT Core provides various tools and services that allow businesses to securely connect, manage, and monitor IoT devices while processing the data they produce. Below is a breakdown of key concepts and tools for managing IoT devices and data effectively using AWS IoT Core.

1. Device Management:

AWS IoT Core offers several features that help manage IoT devices throughout their lifecycle. Device management tools allow for secure registration, provisioning, monitoring, and maintenance of devices.

Device Registration:

- **Thing Registry**: The Thing Registry is a centralized repository in AWS IoT Core that stores metadata about IoT devices. Each device is represented as a "Thing" and is assigned unique identifiers. This registry makes it easy to track, manage, and retrieve information about each device.
  - **Attributes and Tags**: Each device

can have associated metadata (attributes), such as device type, location, or status. You can also use tags for grouping and organizing devices based on categories.

Device Authentication and Authorization:

- **X.509 Certificates**: Devices authenticate to AWS IoT Core using X.509 certificates, ensuring secure communication between the device and the cloud. These certificates can be provisioned manually or dynamically through the **AWS IoT Device Management** service.

- **AWS IoT Identity**: Manage device identities using AWS IoT Core's identity management system. This includes securely associating devices with credentials and ensuring proper access controls.

Over-the-Air (OTA) Updates:

- **Firmware Updates**: AWS IoT Core supports over-the-air (OTA) updates for IoT devices, allowing you to update device firmware remotely. This is essential for maintaining device performance, security, and functionality over time.
  - **AWS IoT Device Management** provides an OTA update

mechanism, allowing you to schedule updates, monitor progress, and rollback if necessary.

Fleet Management:

- **Fleet Indexing and Search**: AWS IoT Core allows you to index your fleet of devices for easy search and retrieval. Using **Fleet Indexing**, you can query device metadata (e.g., status, type, last seen) across large fleets, which helps in managing large-scale IoT deployments.

2. Managing IoT Data:

IoT devices continuously generate data, which needs to be collected, processed, and stored. AWS IoT Core offers several tools to manage and process IoT data efficiently.

Device Shadows:

- **Device Shadow Service**: A "device shadow" is a virtual representation of a device in the cloud. It stores the last known state of the device and allows applications to interact with the device even when it is offline. This helps in synchronizing device data with the cloud, especially for intermittent connectivity scenarios.
  - The device shadow supports both "desired" and "reported" states. The "desired" state is the desired

configuration sent from the cloud to the device, while the "reported" state is the actual state that the device reports back.

Real-Time Data Ingestion:

- **Message Broker (MQTT and HTTPS)**: AWS IoT Core uses a highly scalable MQTT broker for real-time, low-latency communication between devices and the cloud. Devices send messages to AWS IoT Core using the MQTT protocol, which are then processed, stored, or routed to other services.
  - **MQTT Topics**: Devices publish data to specific topics, and applications can subscribe to those topics to receive the data. This decouples devices from applications, ensuring scalability and flexibility.
  - **HTTPS Protocol**: For scenarios where MQTT is not ideal, AWS IoT Core also supports HTTP-based communication.

Data Routing with AWS IoT Core Rules Engine:

- **Rules Engine**: The **AWS IoT Core Rules Engine** allows you to filter, transform, and route incoming device data to other AWS services for further processing. You can create rules based on incoming data and trigger actions, such as:

- Storing data in **Amazon S3** or **Amazon DynamoDB**.
- Sending data to **AWS Lambda** for processing.
- Streaming data to **Amazon Kinesis** for real-time analytics.

Processing and Analyzing IoT Data:

- **AWS IoT Analytics**: Once data is ingested, you can use **AWS IoT Analytics** to process and analyze the data at scale. AWS IoT Analytics provides tools to clean, enrich, and store IoT data for long-term analysis.
  - It integrates with other AWS analytics tools such as **Amazon QuickSight** for visualizing IoT data, or **Amazon SageMaker** for building and deploying machine learning models on IoT data.

3. Device Monitoring and Health Management:

Monitoring the health and status of IoT devices is crucial for maintaining operational efficiency. AWS IoT Core provides several tools to monitor and track device activity.

AWS IoT Device Defender:

- **Security Monitoring**: **AWS IoT Device Defender** continuously audits your device fleet for security risks. It helps you monitor device behavior, check for anomalies, and implement preventive

measures.
- It can detect issues like unauthorized device connections or unusual communication patterns and alert you in real-time.

Device Metrics and Logs with CloudWatch:

- **CloudWatch Integration**: IoT device data can be sent to **AWS CloudWatch** for metrics collection and log analysis. CloudWatch helps you track device performance metrics (e.g., battery status, signal strength) and logs (e.g., device connectivity status, error reports) in real time.
  - You can set up **CloudWatch Alarms** to notify you of any potential issues, such as devices going offline or failing to report data.

AWS IoT Analytics Monitoring:

- **Data Visualization and Analysis**: Use **AWS IoT Analytics** to monitor the data produced by your devices over time. This service allows you to run queries, create dashboards, and visualize trends in your IoT data.

4. Data Storage and Archiving:

Efficiently storing IoT data for long-term analysis and regulatory compliance is another critical aspect of managing IoT systems.

Amazon S3 for Data Storage:

- IoT data can be stored in **Amazon S3**, which is highly scalable, durable, and cost-effective for storing large volumes of data.
    - You can store raw or processed data, logs, and metadata related to IoT devices.
    - **S3 Lifecycle Policies**: Automate the archiving of older data to lower-cost storage options such as **Amazon Glacier**.

Amazon DynamoDB for Device Data Storage:

- **DynamoDB** is ideal for storing device state and metadata in a highly available, low-latency NoSQL database. It allows you to query device data efficiently, even at massive scales.

AWS Glacier for Archiving Data:

- For long-term storage of historical IoT data that is not frequently accessed, **Amazon Glacier** provides a low-cost storage solution with longer retrieval times.

5. Data Privacy and Security:

Ensuring the privacy and security of IoT data is vital for compliance and trust. AWS IoT Core provides multiple security features:

- **Encryption**: Data transmitted between devices and AWS IoT Core is encrypted using **TLS**. Additionally, data can be encrypted at rest using **AWS KMS** (Key Management Service).
- **Access Control**: Fine-grained access control to devices and IoT data is managed via **AWS Identity and Access Management (IAM)** policies and roles.
- **AWS IoT Device Defender** helps ensure that devices follow security best practices and stay secure from threats.

Summary:

Managing IoT devices and data with AWS IoT Core enables businesses to build scalable, secure, and intelligent IoT applications. With features like device registration, shadow management, real-time data ingestion, and seamless integration with AWS analytics and security tools, AWS IoT Core simplifies the challenges of managing large IoT fleets and data flows. Whether you are building a smart city, industrial IoT application, or a health monitoring system, AWS IoT Core provides the tools necessary to connect, manage, and analyze your IoT ecosystem effectively.

CHAPTER 14: SERVERLESS ARCHITECTURE

Advanced Use Cases of AWS Lambda

AWS Lambda is a powerful serverless compute service that allows developers to run code in response to events without provisioning or managing servers. While the basic use cases of AWS Lambda are well-known (e.g., simple event-driven triggers, automated processes), its advanced use cases leverage Lambda's scalability, integration capabilities, and flexibility. Below are some advanced use cases of AWS Lambda that go beyond the basics:

1. Real-Time Data Processing and Analytics

Lambda can be used to process large streams of real-time data and perform analytics tasks like filtering, aggregation, transformation, and enriching data on the fly. This is especially useful for IoT, social media, or financial data.

Use Case: Real-Time Analytics on IoT Data

- **Scenario**: A company collects sensor data from thousands of IoT devices in real-time. Lambda is triggered whenever a new data point is uploaded to Amazon S3 or sent to an **Amazon Kinesis Data Stream**.

- **Implementation**: Lambda processes the incoming data in real time, performs transformations (e.g., data enrichment, filtering), and writes the results to **Amazon DynamoDB** or **Amazon Redshift** for analysis. Additionally, Lambda can trigger **Amazon QuickSight** to visualize the data or invoke **AWS SageMaker** to run machine learning models on the data.

2. Building Microservices with Lambda and API Gateway

Using AWS Lambda in conjunction with **Amazon API Gateway**, you can easily build scalable and cost-effective microservices without managing servers. Each Lambda function can serve a specific API endpoint and perform its own discrete operation, such as data processing, authentication, or querying a database.

Use Case: Serverless Microservices

- **Scenario**: A company is developing a web application with multiple features like user authentication, data retrieval, and notifications. Each feature is encapsulated as a microservice.

- **Implementation**:
    - **API Gateway** acts as a front door for HTTP requests.
    - **Lambda** functions handle the business logic for each endpoint (e.g., user authentication, data fetching, etc.).
    - The microservices interact with databases like **Amazon RDS** or **DynamoDB** and integrate with other services like **S3** or **SNS**.
    - This architecture allows for easy scaling and isolation of different parts of the application.

3. Event-Driven Workflow Automation

Lambda can be used to automate complex workflows triggered by events from other AWS services. This use case is common for tasks such as automating file processing, email notifications, or even integrating external APIs.

Use Case: Automated Image or Video Processing

- **Scenario**: A photo-sharing application allows users to upload images, and upon upload, the images need to be resized, filtered, and analyzed for metadata.
- **Implementation**:
  - **Amazon S3** triggers a Lambda function whenever an image is uploaded.
  - Lambda invokes **Amazon Rekognition** to analyze the image (e.g., detect faces, labels, or text).
  - The function resizes the image using **AWS SDK** and stores the processed images back to S3.
  - Lambda then sends an email or notification via **Amazon SNS** or **SES** to confirm the processing.

4. Real-Time Stream Processing with Kinesis

AWS Lambda integrates seamlessly with **Amazon Kinesis** for stream processing. You can use Lambda to process and analyze data streams, such as social media feeds, website logs, or sensor data in real-time.

Use Case: Real-Time Log Analysis

- **Scenario**: A company collects logs from its web servers, and it needs to process these logs in real-time to detect anomalies or errors.
- **Implementation**:
  - Logs are sent to **Amazon Kinesis**

Data Streams.
- Lambda processes these logs in real-time, looking for specific patterns (e.g., error codes or unusual request spikes).
- Lambda then triggers alerts via **Amazon SNS** or stores the processed data in **Amazon Elasticsearch Service** for visualization and analysis in **Kibana**.

5. Serverless ETL (Extract, Transform, Load)

Lambda can be used as part of a serverless ETL pipeline, where it extracts data from sources, transforms it according to business logic, and loads it into the desired destination (such as data lakes, warehouses, or databases).

Use Case: Data Migration and Transformation

- **Scenario**: A company is migrating its data from an on-premises database to AWS, and the data needs to be transformed before storing it in **Amazon Redshift**.
- **Implementation**:
    - Lambda is triggered by **Amazon S3** events whenever new data is uploaded or moved to S3 buckets.
    - The function extracts the data, transforms it (e.g., cleaning, aggregation, or enrichment), and then loads the results into

Amazon Redshift or **Amazon S3** for further processing.

- You can also use **AWS Glue** with Lambda for more complex transformations or orchestrate workflows with **AWS Step Functions**.

6. Automating Security and Compliance Monitoring

Lambda is ideal for automating security checks, vulnerability scanning, and ensuring compliance with regulatory requirements.

Use Case: Security Auditing and Remediation

- **Scenario**: A company needs to ensure that its AWS environment is compliant with security best practices (e.g., checking for open security groups or improper IAM permissions).

- **Implementation**:
    - Lambda is triggered by **Amazon CloudWatch Events** (for scheduled checks) or by configuration changes in **AWS Config**.
    - Lambda runs security checks on resources like **IAM roles**, **S3 buckets**, **security groups**, etc.
    - If Lambda detects an issue (e.g., a security group with inbound HTTP access), it can trigger an automated remediation action,

such as restricting access or notifying the security team through **Amazon SNS**.

7. AI and ML Model Inference with Lambda

AWS Lambda can be used to run machine learning models and provide real-time inference for applications. This is useful for building applications that require low-latency predictions and scalable deployment without managing dedicated infrastructure.

Use Case: Real-Time Fraud Detection

- **Scenario**: An e-commerce platform needs to detect fraud in real-time for every transaction made by users.
- **Implementation**:
    - Lambda is triggered by **Amazon API Gateway** or **Amazon SNS** whenever a new transaction is initiated.
    - It invokes a pre-trained **AWS SageMaker** model or calls an ML model deployed on **Amazon Lambda** to predict if a transaction is fraudulent.
    - Based on the prediction, Lambda can take immediate action, such as flagging the transaction for review or blocking it, and send alerts to the security team.

8. Automated Backup and Disaster Recovery

Lambda can automate backup processes and orchestrate disaster recovery procedures to ensure data integrity and availability.

Use Case: Scheduled Backup of Critical Data

- **Scenario**: A company needs to back up critical files stored in Amazon S3 regularly to **Amazon Glacier** for cost-effective long-term storage.
- **Implementation**:
    - Lambda is scheduled using **Amazon CloudWatch Events** to run at specific intervals (e.g., daily, weekly).
    - The Lambda function copies files from S3 to Glacier, ensuring that important data is stored securely and cost-effectively.
    - Additionally, Lambda can track and log backup status using **Amazon CloudWatch Logs**.

9. Serverless Chatbots and Voice Assistants

AWS Lambda can be used to build serverless chatbots or voice assistants that process input and respond dynamically.

Use Case: Building a Serverless Chatbot

- **Scenario**: A company wants to create a customer support chatbot using **Amazon Lex** (a service for building conversational interfaces).

- **Implementation**:
  - Lambda functions are invoked by **Amazon Lex** whenever a user interacts with the chatbot.
  - The Lambda function processes the request, interacts with back-end services (e.g., querying a database, accessing APIs), and sends a dynamic response back to the user through **Lex**.
  - This architecture allows you to scale interactions without worrying about server management.

Summary:

AWS Lambda's advanced capabilities extend far beyond simple event-driven triggers. It is highly versatile and can be integrated with a variety of AWS services to solve complex challenges in real-time data processing, serverless architectures, AI/ML, security, and much more. Leveraging Lambda for these advanced use cases enables businesses to build efficient, scalable, and cost-effective solutions while focusing on innovation rather than infrastructure management.

AWS Step Functions: Orchestrating Workflows

AWS Step Functions is a fully managed service that enables the orchestration of complex workflows across multiple AWS services. It allows you to coordinate the components of distributed applications, microservices, and serverless workflows, ensuring that tasks are executed in the correct order and that errors are handled efficiently. Step Functions simplifies the management of workflows by providing a visual interface for designing and monitoring processes, as well as integrating seamlessly with other AWS services. Here's a breakdown of **AWS Step Functions** and its key features:

Key Features of AWS Step Functions

1. **Visual Workflow Design**

   AWS Step Functions provides a graphical interface for defining workflows as state machines. You can easily design, visualize, and troubleshoot complex processes by creating a flowchart of tasks and specifying how they interact. Each state in the workflow can perform an action, wait for a response, or transition to another state based on conditions.

2. **State Machines**

   The core concept of Step Functions is the state machine. A state machine is a collection of states, each of which performs an action or makes a decision. States can be of different types, such as:
   - **Task**: Executes a specific action, such as invoking a Lambda function.
   - **Choice**: Directs the workflow based on conditions.
   - **Wait**: Pauses the workflow for a specified duration.
   - **Parallel**: Runs multiple tasks simultaneously.
   - **Succeed**: Marks the successful completion of a workflow.
   - **Fail**: Ends the workflow with a failure status.

3. **Error Handling and Retries**

   Step Functions provides built-in error handling and retry mechanisms to ensure workflows continue even in the face of failures. You can define custom retry policies (e.g., exponential backoff) and specify how errors are handled at the task level.

4. **Integration with AWS Services**

   Step Functions can integrate with over

200 AWS services, including:
- **AWS Lambda** for executing serverless functions.
- **Amazon SNS** for notifications.
- **Amazon S3** for file storage.
- **Amazon DynamoDB** for NoSQL databases.
- **Amazon SQS** for message queuing.
- **AWS Glue** for ETL workflows. This deep integration allows you to automate, orchestrate, and scale workflows across a wide range of AWS services.

5. **Workflow Monitoring**
Step Functions provides detailed logs and visual workflows for monitoring the progress of each execution. You can view the history of workflows, trace the execution path, and examine the input/output for each step. This helps in identifying issues and improving workflows.

6. **Serverless Workflow Automation**
As part of the serverless ecosystem, Step Functions enables the automation of serverless applications without managing infrastructure. You can build highly scalable, resilient applications

that automatically scale based on demand.

Common Use Cases for AWS Step Functions

1. **Serverless Applications** Step Functions is ideal for orchestrating serverless workflows. You can create an end-to-end application by chaining Lambda functions, integrating them with other AWS services like S3, DynamoDB, and SNS to create powerful workflows that run in the cloud.

Example: A serverless image processing pipeline that:

- Receives an image upload event from S3.
- Triggers a Lambda function for image resizing.
- Stores the resized image in another S3 bucket.
- Sends a notification via SNS when the processing is complete.

2. **Microservices Orchestration** In a microservices architecture, Step Functions can coordinate the different services by controlling the flow of data between them. This is essential for managing complex, multi-step processes that require multiple

microservices to interact.

Example: An e-commerce order processing system:

- The order service processes a new customer order.
- The payment service verifies and processes payment.
- The shipping service arranges delivery once payment is confirmed.

3. **Data Processing Workflows** AWS Step Functions can be used for ETL (Extract, Transform, Load) jobs by orchestrating the flow of data through multiple steps, such as extraction, transformation, and loading into data warehouses or other storage systems.

Example: A data pipeline that:

- Extracts data from a database.
- Processes the data using AWS Lambda or AWS Glue.
- Loads the results into **Amazon Redshift** or **Amazon S3**.

4. **Machine Learning Workflows** Step Functions simplifies machine learning workflows by chaining different steps like data preprocessing, model training, model evaluation, and inference. It integrates well with **Amazon**

SageMaker, making it easier to automate the process of model deployment and management.

Example: A machine learning pipeline that:

- Loads and preprocesses data.
- Trains a machine learning model using SageMaker.
- Evaluates the model's performance.
- Deploys the trained model to an endpoint for real-time inference.

5. **Business Process Automation** Step Functions is also used for automating business processes like approval workflows, payment processing, or content moderation. By combining conditional logic and task states, you can model real-world workflows with complex decisions and multiple outcomes.

Example: An approval workflow:

- A request is submitted by a user.
- An approval process is triggered where different managers review and approve or deny the request.
- Notifications are sent depending on the outcome of the review.

6. **Batch Processing and Job Scheduling**

AWS Step Functions can automate and manage batch processing tasks that need to be executed on a regular schedule, making it easy to integrate with other AWS services like S3, DynamoDB, and SQS.

Example: A batch data processing job that:

- Runs at scheduled intervals using **Amazon CloudWatch Events**.
- Extracts data from S3.
- Processes and stores it in a database or data warehouse.

Step Functions vs. AWS Lambda: When to Use Each

While both AWS Step Functions and AWS Lambda are used for building scalable applications, they serve different purposes:

- **AWS Lambda** is best suited for executing short-lived, discrete tasks. It's used when you need to execute code in response to events, but you do not require complex coordination or long-running workflows.

- **AWS Step Functions** is used when you need to orchestrate multiple tasks, integrate various AWS services, and manage complex workflows. It's ideal for long-running workflows that involve multiple tasks and decision points.

In many cases, **AWS Step Functions** and **AWS Lambda** work together, with Lambda performing the task executions and Step Functions managing the workflow.

How to Get Started with AWS Step Functions

1. **Define State Machine**: Use the AWS Step Functions console or the **Amazon States Language** (ASL) to define your workflow.

2. **Create Resources**: Set up the AWS services that Step Functions will invoke (e.g., Lambda functions, SNS topics).

3. **Test the Workflow**: Test the state machine to ensure that the tasks are performed in the correct order and that error handling works as expected.

4. **Monitor and Optimize**: Use AWS CloudWatch to monitor the performance of your workflows and optimize them for better cost-efficiency and scalability.

Summary

AWS Step Functions simplifies the orchestration of complex workflows and automates business processes, making it an essential tool for building scalable, distributed, and serverless applications. With its visual interface, error handling, integration with AWS services, and support for microservices, Step Functions helps developers streamline the design and management of workflows, significantly reducing the complexity of coordinating multiple services and tasks. Whether you're building a serverless application, automating a business process, or orchestrating data pipelines, AWS Step Functions provides the tools you need to scale and manage your workflows effectively.

PART 5: CASE STUDIES AND REAL-WORLD APPLICATIONS

CHAPTER 15: BUILDING SCALABLE WEB APPLICATIONS

End-to-End Application Deployment with AWS

Deploying an application end-to-end in AWS involves managing various components, from infrastructure setup to application configuration and scaling. AWS provides a comprehensive suite of tools and services to streamline this process, whether you're deploying a simple web application or a complex distributed system.

Here's a guide to understanding **End-to-End**

Application Deployment in AWS:

Key Phases in End-to-End Deployment

1. **Planning and Design**
    - Define the application architecture, including the choice of compute resources (e.g., EC2, Lambda) and storage services (e.g., S3, RDS).
    - Decide on the network configuration, including VPCs, subnets, and security groups.
    - Choose a deployment strategy, such as blue/green deployments, rolling updates, or canary releases.

2. **Infrastructure Provisioning** AWS offers several tools for infrastructure provisioning:
    - **AWS Management Console**: For manual setup and management.
    - **AWS CloudFormation**: For defining infrastructure as code.
    - **AWS CDK (Cloud Development Kit)**: For using familiar programming languages to define cloud infrastructure.
    - **Terraform**: A third-party tool for infrastructure automation.

3. **Application Development and Packaging**
    - Develop the application using the chosen programming languages and frameworks.
    - Package the application into deployable units, such as container images for **Amazon ECS/EKS** or zip files for **AWS Lambda**.
4. **Application Deployment** AWS provides various services to deploy applications:
    - **AWS Elastic Beanstalk**: Simplifies deployment for web applications and services.
    - **AWS CodePipeline**: Automates the entire deployment pipeline.
    - **Amazon ECS/EKS**: For deploying containerized applications.
    - **AWS Lambda**: For deploying serverless applications.
    - **AWS OpsWorks**: For configuration management and deployment.
5. **Testing and Validation**
    - Conduct automated and manual testing to ensure the application works as expected.

- Validate the deployment process using staging environments before moving to production.

6. **Scaling and Performance Optimization**
    - Use **Elastic Load Balancing (ELB)** and **Auto Scaling** to handle traffic fluctuations.
    - Optimize application performance using **Amazon CloudFront** for content delivery and caching.

7. **Monitoring and Logging**
    - Use **AWS CloudWatch** for monitoring metrics, setting alarms, and logging.
    - Utilize **AWS X-Ray** for application tracing to identify bottlenecks.

8. **Security and Compliance**
    - Implement access controls using **AWS Identity and Access Management (IAM)**.
    - Secure data using **AWS Key Management Service (KMS)** and encryption.
    - Ensure compliance with industry standards and regulations.

9. **Continuous Integration/Continuous Deployment (CI/CD)**
    - Automate the build, test, and deployment processes using AWS services like:
        - **AWS CodePipeline**
        - **AWS CodeBuild**
        - **AWS CodeDeploy**
    - Integrate with version control systems like GitHub or AWS CodeCommit.

AWS Tools and Services for Deployment

1. **Compute Services**
    - **Amazon EC2**: Deploy virtual servers for traditional applications.
    - **AWS Lambda**: Run serverless applications with minimal overhead.
    - **Amazon ECS/EKS**: Deploy and manage containerized applications.

2. **Networking Services**
    - **Amazon VPC**: Define your virtual network and subnets.
    - **Elastic Load Balancer (ELB)**: Distribute traffic across multiple resources.

- **Amazon Route 53**: Manage DNS and domain routing.

3. **Storage Services**
   - **Amazon S3**: Store static assets like images, videos, and HTML files.
   - **Amazon EFS**: For shared file storage.
   - **Amazon RDS/DynamoDB**: Manage relational or NoSQL databases.

4. **Deployment and CI/CD Tools**
   - **AWS CodePipeline**: Automate the deployment pipeline.
   - **AWS Elastic Beanstalk**: Simplify application deployment.
   - **AWS CloudFormation**: Manage infrastructure as code.
   - **AWS CodeDeploy**: Automate deployments for EC2 and on-premises applications.

5. **Monitoring and Optimization**
   - **AWS CloudWatch**: Monitor application metrics and set alarms.
   - **AWS Trusted Advisor**: Optimize performance, security, and cost.
   - **AWS Auto Scaling**:

Automatically adjust capacity to meet demand.

Common Deployment Scenarios

1. **Web Application Deployment**
   - Host static files on **Amazon S3** and serve them via **CloudFront**.
   - Use **EC2** or **Elastic Beanstalk** for backend services.
   - Implement Auto Scaling for dynamic traffic management.

2. **Microservices Deployment**
   - Deploy microservices using **Amazon ECS** or **AWS Lambda**.
   - Use **API Gateway** to expose services securely.
   - Coordinate workflows using **AWS Step Functions**.

3. **Containerized Application Deployment**
   - Use **Amazon ECS** or **Amazon EKS** to deploy containers.
   - Leverage **Fargate** for serverless container orchestration.
   - Use CI/CD pipelines for seamless updates.

4. **Serverless Application Deployment**
   - Deploy functions with **AWS Lambda**.

- Integrate **DynamoDB**, **S3**, and **SNS** for backend processing.
- Use **API Gateway** for frontend integration.

Best Practices for End-to-End Deployment

1. **Automate Everything**
   Use tools like AWS CodePipeline and CloudFormation to automate infrastructure provisioning, application deployment, and testing.

2. **Start Small and Scale Gradually**
   Begin with a small deployment and scale up using Auto Scaling and Elastic Load Balancing.

3. **Monitor Continuously**
   Use AWS CloudWatch to track application health and performance. Implement alarms to handle unexpected events.

4. **Implement Security Best Practices**
   - Use IAM roles and policies for access control.
   - Enable logging and auditing with AWS CloudTrail.

5. **Optimize Costs**
   Use **AWS Cost Explorer** to monitor expenses and optimize resource usage.

Example Workflow for End-to-End Deployment

Scenario: Deploying a web application.

1. **Set Up Infrastructure**
   - Define a VPC with public and private subnets.
   - Configure an Internet Gateway and security groups.

2. **Deploy Application**
   - Host static files on **Amazon S3** with CloudFront.
   - Use **AWS Elastic Beanstalk** to deploy the backend.

3. **Set Up CI/CD**
   - Create a pipeline in **AWS CodePipeline**.
   - Use **AWS CodeBuild** to compile and test the application.
   - Deploy the application using **AWS CodeDeploy**.

4. **Enable Monitoring**
   - Set up **CloudWatch** dashboards and alarms.
   - Use **X-Ray** to trace application performance.

5. **Optimize and Scale**
   - Enable Auto Scaling to manage traffic spikes.
   - Use Trusted Advisor to identify

cost-saving opportunities.

Summary

AWS provides a robust ecosystem of services for deploying applications end-to-end. By leveraging AWS tools for compute, storage, networking, CI/CD, and monitoring, you can build scalable, resilient, and cost-effective applications. Whether you're deploying a simple website or a complex enterprise solution, AWS makes it easier to manage every step of the deployment lifecycle.

Auto Scaling and Load Balancing in AWS

Auto Scaling and Load Balancing are essential components for building scalable, highly available, and cost-efficient applications in AWS. These features work together to handle fluctuations in traffic, ensure application reliability, and optimize resource usage.

1. Elastic Load Balancing (ELB)

Overview

Elastic Load Balancing (ELB) automatically distributes incoming application traffic across multiple targets, such as Amazon EC2 instances, containers, or Lambda functions. It ensures fault tolerance and improves the availability of your application.

Types of Elastic Load Balancers

1. **Application Load Balancer (ALB)**
   - Operates at Layer 7 (Application Layer).
   - Ideal for HTTP and HTTPS traffic.
   - Supports advanced routing, such as path-based and host-based routing.
   - Integrates with AWS WAF for web application security.

2. **Network Load Balancer (NLB)**
   - Operates at Layer 4 (Transport Layer).
   - Designed for high-performance, low-latency traffic.
   - Suitable for TCP/UDP traffic and long-lived connections.

3. **Gateway Load Balancer (GWLB)**
   - Works at Layer 3 (Network Layer).
   - Used for deploying third-party virtual appliances like firewalls and intrusion detection systems.

4. **Classic Load Balancer (CLB)**
    - Operates at Layers 4 and 7.
    - Legacy option, suitable for basic load balancing needs.

Key Features

- **Health Checks**: Monitors the health of targets and routes traffic only to healthy instances.
- **Sticky Sessions**: Routes requests from a client to the same target.
- **SSL Termination**: Offloads SSL/TLS processing to the load balancer.
- **Cross-Zone Load Balancing**: Distributes traffic evenly across multiple Availability Zones.

Use Cases

- Hosting scalable web applications.
- Distributing API requests.
- Managing workloads for microservices architectures.

2. Auto Scaling

Overview

AWS Auto Scaling automatically adjusts the number of resources in your application to maintain performance while optimizing costs. It can scale in (reduce resources) during low demand and scale out (add resources) during high demand.

Types of Auto Scaling

1. **Amazon EC2 Auto Scaling**
   - Adjusts the number of EC2 instances in an Auto Scaling group.
   - Based on pre-defined scaling policies or dynamic conditions.

2. **Application Auto Scaling**
   - Scales resources like Amazon ECS tasks, DynamoDB tables, Lambda functions, and Aurora DB clusters.

3. **AWS Auto Scaling**
   - Provides a unified interface to manage scaling across multiple AWS services.

Key Features

- **Scaling Policies**:
   - **Target Tracking Scaling**: Adjusts resources to maintain a target metric, such as CPU utilization.
   - **Step Scaling**: Adds or removes resources based on metric thresholds.
   - **Scheduled Scaling**: Scales resources at specified times.
- **Dynamic Scaling**: Automatically reacts to changing demand using monitoring

data from **Amazon CloudWatch**.

- **Predictive Scaling**: Uses machine learning to anticipate future demand and scales resources in advance.

Use Cases

- Managing traffic spikes for e-commerce platforms.
- Scaling microservices based on API request rates.
- Optimizing compute capacity for cost efficiency.

3. How Auto Scaling and Load Balancing Work Together

Integration Flow

1. **Traffic Distribution**:
   - ELB distributes incoming traffic across targets in different Availability Zones.

2. **Scaling Resources**:
   - Auto Scaling monitors application demand using metrics from **CloudWatch** and dynamically adjusts resources in the Auto Scaling group.

3. **Health Management**:
   - ELB checks the health of targets.
   - If an instance becomes

unhealthy, Auto Scaling terminates it and launches a new instance.

4. **Improved Availability**:
    - ELB ensures traffic is routed only to healthy instances, while Auto Scaling ensures enough instances are available to handle demand.

4. Setting Up Auto Scaling and Load Balancing

Step 1: Create a Load Balancer

- Use the AWS Management Console, CLI, or SDK to configure an ALB, NLB, or CLB.
- Define target groups and attach EC2 instances, containers, or Lambda functions.

Step 2: Configure an Auto Scaling Group

- Specify a launch template or configuration for EC2 instances.
- Define the desired capacity, minimum size, and maximum size.

Step 3: Set Up Scaling Policies

- Use target tracking or step scaling to adjust the number of instances based on metrics like CPU utilization or request count.

Step 4: Monitor and Optimize

- Use **CloudWatch** dashboards to monitor performance.
- Adjust scaling policies and load balancer configurations based on usage patterns.

5. Benefits

Elastic Load Balancing

- Distributes traffic efficiently across resources.
- Ensures fault tolerance and high availability.
- Offloads tasks like SSL termination and health checks.

Auto Scaling

- Optimizes resource utilization and reduces costs.
- Responds dynamically to changes in demand.
- Improves resilience by replacing unhealthy instances.

6. Real-World Example

Scenario: A high-traffic e-commerce website.

- **Challenge**: Handle sudden spikes during flash sales.
- **Solution**:
    - Use an ALB to route traffic to EC2 instances in multiple Availability Zones.

- Configure Auto Scaling to maintain a CPU utilization target of 70%.
- During sales, Auto Scaling scales out EC2 instances to handle the surge in traffic.
- After the sale, Auto Scaling scales in to minimize costs.

7. Best Practices

1. **Enable Cross-Zone Load Balancing**: Distribute traffic evenly across all instances in different zones.

2. **Use Health Checks**: Configure detailed health checks for the load balancer to detect unresponsive targets.

3. **Optimize Scaling Policies**: Fine-tune target metrics and thresholds based on application behavior.

4. **Monitor Costs**: Use **AWS Cost Explorer** to track the costs of scaling events.

5. **Test in Staging**: Simulate scaling scenarios in a staging environment to identify potential issues.

Summary

Auto Scaling and Load Balancing are foundational services for building robust, cost-effective, and highly available applications in AWS. By combining ELB for efficient traffic distribution and Auto Scaling for dynamic resource management, you can ensure optimal performance and resilience for your workloads.

CHAPTER 16: DISASTER RECOVERY AND BACKUP

Designing Backup Strategies with AWS

Creating an effective backup strategy is critical to ensuring data integrity, availability, and disaster recovery. AWS offers a wide range of services and tools to design and implement robust backup solutions for diverse workloads.

1. Importance of Backup Strategies

- **Data Protection**: Safeguards against accidental deletion, corruption, or cyberattacks.

- **Disaster Recovery**: Ensures business continuity during outages or failures.
- **Regulatory Compliance**: Meets data retention and protection requirements.
- **Cost Efficiency**: Balances storage and recovery costs effectively.

2. AWS Backup Services Overview

AWS provides dedicated services and features to facilitate automated, secure, and cost-effective backups:

AWS Backup

- Centralized service for managing and automating backup processes across AWS services.
- Supports resources like Amazon RDS, DynamoDB, EBS, EFS, and EC2 instances.
- Offers features like backup scheduling, retention policies, and encryption.

Amazon S3

- Cost-efficient and scalable object storage ideal for backups.
- Integrates with features like **S3 Versioning**, **Lifecycle Policies**, and **Glacier** for archiving.

Amazon Glacier and Glacier Deep Archive

- Designed for long-term, low-cost data archiving.
- Suitable for infrequently accessed backups.
- Supports retrieval options from minutes to hours.

AWS Storage Gateway

- Hybrid cloud storage service enabling on-premises backups to AWS.
- Offers Tape Gateway for virtual tape backups and File Gateway for NFS/SMB-based storage.

Amazon RDS Snapshots and Automated Backups

- Built-in snapshot functionality for relational databases.
- Automated backups with configurable retention periods.

AWS Elastic Block Store (EBS) Snapshots

- Point-in-time backups of EBS volumes.
- Enables incremental backups to save storage costs.

3. Designing an Effective Backup Strategy

Step 1: Define Backup Objectives

- **Recovery Point Objective (RPO)**: How much data loss is acceptable.

- **Recovery Time Objective (RTO)**: How quickly data needs to be restored.
- **Retention Requirements**: How long backups must be retained.

Step 2: Identify Data and Resources to Back Up

- Identify critical workloads, databases, and files that need regular backups.
- Consider all AWS services in use, such as EC2, RDS, S3, DynamoDB, etc.

Step 3: Choose Backup Frequency

- **Daily**: For production databases and frequently changing files.
- **Weekly**: For less critical data or stable environments.
- **Monthly/Yearly**: For long-term archival.

Step 4: Select Backup Storage Solutions

- **Short-Term Storage**: Use **Amazon S3** or **EBS Snapshots** for quick recovery.
- **Long-Term Storage**: Use **Amazon Glacier** or **Glacier Deep Archive** for archival.

Step 5: Automate Backup Processes

- Use **AWS Backup** to schedule and automate backups across services.
- Leverage Lambda functions for custom automation workflows.

Step 6: Monitor and Test Backups
- Regularly verify backup integrity.
- Conduct disaster recovery simulations to validate recovery times and processes.

4. AWS Backup Best Practices

1. **Enable Encryption**:
    - Use AWS-managed or customer-managed keys in **AWS Key Management Service (KMS)**.

2. **Implement Versioning**:
    - Enable versioning in S3 to protect against accidental overwrites and deletions.

3. **Follow the 3-2-1 Backup Rule**:
    - Keep three copies of your data: two on different storage mediums and one offsite.

4. **Optimize Costs**:
    - Use **Lifecycle Policies** to move infrequently accessed backups to lower-cost storage tiers like Glacier.

5. **Utilize Tags for Organization**:
    - Tag resources to group backups by project, environment, or department.

6. **Geographic Redundancy**:
    - Store backups in multiple AWS

Regions using **Cross-Region Replication**.

5. Backup Strategies for Common AWS Services

Amazon S3

- Enable **S3 Versioning** for automatic backup of object changes.
- Use **Cross-Region Replication (CRR)** for disaster recovery.
- Set up **Lifecycle Rules** to archive data to Glacier.

Amazon RDS

- Enable **Automated Backups** and configure the retention period.
- Create manual **DB Snapshots** before major updates.
- Use **Cross-Region Read Replicas** for additional redundancy.

Amazon DynamoDB

- Enable **Point-in-Time Recovery (PITR)** for continuous backups.
- Export tables to Amazon S3 for additional backup redundancy.

EC2 and EBS

- Schedule **EBS Snapshots** for persistent volume backups.
- Use **AWS Backup** to manage EC2

instance and volume backups together.

AWS Storage Gateway

- Deploy **Tape Gateway** to replace on-premises tape libraries.
- Configure **File Gateway** for seamless NFS/SMB file backups to S3.

6. Real-World Scenario

Use Case: A SaaS company requires robust backup solutions to protect user data and ensure uptime.

- **RPO**: 15 minutes.
- **RTO**: 2 hours.
- **Solution**:
    - Use EBS Snapshots for EC2 instances with daily backups.
    - Enable RDS Automated Backups with a 7-day retention policy.
    - Store long-term archives in Glacier with lifecycle transitions from S3.
    - Implement Cross-Region Replication for critical S3 data.
    - Monitor backup activities using **AWS Backup Audit Manager**.

7. Challenges and Mitigations

Challenge	Mitigation
High Backup Costs	Use incremental backups and lifecycle

	policies to minimize storage expenses.
Recovery Time Constraints	Use high-performance tiers like S3 Standard for faster recovery.
Compliance Requirements	Leverage AWS Backup Audit Manager for tracking and reporting compliance.
Data Corruption Risks	Test backups regularly to ensure data integrity.

Summary

AWS offers a robust suite of services for designing effective backup strategies, ensuring data availability and compliance. By leveraging features like automated backups, cross-region replication, and cost-optimized storage tiers, businesses can build resilient systems that meet operational and regulatory needs. Regular monitoring and testing further ensure that backup strategies remain reliable and aligned with organizational goals.

Multi-Region Disaster Recovery Solutions

Multi-Region Disaster Recovery (DR) ensures the continuity of critical operations during outages by replicating resources and data across multiple AWS Regions. This strategy minimizes downtime, protects against regional failures, and enhances application resilience.

1. Why Multi-Region Disaster Recovery?

- **Resilience Against Regional Failures**: Protects against natural disasters, power outages, and network disruptions.

- **Global Reach**: Ensures applications are available closer to users worldwide.

- **Compliance**: Meets regulatory requirements for redundancy and data sovereignty.

- **Business Continuity**: Reduces downtime and protects critical operations.

2. Key AWS Services for Multi-Region DR

Amazon Route 53

- **DNS Failover**: Automatically redirects traffic to healthy endpoints in other regions using health checks.

- **Latency-Based Routing**: Ensures traffic is routed to the closest or fastest region.

Amazon S3 and Cross-Region Replication (CRR)

- Automatically replicates objects to a bucket in another region for redundancy.
- Ensures compliance with data residency and disaster recovery requirements.

Amazon RDS Multi-Region Read Replicas

- Provides read replicas in secondary regions for failover support.
- Promotes read replicas to standalone databases during regional outages.

Amazon DynamoDB Global Tables

- Offers fully managed, multi-region, multi-active database replication.
- Ensures low-latency access and automatic conflict resolution across regions.

AWS Global Accelerator

- Improves application availability by routing traffic to healthy endpoints across multiple regions.
- Automatically adjusts to regional failures.

Amazon EC2 and EBS Snapshots

- Replicates EBS snapshots to other regions for disaster recovery.
- Enables quick instance recovery in alternate regions.

AWS Elastic Load Balancer (ELB) with Global Load Balancing

- Routes traffic across regions using global load balancing for high availability.

3. Multi-Region DR Architectures

1. Backup and Restore

- **Overview**: Stores backups in a secondary region and restores resources when needed.
- **Advantages**: Low cost, suitable for non-critical workloads.
- **Disadvantages**: Longer recovery time.

2. Pilot Light

- **Overview**: A minimal version of the production environment runs in the secondary region, ready for scaling during failover.
- **Advantages**: Faster recovery time than backup and restore.
- **Disadvantages**: Increased costs for maintaining the minimal infrastructure.

3. Warm Standby

- **Overview**: A scaled-down version of the production environment runs in the secondary region, ready to scale up during failover.
- **Advantages**: Faster failover and recovery than pilot light.
- **Disadvantages**: Higher costs compared to pilot light.

4. Active-Active

- **Overview**: Fully operational production environments run in multiple regions, with traffic distributed across them.
- **Advantages**: Near-instant failover, improved latency, and continuous availability.
- **Disadvantages**: High cost and complexity.

4. Implementing Multi-Region DR

Step 1: Define RPO and RTO

- **Recovery Point Objective (RPO)**: Maximum acceptable data loss (e.g., last 15 minutes).
- **Recovery Time Objective (RTO)**: Maximum acceptable downtime (e.g., 5 minutes).

Step 2: Identify Critical Resources

- Identify databases, applications,

and services requiring multi-region redundancy.

Step 3: Select Appropriate Architecture

- Choose between backup/restore, pilot light, warm standby, or active-active based on workload requirements and budget.

Step 4: Automate Replication

- Use services like S3 CRR, RDS Read Replicas, and DynamoDB Global Tables for automated data replication.

Step 5: Enable Failover Mechanisms

- Configure Route 53 health checks and failover policies to redirect traffic automatically during outages.

Step 6: Test the DR Plan

- Regularly simulate disaster scenarios to validate failover mechanisms and recovery processes.

5. Best Practices for Multi-Region DR

1. **Use Infrastructure as Code (IaC):**
   - Use **AWS CloudFormation** or **Terraform** to replicate infrastructure in multiple regions.

2. **Automate Failover Processes:**
   - Leverage Route 53, AWS Lambda,

and Global Accelerator for automated failover.

3. **Implement Data Encryption**:
    - Use **AWS Key Management Service (KMS)** to secure data in transit and at rest across regions.

4. **Monitor Resources Across Regions**:
    - Use **AWS CloudWatch** for unified monitoring and **CloudTrail** for auditing.

5. **Optimize Costs**:
    - Use reserved instances or spot instances in secondary regions to reduce expenses.

6. **Ensure Consistency**:
    - Use tools like **AWS Config** and **AWS Systems Manager** to maintain configuration consistency across regions.

6. Real-World Example

Scenario: An e-commerce company with a global customer base requires a multi-region DR solution to ensure 99.99% availability.

Solution:

- **Active Regions**: Deploy production environments in the US East and EU West regions.
- **Data Replication**: Use DynamoDB

Global Tables and S3 CRR for data synchronization.

- **Traffic Management**: Configure Route 53 with latency-based routing for global traffic.
- **Failover Plan**: Use Global Accelerator and Route 53 health checks to redirect traffic during outages.
- **Monitoring**: Enable CloudWatch alarms and CloudTrail for operational visibility.

7. Challenges and Mitigations

Challenge	Mitigation
High Costs	Use cost optimization tools like **AWS Budgets** and spot instances.
Complexity of Data Synchronization	Leverage managed services like DynamoDB Global Tables for seamless replication.
Latency Concerns	Use **Global Accelerator** for improved routing and reduced latency.
Configuration Drift	Use **AWS Config** to enforce consistent configurations across regions.

Summary

Multi-Region Disaster Recovery is a crucial strategy for organizations seeking to ensure high availability and resilience. By leveraging AWS's diverse suite of services and best practices, businesses can build robust DR architectures that minimize downtime, protect data, and maintain user trust during disruptions.

CHAPTER 17: MIGRATION TO AWS

AWS Migration Hub

AWS Migration Hub is a central platform that simplifies the migration process by allowing users to track the progress of their application migrations across multiple AWS and partner tools. It provides visibility into the status and metrics of migrations, helping organizations efficiently manage and orchestrate their migration projects.

1. Key Features of AWS Migration Hub

1. **Centralized Tracking**:
    - Tracks migrations in one dashboard, regardless of the tools or services used.

- Integrates with AWS-native and third-party migration tools.

2. **Application-Level View**:
   - Groups resources into applications to monitor migration progress holistically.
   - Provides a comprehensive status for each application, not just individual resources.

3. **Integration with AWS Migration Services**:
   - Works with services like **AWS Application Migration Service (MGN)**, **AWS Database Migration Service (DMS)**, and **AWS Server Migration Service (SMS)**.

4. **Support for Third-Party Tools**:
   - Compatible with popular third-party migration tools, allowing flexibility in tool choice.

5. **Customizable Reporting**:
   - Offers detailed reports to help stakeholders track key performance indicators (KPIs).

6. **Cost Efficiency**:
   - The service is free; you only pay for the AWS resources used during migration.

2. Benefits of Using AWS Migration Hub

1. **Simplified Management**:
   - A single pane of glass for tracking all migration activities.
   - Reduces the complexity of managing multiple tools and workflows.

2. **Improved Visibility**:
   - Provides real-time updates on migration progress.
   - Identifies bottlenecks or delays, enabling faster resolution.

3. **Enhanced Collaboration**:
   - Teams can collaborate effectively with a unified view of migration tasks and statuses.

4. **Flexibility**:
   - Supports a variety of migration tools, allowing organizations to choose the best fit for their workloads.

5. **Reduced Risk**:
   - Centralized tracking ensures no resource is overlooked during migration.

3. How AWS Migration Hub Works

1. **Assessment**:
   - Discover and assess the

resources to be migrated using tools like AWS Application Discovery Service.

2. **Planning**:
   - Group resources into applications for better tracking.
   - Set migration timelines and allocate resources.

3. **Migration**:
   - Use supported tools (e.g., AWS MGN, DMS, or SMS) to migrate resources.
   - Monitor progress through the Migration Hub dashboard.

4. **Tracking and Reporting**:
   - Continuously monitor migration status, detect issues, and generate reports.
   - Adjust strategies based on real-time insights.

5. **Post-Migration Optimization**:
   - Optimize workloads using AWS tools like Cost Explorer and Trusted Advisor.

4. Common Use Cases

1. **Data Center to Cloud Migration**:
   - Simplify tracking of server, database, and application

migrations to AWS.

2. **Multi-Cloud and Hybrid Migrations**:
   - Monitor migrations that involve on-premises, multi-cloud, or hybrid environments.

3. **Database Modernization**:
   - Manage database migrations using **AWS DMS** to move from legacy systems to modern cloud-native databases.

4. **Application Rehosting**:
   - Track lift-and-shift migrations using AWS MGN or SMS.

5. Supported Migration Tools

AWS Tools	Description
AWS Application Migration Service	Automates lift-and-shift migrations for applications and servers.
AWS Database Migration Service	Migrates and replicates databases to and from AWS.
AWS Server Migration Service	Simplifies the migration of on-premises servers to AWS.
AWS Application Discovery Service	Discovers on-premises applications

and dependencies to plan migrations.

Third-Party Tools	Description
CloudEndure Migration	Accelerates large-scale migrations to AWS.
RiverMeadow	Enables live migrations of workloads to AWS.

6. Steps to Use AWS Migration Hub

1. **Set Up Migration Hub**:
     - Access Migration Hub via the AWS Management Console.

2. **Discover Applications**:
     - Use AWS Application Discovery Service to gather information on on-premises resources.

3. **Group Resources into Applications**:
     - Organize resources based on application dependencies for streamlined tracking.

4. **Select Migration Tools**:
     - Choose appropriate tools based on the type of workload (e.g., databases, virtual machines).

5. **Migrate Applications**:
     - Start migration and monitor

progress in real-time within Migration Hub.

6. **Review and Optimize**:
    - Post-migration, review the applications for performance and cost optimization.

7. Best Practices

1. **Pre-Migration Assessment**:
    - Use discovery tools to assess workloads and identify dependencies before migration.

2. **Application Grouping**:
    - Always group resources by application for better monitoring and troubleshooting.

3. **Leverage Automation**:
    - Automate repetitive tasks with AWS CLI or SDK to reduce manual intervention.

4. **Regular Reporting**:
    - Generate progress reports to keep stakeholders informed and address issues early.

5. **Test Migration Plans**:
    - Perform dry runs to validate migration strategies and tools.

8. Real-World Example

Scenario: A financial institution plans to migrate its on-premises data center to AWS.

Solution:

- **Discovery**: Used AWS Application Discovery Service to identify resources and dependencies.
- **Planning**: Grouped workloads into applications (e.g., web servers, databases).
- **Migration**: Leveraged AWS DMS for databases and AWS MGN for servers.
- **Tracking**: Monitored the migration status in AWS Migration Hub.
- **Outcome**: Achieved seamless migration with minimal downtime and real-time tracking.

Summary

AWS Migration Hub simplifies the migration process by providing a unified platform to track and manage migrations. With its integration of AWS and third-party tools, it offers unparalleled flexibility and visibility, making it an essential service for organizations transitioning to the cloud.

Best Practices for Moving to the Cloud

Transitioning to the cloud can be a complex process, but following best practices ensures a smoother migration, optimized performance, and reduced risks. Below is a comprehensive guide to best practices for moving workloads to the cloud, particularly on AWS.

1. Plan and Prepare Thoroughly

1. **Define Clear Goals**:
    - Identify why you are migrating to the cloud (e.g., cost reduction, scalability, or performance improvement).
    - Establish measurable success criteria for the migration.

2. **Perform a Cloud Readiness Assessment**:
    - Evaluate your organization's infrastructure, applications, and staff readiness for the cloud.
    - Identify gaps in skills and tools.

3. **Choose the Right Cloud Migration Strategy**:
    - Common approaches include **Rehosting (Lift-and-Shift)**,

Replatforming, **Repurchasing**, **Refactoring**, **Retiring**, and **Retaining**.

4. **Prioritize Applications for Migration**:
   - Start with non-critical or less complex workloads to gain confidence and experience.
   - Group applications by dependencies for seamless migration.

2. Establish a Cloud Governance Framework

1. **Define Policies and Guidelines**:
   - Set clear guidelines for cloud usage, resource provisioning, and cost management.

2. **Implement Role-Based Access Control (RBAC)**:
   - Use AWS Identity and Access Management (IAM) to enforce the principle of least privilege.

3. **Monitor Compliance**:
   - Utilize AWS Config and AWS CloudTrail to ensure continuous compliance with organizational policies.

3. Optimize Costs

1. **Understand AWS Pricing Models**:
   - Take advantage of **On-Demand**,

Reserved Instances, and **Spot Instances** to reduce costs.

2. **Use AWS Budgets and Cost Explorer**:
   - Set spending limits and monitor cost trends in real time.

3. **Implement Resource Tagging**:
   - Tag resources for better tracking and accountability.

4. Secure Your Cloud Environment

1. **Enable Multi-Factor Authentication (MFA)**:
   - Protect user accounts with MFA, especially for root accounts.

2. **Encrypt Data**:
   - Use AWS Key Management Service (KMS) for encrypting data at rest and in transit.

3. **Monitor and Audit**:
   - Continuously monitor security logs using AWS CloudWatch and AWS Security Hub.

4. **Implement a Shared Responsibility Model**:
   - Understand and fulfill your responsibilities under AWS's shared security model.

5. Use Automation and Tools

1. **Leverage Automation**:

- Use AWS tools like AWS CloudFormation, AWS Elastic Beanstalk, or AWS OpsWorks to automate infrastructure provisioning.

2. **Adopt CI/CD Pipelines**:
    - Use AWS CodePipeline and CodeBuild to automate application deployment and updates.

3. **Utilize Monitoring Tools**:
    - Set up monitoring and alerts with AWS CloudWatch and AWS Trusted Advisor.

6. Ensure High Availability and Resilience

1. **Design for Fault Tolerance**:
    - Distribute applications across multiple Availability Zones (AZs) and Regions.

2. **Implement Elastic Load Balancing (ELB)**:
    - Ensure automatic distribution of traffic to healthy instances.

3. **Set Up Auto Scaling**:
    - Use Auto Scaling to handle traffic spikes and maintain optimal performance.

7. Test and Validate Migration Plans

1. **Run Proof of Concepts (PoC):**
    - Test workloads in a cloud sandbox before full migration.
2. **Conduct Dry Runs:**
    - Validate the migration process in a staging environment to identify and fix issues.
3. **Monitor Performance Post-Migration:**
    - Use AWS CloudWatch to ensure that migrated applications meet performance benchmarks.

8. Train and Upskill Teams

1. **Invest in AWS Training:**
    - Enroll teams in AWS certification programs like Solutions Architect or Developer Associate.
2. **Encourage Hands-On Learning:**
    - Use AWS Free Tier or sandbox environments for practice.
3. **Establish a Cloud Center of Excellence (CCoE):**
    - Create a dedicated team to drive cloud adoption and share best practices.

9. Plan for Data Migration

1. **Choose the Right Data Transfer Method:**
    - Use tools like **AWS DataSync**,

AWS Snowball, or **AWS Storage Gateway** depending on data volume.

2. **Minimize Downtime**:
   - Use incremental data transfers or hybrid models to ensure smooth transitions.

3. **Validate Data Integrity**:
   - Verify that data is transferred accurately using checksum tools or AWS tools.

10. Leverage AWS Services for Optimization

1. **Use AWS Trusted Advisor**:
   - Get insights and recommendations for improving cost, performance, and security.

2. **Implement Elasticity**:
   - Use services like Amazon EC2 Auto Scaling, AWS Lambda, and Amazon Aurora to scale resources dynamically.

3. **Monitor with AWS CloudTrail**:
   - Track all API activity for auditing and troubleshooting purposes.

11. Post-Migration Practices

1. **Monitor Workloads Continuously**:
   - Use AWS CloudWatch and third-party tools for ongoing

performance monitoring.

2. **Optimize for the Cloud**:
    - Refactor applications post-migration to take full advantage of cloud-native services like AWS Lambda or DynamoDB.

3. **Review and Iterate**:
    - Conduct regular reviews to identify areas for further optimization or cost savings.

12. Common Challenges and How to Address Them

Challenge	Solution
Resistance to Change	Engage stakeholders early, and demonstrate the value of cloud adoption.
Skill Gaps	Invest in AWS training and certifications for your teams.
Security Concerns	Adopt robust security policies and tools like AWS Security Hub.
Unexpected Costs	Use AWS Budgets and Cost Explorer to monitor and control expenses.
Downtime During	Plan incremental

| Migration | migrations and validate with thorough testing. |

Summary

Adopting these best practices ensures a smooth transition to the cloud while minimizing risks and maximizing benefits. With AWS's robust ecosystem of tools and services, organizations can streamline their migration process, optimize resources, and achieve their cloud goals efficiently.

CONCLUSION

The Future of AWS and Cloud Computing

As technology evolves, the role of AWS and cloud computing will become even more pivotal in shaping how businesses operate, innovate, and grow. This chapter explores the anticipated trends, advancements, and emerging opportunities in AWS and the broader cloud ecosystem.

1. The Expanding Role of Cloud Computing

1. **Cloud as the Default IT Infrastructure**:
    - More businesses will adopt a cloud-first or cloud-only strategy, moving away from on-premises data centers entirely.
    - Hybrid cloud models will mature, integrating public cloud services like AWS

with on-premises infrastructure seamlessly.

2. **Increased Adoption by SMEs and Startups**:
   - Small and medium enterprises (SMEs) will leverage AWS for affordable, scalable IT solutions.
   - Startups will continue to innovate faster using cloud-native services like AWS Lambda and Amazon SageMaker.

3. **Global Reach and Accessibility**:
   - AWS will expand its global infrastructure, introducing more **Regions**, **Availability Zones**, and **Local Zones** to enhance performance and compliance with local regulations.

2. Emerging Technologies and Their Impact

1. **Artificial Intelligence (AI) and Machine Learning (ML)**:
   - AWS will continue investing in AI/ML services like SageMaker and AI-powered solutions such as Amazon Rekognition, Polly, and Lex.
   - AI will drive innovations in predictive analytics,

automation, and personalized user experiences.

2. **Quantum Computing**:
    - AWS Braket will play a significant role in democratizing quantum computing, enabling researchers and developers to solve complex problems previously beyond reach.

3. **Edge Computing and IoT**:
    - Services like **AWS IoT Core** and **AWS Outposts** will support real-time processing closer to devices, reducing latency and enabling new use cases in autonomous vehicles, healthcare, and smart cities.

4. **5G Integration**:
    - The combination of AWS and 5G networks will enhance the potential of edge computing, enabling ultra-low latency applications such as augmented reality (AR), virtual reality (VR), and industrial automation.

3. Sustainability and Green Cloud Computing

1. **Energy-Efficient Data Centers**:
    - AWS is already committed to sustainability, with initiatives to

power its operations using 100% renewable energy by 2025.
- Future data centers will incorporate cutting-edge cooling technologies and AI-driven energy management systems.

2. **Carbon Footprint Reduction**:
    - AWS will provide more tools like the **AWS Customer Carbon Footprint Tool** to help organizations measure and minimize their environmental impact.
    - Serverless computing models and elastic scaling will further reduce resource wastage.

4. Democratization of Technology

1. **Low-Code and No-Code Platforms**:
    - AWS will expand its offerings in this space, allowing non-developers to build applications using drag-and-drop interfaces.
    - Tools like **AWS Honeycode** will empower businesses to automate processes without deep technical expertise.

2. **Access to Advanced Analytics**:
    - Services like Amazon QuickSight and AWS Data Exchange will

make advanced analytics more accessible to organizations of all sizes.

5. Security and Compliance

1. **Enhanced Security Models**:
    - AWS will continue innovating with tools like **AWS Security Hub**, **Amazon Macie**, and **AWS GuardDuty** to address evolving security threats.
    - Zero Trust architecture will become a standard approach for securing cloud environments.

2. **Regulatory Compliance**:
    - AWS will offer more localized compliance frameworks and services to address stricter global data privacy laws, such as GDPR and CCPA.

6. The Workforce of the Future

1. **Upskilling and Certifications**:
    - AWS will expand training and certification programs to address the growing demand for cloud professionals.
    - Future skills will focus on AI/ML, DevOps, and cloud-native application development.

2. **Automation and Productivity Tools**:
   - AWS will introduce more tools that simplify IT operations and reduce manual intervention, empowering teams to focus on innovation.

7. Anticipated AWS Developments

1. **New Services and Features**:
   - AWS will launch industry-specific solutions, tailored for sectors like healthcare, finance, and education.
   - Continuous improvements in existing services will enhance scalability, reliability, and usability.

2. **Greater Focus on Multi-Cloud Interoperability**:
   - Although AWS remains a dominant player, there will be more emphasis on seamless integration with other cloud providers like Azure and Google Cloud.

3. **AI-Powered Automation**:
   - Expect AI to automate tasks like infrastructure management, security monitoring, and application scaling.

8. Future Challenges

1. **Data Sovereignty Issues**:
   - As governments enforce stricter data localization laws, AWS will face the challenge of building more localized infrastructure.

2. **Cybersecurity Threats**:
   - AWS must stay ahead of increasingly sophisticated cyberattacks by continuously improving its security offerings.

3. **Rising Competition**:
   - With the cloud market expanding, AWS will need to innovate to maintain its leadership position amidst competitors like Microsoft and Google.

Summary

The future of AWS and cloud computing is bright, with transformative technologies reshaping how businesses and individuals leverage IT resources. AWS's focus on innovation, sustainability, and democratization ensures it will remain at the forefront of this evolution. By embracing these advancements and preparing for challenges, businesses can unlock the full potential of the cloud and stay ahead in a competitive, digital-first world.

Learning Resources and Certification Paths

Mastering AWS requires a combination of practical experience, theoretical knowledge, and formal training. AWS provides a wealth of resources to help individuals and organizations learn and grow their cloud skills. This chapter outlines the most effective learning materials, training platforms, and certification paths to guide your AWS learning journey.

1. AWS Learning Resources

a. Official AWS Training

- **AWS Training Portal**:
  AWS offers an extensive catalog of free and paid courses through its official website, catering to various skill levels and roles.
    - Topics include foundational cloud computing, advanced architectural designs, and DevOps best practices.
    - Hands-on labs allow learners to practice real-world scenarios.
- **AWS Skill Builder**:

An interactive platform featuring over 500 free and premium digital training modules, including game-based learning.

b. AWS Documentation

- Comprehensive technical guides and API references are available for every AWS service.
- Includes tutorials, FAQs, and troubleshooting tips.

c. AWS Blogs

- Official AWS blogs provide updates on new services, use cases, and best practices.
- Categories include compute, databases, machine learning, and security.

d. AWS Whitepapers

- In-depth technical papers on AWS architecture, security, and optimization strategies.
- Recommended whitepapers: *AWS Well-Architected Framework* and *AWS Cloud Best Practices*.

e. YouTube Channels

- **AWS Official Channel**: Regularly updated with webinars, tutorials, and customer stories.

- Independent creators and experts also share tutorials and case studies on platforms like YouTube.

f. AWS Events

- **AWS re:Invent**: The largest annual AWS conference, featuring hands-on labs, workshops, and keynote presentations.
- Regional summits and webinars for localized learning.

2. Third-Party Learning Platforms

a. Online Course Platforms

- **Coursera, Udemy, and LinkedIn Learning**:
  Offer affordable and detailed AWS courses tailored for different skill levels.
    - Popular courses include "AWS Certified Solutions Architect – Associate" and "AWS Developer – Associate."
- **A Cloud Guru and Pluralsight**:
  Dedicated platforms for cloud learning, offering practice exams, labs, and certification prep.

b. Hands-On Learning

- **AWS Free Tier**:
  A great way to explore and practice AWS services without incurring costs.
    - Examples: Amazon EC2, S3, RDS, and Lambda.

- **Qwiklabs**:
  Hands-on labs focused on real-world AWS use cases, ideal for practical learners.
- **Cloud Academy**:
  Offers labs, exams, and interactive courses specifically for AWS.

3. AWS Certification Paths

AWS certifications validate your cloud expertise and are highly regarded in the industry. AWS certifications are divided into four levels:

a. Foundational Level

- **AWS Certified Cloud Practitioner**:
  Ideal for beginners, covering basic AWS concepts, pricing, and architecture.
    - **Recommended For**: Business professionals and entry-level IT staff.

b. Associate Level

- **AWS Certified Solutions Architect – Associate**:
  Focuses on designing cost-effective, scalable, and secure solutions.
    - **Recommended For**: Solution architects and system engineers.
- **AWS Certified Developer – Associate**:
  Emphasizes developing applications and optimizing performance using AWS services.

- **Recommended For**: Developers and software engineers.
- **AWS Certified SysOps Administrator – Associate**:
Focuses on deploying, managing, and operating workloads on AWS.
  - **Recommended For**: System administrators and DevOps professionals.

c. Professional Level

- **AWS Certified Solutions Architect – Professional**:
Advanced certification for designing complex AWS solutions.
  - **Recommended For**: Experienced architects.
- **AWS Certified DevOps Engineer – Professional**:
Focuses on CI/CD pipelines, automation, and deployment best practices.
  - **Recommended For**: Senior DevOps engineers.

d. Specialty Certifications

For professionals seeking expertise in specific domains:

- **AWS Certified Advanced Networking**
- **AWS Certified Big Data**
- **AWS Certified Security**
- **AWS Certified Machine Learning**

- **AWS Certified Database**

4. Tips for Certification Success

a. Start with Hands-On Practice

- Use the AWS Free Tier to explore core services and build small projects.

b. Join AWS Communities

- Participate in local meetups, forums, and online groups to exchange knowledge.
- Recommended platforms: **AWS Forums**, **Reddit (r/aws)**, and LinkedIn groups.

c. Simulate Exam Environments

- Use platforms like **Whizlabs** or **ExamTopics** for mock exams.
- Focus on understanding the reasoning behind correct answers.

d. Build Real-World Projects

- Develop applications, implement security policies, or design networks using AWS to enhance practical understanding.

e. Leverage Study Groups

- Join study groups on platforms like Discord or Slack for collaborative learning and accountability.

5. Lifelong Learning with AWS

AWS evolves constantly, introducing new services and updates. Staying current requires:

- Regularly revisiting AWS training platforms.
- Keeping up with certifications by taking recertification exams every two years.
- Exploring advanced tools and services as you grow in your cloud expertise.

By utilizing these resources and following the structured certification paths, you can effectively master AWS, unlocking new career opportunities and enhancing your ability to build scalable, secure, and innovative solutions.

Final Tips for Mastery

Achieving mastery in AWS requires a blend of consistent learning, practical application, and a proactive mindset to adapt to the rapidly evolving cloud landscape. Here are the final tips to help you excel in AWS and become an expert in cloud computing:

1. Focus on Hands-On Experience

- **Practice Regularly**: Use the AWS Free Tier to explore new services and experiment with configurations.

- **Work on Real Projects**: Build solutions for real-world problems, such as hosting a website, setting up a serverless application, or creating a backup strategy.
- **Leverage Sandboxes**: Platforms like Qwiklabs and A Cloud Guru offer safe environments for practicing advanced AWS services without affecting live systems.

2. Stay Updated with AWS Innovations

- **Follow AWS Announcements**: Subscribe to the AWS blog and updates to keep track of new services and features.
- **Attend AWS Events**: Participate in AWS re:Invent, summits, and webinars to gain insights from AWS experts and industry leaders.
- **Explore AWS Labs**: Stay ahead by experimenting with beta features and tools provided by AWS Labs.

3. Adopt a Problem-Solving Mindset

- **Understand Use Cases**: Familiarize yourself with common AWS use cases to better identify the right tools and services for specific scenarios.
- **Optimize Solutions**: Continuously evaluate and refine your AWS solutions

for performance, cost, and scalability.

- **Learn from Failures**: Analyze mistakes and failures in your projects to deepen your understanding of AWS limitations and best practices.

4. Deepen Your Knowledge in Key Areas

- **Security and Compliance**: Master AWS Identity and Access Management (IAM), Key Management Service (KMS), and other security tools to build robust and compliant systems.
- **Cost Management**: Learn to optimize costs using AWS Cost Explorer, Budgets, and Reserved Instances.
- **Scalability and Performance**: Dive into Auto Scaling, Elastic Load Balancing, and other services that ensure application resilience under varying workloads.

5. Build a Strong Foundation

- **Master Core Services**: Focus on services like EC2, S3, Lambda, RDS, and DynamoDB as they are the backbone of most AWS solutions.
- **Understand Networking**: Gain proficiency in Amazon VPC, Route 53, and CloudFront to design efficient and secure networks.

- **Embrace Serverless Architectures**: Explore serverless computing to develop highly scalable and cost-efficient applications.

6. Engage with the AWS Community

- **Join User Groups**: Connect with local and global AWS enthusiasts through meetups, forums, and online groups.
- **Participate in Open Source Projects**: Contribute to open-source projects built on AWS to gain exposure to diverse use cases and architectures.
- **Network with Experts**: Collaborate with experienced professionals to exchange ideas and gain mentorship.

7. Pursue Continuous Learning

- **Certify Your Skills**: Follow the AWS certification paths to validate your expertise and enhance your career opportunities.
- **Explore Advanced Topics**: Delve into areas like machine learning (SageMaker), big data (Redshift), and IoT (AWS IoT Core) to expand your knowledge.
- **Utilize Third-Party Resources**: Enroll in courses, read books, and watch tutorials to supplement your AWS training.

8. Develop Soft Skills

- **Document Your Work**: Maintain clear documentation for every project to enhance your problem-solving approach and aid future troubleshooting.
- **Improve Presentation Skills**: Learn to effectively communicate your AWS solutions to stakeholders and teams.
- **Be Solution-Oriented**: Focus on delivering business value through AWS by aligning technical capabilities with organizational goals.

9. Build a Portfolio

- **Showcase Your Projects**: Create a portfolio of AWS projects that demonstrate your skills, such as web apps, data pipelines, or security architectures.
- **Contribute Case Studies**: Share your experiences and solutions in AWS forums or blogs to establish your expertise in the community.

10. Adopt a Growth Mindset

- **Embrace Challenges**: Tackle complex AWS scenarios and push yourself out of your comfort zone to accelerate learning.
- **Stay Curious**: Continuously explore new AWS services, even those outside your

immediate needs.

- **Never Stop Learning**: Cloud computing is dynamic; stay committed to lifelong learning to maintain your edge in the industry.

By applying these tips, you'll not only master AWS but also position yourself as a thought leader in cloud computing. AWS mastery is a journey, not a destination—stay passionate, persistent, and proactive in your learning and practice.

APPENDICES

Appendix A: AWS Certification Paths and Study Tips

AWS certifications validate your expertise in specific areas of cloud computing and can significantly boost your career. This appendix provides an overview of the available certifications and study tips to help you prepare effectively.

AWS Certification Paths

AWS certifications are divided into **Foundational**, **Associate**, **Professional**, and **Specialty** levels. Each level targets specific expertise and roles.

1. Foundational Level

- **AWS Certified Cloud Practitioner**
    - **Target Audience**: Beginners and

non-technical roles (e.g., sales, marketing).
- **Focus Areas**: Cloud basics, AWS services, security, and pricing models.

2. Associate Level

- **AWS Certified Solutions Architect – Associate**
  - **Target Audience**: Cloud architects and engineers.
  - **Focus Areas**: Designing cost-effective, scalable, and secure AWS solutions.
- **AWS Certified Developer – Associate**
  - **Target Audience**: Developers building and deploying AWS-based applications.
  - **Focus Areas**: Programming, SDK usage, and serverless applications.
- **AWS Certified SysOps Administrator – Associate**
  - **Target Audience**: System administrators and operations professionals.
  - **Focus Areas**: Deployment, management, and operational tasks on AWS.

3. Professional Level

- **AWS Certified Solutions Architect – Professional**

- **Target Audience**: Advanced architects designing complex AWS solutions.
- **Focus Areas**: Multi-tier architectures, cost optimization, and migration strategies.

- **AWS Certified DevOps Engineer – Professional**
  - **Target Audience**: DevOps engineers focusing on automation and CI/CD pipelines.
  - **Focus Areas**: Infrastructure as code, monitoring, and security.

4. Specialty Certifications

- **AWS Certified Advanced Networking – Specialty**
  - **Focus Areas**: Complex networking tasks and hybrid architectures.

- **AWS Certified Security – Specialty**
  - **Focus Areas**: Data protection, incident response, and compliance.

- **AWS Certified Machine Learning – Specialty**
  - **Focus Areas**: Designing, implementing, and maintaining ML solutions.

- **AWS Certified Database – Specialty**
  - **Focus Areas**: Database design, migration, and troubleshooting.

- **AWS Certified Data Analytics – Specialty**
  - **Focus Areas**: Data lakes, analytics services, and visualization.
- **AWS Certified SAP on AWS – Specialty**
  - **Focus Areas**: Managing SAP workloads on AWS.

Study Tips for AWS Certification Exams

1. Understand the Exam Blueprint

- Review the **exam guide** to understand the domains and percentage weights.
- Focus more on high-weighted sections during your preparation.

2. Use Official AWS Learning Resources

- **AWS Training and Certification Portal**: Access free digital courses and hands-on labs.
- **AWS Whitepapers**: Read key whitepapers, such as the *Well-Architected Framework* and *Security Best Practices*.

3. Leverage Hands-On Practice

- Use the **AWS Free Tier** to gain practical experience with services.
- Practice building, configuring, and managing AWS solutions similar to exam scenarios.

4. Take Practice Exams

- Use official and third-party practice exams to familiarize yourself with the question format.
- Analyze your results to identify weak areas and improve.

5. Join Study Groups and Communities

- Participate in online forums, such as the AWS subreddit, Discord channels, or LinkedIn groups.
- Engage with peers preparing for the same certification for knowledge-sharing.

6. Create a Study Schedule

- Allocate specific times for learning each domain.
- Stick to your schedule and track your progress consistently.

7. Explore Third-Party Study Platforms

- Platforms like A Cloud Guru, Linux Academy, and Whizlabs provide excellent courses and mock exams tailored to AWS certifications.

8. Read and Experiment

- Experiment with services mentioned in the exam objectives.
- Build small projects like a WordPress site, a Lambda function, or a data

pipeline to deepen your understanding.

9. Focus on Best Practices

- Learn AWS best practices for security, performance optimization, and cost management.
- Understand the **Shared Responsibility Model** for securing AWS resources.

10. Stay Calm and Confident During the Exam

- Read each question carefully and eliminate incorrect options.
- Manage your time effectively—don't dwell too long on challenging questions.

Certification Renewal

AWS certifications are valid for three years. To maintain your certification, you must pass a recertification exam or earn a higher-level certification in the same track.

By following these paths and tips, you'll be well-prepared to excel in AWS certifications and demonstrate your cloud expertise effectively.

Appendix B: Troubleshooting Common Issues

This appendix provides guidance on troubleshooting common issues encountered when using AWS services. Whether you're new to AWS or an experienced user, knowing how to effectively diagnose and resolve problems can save you time and ensure your applications run smoothly.

1. EC2 Instance Issues

Issue: EC2 Instance is Not Starting

- **Possible Causes**:
    - Insufficient instance capacity in the selected region.
    - Instance type mismatch or lack of compatible AMI (Amazon Machine Image).
    - Issues with the instance's security group or network configuration.
- **Troubleshooting Steps**:
    - Verify that there is available capacity in your chosen region.
    - Check the instance type and AMI compatibility.
    - Review the instance's security group to ensure appropriate inbound/outbound rules.

- Inspect CloudWatch logs for any instance startup errors.

Issue: EC2 Instance is Unreachable (No SSH/RDP)

- **Possible Causes**:
  - Incorrect security group settings blocking SSH (port 22) or RDP (port 3389).
  - Network ACLs or routing tables misconfigured.
  - Missing or incorrect key pair for SSH access.

- **Troubleshooting Steps**:
  - Confirm that the security group allows access to the required ports (SSH for Linux or RDP for Windows).
  - Check network ACLs and route tables for appropriate configuration.
  - Verify that the correct key pair is used for SSH access.

2. Amazon S3 Issues

Issue: Unable to Upload Files to S3

- **Possible Causes**:
  - Bucket policy or IAM user permissions not allowing uploads.
  - Insufficient disk space or invalid file types.

- Object size exceeds the limit for single uploads (5GB).
- **Troubleshooting Steps**:
  - Ensure the IAM user or role has the necessary S3 permissions (e.g., s3:PutObject).
  - Check that the file size is within the limits for direct upload, or use multipart uploads for larger objects.
  - Review the S3 bucket policy for any restrictions that might prevent uploads.

Issue: S3 Bucket is Not Accessible (403 Forbidden)

- **Possible Causes**:
  - Bucket policy is restricting access to specific IPs or users.
  - IAM permissions not properly set for the accessing user.
  - Blocked public access to the bucket (e.g., in bucket settings).
- **Troubleshooting Steps**:
  - Review the bucket's access control list (ACL) and bucket policy for restrictions.
  - Ensure the IAM user has the necessary s3:GetObject permissions.
  - Check the bucket settings for public access restrictions and

adjust as needed.

3. Amazon RDS Issues

Issue: RDS Instance is Unresponsive

- **Possible Causes**:
    - Insufficient resources (e.g., CPU or memory exhaustion).
    - Database connection pool exhaustion.
    - Network connectivity issues between your application and RDS.

- **Troubleshooting Steps**:
    - Check RDS metrics in CloudWatch (CPU, memory, disk I/O) to diagnose resource exhaustion.
    - Scale the RDS instance vertically (larger instance type) or horizontally (read replicas).
    - Verify that your VPC and security group settings allow proper communication between RDS and the application.
    - Enable enhanced monitoring and check for any performance bottlenecks.

Issue: Cannot Connect to RDS Instance

- **Possible Causes**:
    - Misconfigured VPC/subnet or security group rules.

- RDS instance is not publicly accessible (if needed).
- IAM or database credentials are incorrect.

- **Troubleshooting Steps**:
    - Ensure that the VPC/subnet routing and security groups are correctly configured to allow database access.
    - Verify that the instance is set to be publicly accessible (if needed) and the appropriate port is open.
    - Check the database credentials and ensure they match the ones used by your application.

4. Amazon Lambda Issues

Issue: Lambda Function Fails to Execute

- **Possible Causes**:
    - Incorrect function permissions.
    - Timeout settings are too short.
    - Invalid input parameters or malformed event data.

- **Troubleshooting Steps**:
    - Ensure that the Lambda function has the required permissions, such as AWSLambdaBasicExecutionRole.
    - Check the timeout settings in the function configuration and adjust if necessary.
    - Review the event data and logs in

CloudWatch to confirm the input is formatted correctly.

Issue: Lambda Function Performance Is Poor

- **Possible Causes**:
  - Insufficient allocated memory for the Lambda function.
  - Cold starts due to infrequent invocations.
  - Inefficient code or resource access patterns.

- **Troubleshooting Steps**:
  - Increase the function's allocated memory to improve performance.
  - Implement provisioned concurrency if the function experiences frequent cold starts.
  - Review the function code and optimize resource access (e.g., database queries or external API calls).

5. Networking Issues

Issue: Unable to Connect to Resources in a VPC

- **Possible Causes**:
  - Misconfigured route tables, security groups, or network ACLs.
  - VPC peering or Transit Gateway misconfiguration.
  - Incorrect DNS settings or lack of internet gateway for public

access.

- **Troubleshooting Steps**:
    - Check route tables to ensure proper routing between subnets and internet access.
    - Verify security group and network ACL rules for appropriate traffic flow.
    - Ensure that DNS resolution and an internet gateway are configured if needed for external connectivity.

Issue: VPN or Direct Connect Connectivity Issues

- **Possible Causes**:
    - Misconfigured VPN or Direct Connect configuration.
    - Incorrect routing or firewall settings.
    - AWS-side service issues.

- **Troubleshooting Steps**:
    - Check the VPN configuration, including the shared secret, tunnel settings, and customer gateway settings.
    - Verify the network routes in both AWS and on-premise systems.
    - Check the AWS VPN or Direct Connect status for any issues or maintenance activities.

6. Billing and Cost Issues

Issue: Unexpected High AWS Charges

- **Possible Causes**:
  - Unused resources running (e.g., EC2 instances, Elastic IPs).
  - Data transfer costs (e.g., cross-region data transfers).
  - Lack of cost optimization and scaling best practices.

- **Troubleshooting Steps**:
  - Use **AWS Cost Explorer** and **AWS Budgets** to identify which services are consuming the most resources.
  - Check for unused EC2 instances or unattached Elastic IPs that can be terminated.
  - Review data transfer patterns and optimize the architecture for lower cost, such as using CloudFront for caching.

Issue: Unclear Charges for Specific AWS Services

- **Possible Causes**:
  - Complex pricing models for services like S3, EC2, or Lambda.
  - Unfamiliarity with AWS pricing features like reserved instances or data transfer charges.

- **Troubleshooting Steps**:
  - Use **AWS Cost Explorer** and filter by service to understand detailed

billing breakdowns.

- Review the **AWS Pricing Calculator** to estimate costs based on usage patterns.
- Check for any unanticipated charges, such as requests or additional storage, in services like S3 or Lambda.

7. General Troubleshooting Tools

- **AWS CloudWatch Logs**: Use CloudWatch logs to capture detailed error messages and insights into service behavior.

- **AWS CloudTrail**: Use CloudTrail to investigate API calls and identify changes that might have led to issues.

- **AWS Trusted Advisor**: Leverage Trusted Advisor for recommendations on cost optimization, performance, security, and fault tolerance.

- **AWS Support**: If issues persist, consider opening a support ticket with AWS to get expert assistance.

By following these troubleshooting steps and leveraging the AWS tools mentioned, you can efficiently diagnose and resolve common issues within your AWS environment, ensuring better reliability and performance for your applications.

Appendix C: Glossary of AWS Terms and Services

This glossary provides definitions of key AWS terms and services to help you understand the terminology commonly used in the AWS ecosystem. These terms are useful for both beginners and advanced users working with Amazon Web Services.

A

- **Amazon EC2 (Elastic Compute Cloud)**: A web service that provides resizable compute capacity in the cloud. It allows you to run virtual machines (called instances) on-demand.

- **Amazon EBS (Elastic Block Store)**: Provides persistent block storage for Amazon EC2 instances. EBS volumes can be attached to EC2 instances to store data.

- **Amazon S3 (Simple Storage Service)**: An object storage service that offers scalable, high-speed, and low-cost storage for data backup, archival, and analytics.

- **AWS Auto Scaling**: A service that automatically adjusts the number of Amazon EC2 instances in your application based on demand.
- **Amazon Aurora**: A fully managed, MySQL- and PostgreSQL-compatible relational database engine with cloud-native performance and scalability.

B

- **AWS Backup**: A centralized backup service that simplifies the management of backup schedules and retention policies for AWS resources.
- **AWS Batch**: A fully managed service that enables running batch computing workloads at any scale.

C

- **Amazon CloudWatch**: A monitoring service that provides data and actionable insights for AWS resources and applications in real time.
- **AWS CloudFormation**: A service that helps you model and set up AWS resources so that you can spend less time managing those resources and more time focusing on your application.
- **AWS CloudTrail**: A service that enables governance, compliance, and

operational and risk auditing of your AWS account by logging all API calls made in your account.

- **Amazon CloudFront**: A content delivery network (CDN) that distributes content globally with low latency and high transfer speeds.

D

- **Amazon DynamoDB**: A fully managed NoSQL database service that provides fast and predictable performance with seamless scalability.

- **AWS Direct Connect**: A network service that provides a dedicated connection from your premises to AWS.

- **AWS Data Pipeline**: A web service that helps you reliably process and move data between different AWS compute and storage services.

E

- **Amazon Elastic Beanstalk**: A platform-as-a-service (PaaS) for deploying and managing web applications and services without worrying about infrastructure.

- **Amazon EFS (Elastic File System)**: A fully managed network file system that can be accessed from multiple EC2 instances.

- **Amazon EMR (Elastic MapReduce)**: A cloud-native big data platform for processing large amounts of data quickly and cost-effectively using open-source tools like Hadoop, Spark, and Hive.

F

- **AWS Fargate**: A serverless compute engine for containers that works with Amazon ECS and Amazon EKS to run containers without managing servers.
- **AWS Fault Injection Simulator**: A fully managed service for running chaos engineering experiments to test the resilience of your applications.

G

- **Amazon Glacier**: A low-cost cloud storage service designed for data archiving and long-term backup.
- **AWS Glue**: A fully managed ETL (extract, transform, load) service for preparing data for analytics.

I

- **Amazon IAM (Identity and Access Management)**: A service that helps you securely control access to AWS services and resources for your users and applications.

- **AWS IoT Core**: A service that allows you to connect Internet of Things (IoT) devices to AWS services and other devices.
- **Amazon Inspector**: An automated security assessment service to help improve the security and compliance of applications deployed on AWS.

K

- **AWS KMS (Key Management Service)**: A fully managed service for creating and controlling encryption keys used to encrypt your data.
- **Amazon Kinesis**: A platform for streaming data on AWS, enabling real-time analytics and data processing.

L

- **AWS Lambda**: A serverless compute service that runs your code in response to events such as changes in data or user actions, automatically managing the compute resources for you.
- **Amazon Lightsail**: A simplified cloud platform that provides virtual private servers (VPS) for developers and small businesses.

M

- **AWS Managed Services**: A suite of

services designed to help manage your AWS environment and ensure efficient operation.

- **Amazon Machine Image (AMI)**: A pre-configured virtual machine image used to create EC2 instances.

N

- **Amazon Network Load Balancer (NLB)**: A highly scalable load balancer designed to handle millions of requests per second while maintaining high throughput at ultra-low latency.
- **AWS NAT Gateway**: A service that enables instances in a private subnet to access the internet while remaining private.

P

- **AWS Pricing Calculator**: A tool to help estimate the cost of AWS services based on your expected usage.
- **AWS Polling**: The process of regularly checking a service for updates or changes, often used in event-driven systems.
- **Amazon Polly**: A text-to-speech service that converts text into lifelike speech using deep learning models.

R

- **Amazon RDS (Relational Database Service)**: A managed relational database service that simplifies setting up, operating, and scaling databases like MySQL, PostgreSQL, Oracle, and SQL Server.

- **AWS Redshift**: A fully managed, petabyte-scale data warehouse service designed for large-scale data analytics.

S

- **Amazon S3 Glacier**: A low-cost, long-term storage service for data archiving.

- **AWS Secrets Manager**: A service for securely storing, managing, and accessing secrets such as API keys, database credentials, and other sensitive information.

- **AWS Security Hub**: A service that provides a comprehensive view of your security state within AWS and helps you manage security alerts.

T

- **Amazon Timestream**: A time-series database service optimized for storing and analyzing time-series data, such as IoT telemetry, application monitoring data, and real-time analytics.

- **AWS Transit Gateway**: A service that

allows you to connect multiple VPCs and on-premises networks to a central hub, simplifying network management.

V

- **Amazon VPC (Virtual Private Cloud)**: A logically isolated network that allows you to launch AWS resources in a virtual network you define.
- **AWS VPN**: A service that securely connects your on-premises network to AWS using an encrypted tunnel.

W

- **AWS WAF (Web Application Firewall)**: A service that helps protect web applications from common web exploits that could affect availability, compromise security, or consume excessive resources.
- **AWS WorkSpaces**: A managed, secure cloud desktop service that allows you to provision virtual desktops for your users.

Z

- **AWS Zocalo**: (Now known as Amazon WorkDocs) A secure document collaboration service that helps teams collaborate and share documents in real-time.

This glossary should serve as a quick reference to help you navigate AWS services and their functions. It's important to familiarize yourself with these terms as you continue to explore the AWS ecosystem.

AFTERWORD

As we close the final chapter of Mastering AWS, I want to take a moment to reflect on the journey we've undertaken together. Cloud computing, and AWS in particular, has transformed the way businesses and individuals approach technology, and I am grateful to have had the opportunity to share my knowledge and experiences with you throughout this book.

When I first began using AWS, it was with the belief that the cloud had immense potential, but I never could have fully anticipated the speed at which the technology would evolve, nor the magnitude of its impact on the world. From hosting simple web applications to orchestrating large-scale, complex global systems, AWS has proven time and again that its capabilities can support virtually any use case—if you know how to harness them.

But Mastering AWS is not just a technical guide. It's about empowering you to think critically, creatively, and strategically when approaching the cloud. As you apply the skills and knowledge from this book, I encourage you to keep a few things in mind:

Experiment and Explore: AWS is vast, and the only way to truly master it is through experimentation. Don't be afraid to try out new services, test different architectures, and find what works best for your unique needs.

Stay Curious: Cloud technology is always evolving. AWS frequently releases new features and services, many of which can radically change how we approach old challenges. Stay engaged with AWS's updates and the broader cloud community to stay ahead of the curve.

Never Stop Learning: The cloud is a journey, not a destination. While this book has provided a comprehensive foundation, there will always be more to learn and explore. As you continue to grow your AWS expertise, take advantage of AWS's certification programs, online resources, and community forums to deepen your knowledge.

Build for the Future: AWS empowers you to build scalable, secure, and innovative solutions that can withstand the test of time. Whether you're working on a small side project or a mission-critical application, remember that cloud infrastructure isn't just about today—it's about setting yourself up for success in the future.

Finally, I want to express my gratitude to you, the reader, for taking the time to embark on this journey with me. Whether you're just starting out with AWS or you're an experienced user looking to refine your skills, I hope that this book has provided you with the tools, knowledge, and inspiration to continue your journey in the cloud.

AWS offers an incredible range of possibilities, and now it's your turn to explore them. The world of cloud computing is yours to shape. I look forward to seeing the amazing things you will build, innovate, and create.

Thank you for being part of this journey. Here's to your continued success with AWS.

— Edwin Cano

ACKNOWLEDGEMENT

Writing Mastering AWS has been a rewarding and challenging experience, and I could not have completed this project without the support and encouragement of many wonderful people. I would like to take this opportunity to express my heartfelt gratitude to those who helped bring this book to life.

First and foremost, I would like to thank my family and friends. Your unwavering support, patience, and belief in me were invaluable throughout this process. Your encouragement kept me focused and motivated during the long hours of writing and research.

To my colleagues and mentors in the cloud computing field, thank you for sharing your insights and experiences with me.

Your expertise, feedback, and passion for technology have inspired and shaped my own understanding of AWS. I am grateful for the knowledge you've passed on to me and the conversations that pushed my thinking further.

A special thank you goes to the AWS community, whose vast network of cloud practitioners, developers, and experts provided both inspiration and practical guidance. Whether through forums, webinars, blogs, or open-source contributions, your generosity in sharing knowledge helped me craft this book and made the cloud a much more accessible space for all.

To the AWS team, thank you for continually innovating and expanding the AWS ecosystem. Your dedication to excellence in cloud computing and your user-first approach have made AWS an indispensable tool for businesses and individuals alike. It's been a privilege to work with such a powerful and ever-evolving platform.

I also want to extend my deepest appreciation to my editor, publisher, and the production team who worked tirelessly to ensure this book reached its full potential. Your professionalism, attention to detail, and constructive feedback have made this book what it is today.

Finally, to you, the reader, I offer my sincere thanks. Without your interest, curiosity, and desire to learn, this book wouldn't have a purpose. I hope the knowledge shared here has helped you take the next step in your AWS journey and empowered you to build, innovate, and lead with cloud technologies.

Thank you all for being part of this journey. Your contributions—big and small—have made this project possible, and I am forever grateful.

— Edwin Cano

ABOUT THE AUTHOR

Edwin Cano

Edwin Cano is an experienced cloud enthusiast, technology consultant, and AWS practitioner with a passion for helping individuals and organizations harness the power of cloud computing. With years of hands-on experience across various industries, Edwin has witnessed firsthand the transformative potential of AWS, making it an essential part of his professional toolkit.

As an AWS user, Edwin has worked with a diverse range of AWS services, from compute and storage solutions to advanced machine learning and data analytics. His journey with AWS began several years ago when he saw the potential to simplify and scale IT infrastructure using cloud technologies. Since then, he has been deeply involved in deploying and managing applications in the AWS ecosystem, driving innovation and efficiency for businesses of all sizes.

Edwin's expertise spans various domains, including cloud architecture, serverless computing, data analytics, and DevOps practices. His deep understanding of AWS is complemented by his commitment to exploring new technologies and staying up-to-date with the latest advancements in cloud computing. His ability to explain complex AWS concepts in an accessible and practical manner has earned him recognition as a trusted resource among his peers and clients.

In addition to his professional experience, Edwin is a passionate educator and mentor. He has guided many aspiring cloud professionals and businesses through the intricacies of AWS, helping them adopt cloud services to solve real-world challenges. His goal is to empower others to use AWS effectively, maximizing the benefits of the cloud for both personal and organizational success.

This book is a culmination of Edwin's journey as an AWS user, where he has combined his technical expertise with his desire to share knowledge with others. Whether you are a beginner or an experienced cloud practitioner, Edwin's insights and practical tips will help you navigate the AWS ecosystem with confidence and mastery.

When he's not working with cloud technologies, Edwin enjoys exploring new technological innovations, reading about the future of computing, and contributing to the cloud community. He is a firm believer in the transformative power of technology and the cloud, and he is excited to help others unlock their potential with AWS.

Connect with Edwin Cano
Instagram: @imceowin
Website: www.imceowin.com
Email: author@imceowin.com

PRAISE FOR AUTHOR

"Edwin Cano is a seasoned cloud technology expert whose deep understanding of AWS has helped countless individuals and organizations harness the power of the cloud. His unique ability to explain complex cloud concepts in an easy-to-understand manner is what sets him apart. Mastering AWS is not only a comprehensive guide but also a testament to Edwin's dedication to empowering others to succeed in the ever-evolving world of cloud computing."

- — DANIEL K., CLOUD ARCHITECT

"Edwin's expertise in AWS shines through in this book. His practical insights, clear explanations, and real-world examples make learning AWS both enjoyable and impactful. Whether you're just starting out or looking to refine your skills, Edwin's

approach will help you master AWS and make the most of its powerful features."

- — RAYMOND D., SENIOR CLOUD DEVELOPER

"Mastering AWS is an exceptional resource for anyone seeking to gain expertise in cloud computing. Edwin's ability to take complex AWS topics and break them down into accessible and digestible lessons is unparalleled. His knowledge and passion for cloud technology are evident on every page."

- — MICHAEL S., CTO

"Edwin Cano is an educator at heart, and it's clear from this book that his mission is to make AWS accessible to everyone. His hands-on approach to explaining AWS services ensures that even the most challenging topics are easy to understand. This book is a must-have for anyone serious about mastering AWS."

- — SAMANTHA P., CLOUD SOLUTIONS ARCHITECT

"With a clear and straightforward approach, Edwin Cano delivers a masterpiece in Mastering AWS. This book is packed with essential knowledge that not only covers the breadth of AWS but also dives deep into the real-world applications of cloud technologies. Edwin's passion for AWS is evident, making this an indispensable resource for both beginners and seasoned professionals."

- — ANTHONY Y., AWS SOLUTIONS ARCHITECT

"Edwin Cano is one of the brightest minds in the world of cloud computing. His ability to make AWS approachable and practical has helped me and my team enhance our cloud strategy. Mastering AWS provides an invaluable blueprint for anyone looking to optimize their use of AWS and make the most of what the cloud has to offer."

- — SHERRYL S., HEAD OF IT OPERATIONS